Britain's Sterling Colonial Policy and Decolonization, 1939–1958

Recent Titles in
Contributions in Comparative Colonial Studies

Journalists for Empire: The Imperial Debate in the Edwardian Stately Press, 1903–1913
James D. Startt

Imperial Diplomacy in the Era of Decolonization: The Sudan and Anglo-Egyptian Relations, 1945-1956
W. Travis Hanes III

The Man on the Spot: Essays on British Empire History
Roger D. Long, editor

Imperialism and Colonialism: Essays on the History of European Expansion
H. L. Wesseling

The Racial Dimension of American Overseas Colonial Policy
Hazel M. McFerson

Meeting Technology's Advance: Social Change in China and Zimbabwe in the Railway Age
James Zheng Gao

U.S. Imperialism in Latin America: Bryan's Challenges and Contributions, 1900–1920
Edward S. Kaplan

The Kingdom of Swaziland: Studies in Political History
D. Hugh Gillis

The Bringing of Wonder: Trade and the Indians of the Southeast, 1700–1783
Michael P. Morris

Policing Islam: The British Occupation of Egypt and the Anglo-Egyptian Struggle over Control of the Police, 1882–1914
Harold Tollefson

India: The Seductive and Seduced "Other" of German Orientalism
Kamakshi P. Murti

The Betrothed of Death: The Spanish Foreign Legion During the Rif Rebellion, 1920–1927
Jose E. Alvarez

Britain's Sterling Colonial Policy and Decolonization, 1939–1958

Allister Hinds

Contributions in Comparative Colonial Studies, Number 42

GREENWOOD PRESS
Westport, Connecticut • London

Library of Congress Cataloging-in-Publication Data

Hinds, Allister, 1957–
    Britain's sterling colonial policy and decolonization, 1939–1958 / Allister Hinds.
      p. cm.—(Contributions in comparative colonial studies, ISSN 0163–3813 ; no. 42)
    Includes bibliographical references and index.
    ISBN 0–313–31953–7 (alk. paper)
    1. Decolonization—Great Britain—Colonies—History—20th century. 2. Great
Britain—Colonies—History—20th century. 3. Great Britain—Foreign economic relations.
4. Sterling area. I. Title. II. Series.
    DA16.H55 2001
    325.341′09′044—dc21   2001018222

British Library Cataloguing in Publication Data is available.

Library of Congress Catalog Card Number: 2001018222
ISBN: 0–313–31953–7
ISSN: 0163–3813

First published in 2001

Greenwood Press, 88 Post Road West, Westport, CT 06881
An imprint of Greenwood Publishing Group, Inc.
www.greenwood.com

Printed in the United States of America

The paper used in this book complies with the
Permanent Paper Standard issued by the National
Information Standards Organization (Z39.48–1984).

10 9 8 7 6 5 4 3 2 1

DEDICATION

To My Parents

Barbara and Victor Hinds

and

Akeem

My "Bumble Bee"

Contents

List of Tables

Preface

This study was prompted by my concern that the current literature does not adequately explore the nature of economic relations between Britain and its colonial territories between 1939 and 1958 and the impact of these relations on decolonization in the British empire. It focuses primarily on the connection between Britain's sterling and balance of payments policy, colonial economic policy and the British government's decision to transfer power to colonial peoples. This book examines the factors that underpinned the debate in British and colonial government circles over colonial economic policy during the war and the postwar reconstruction period in Britain. In particular, it explores the extent to which the requirements of Britain's sterling policy and the general demands of the British economy influenced Britain's colonial policy, especially its policy toward colonial development and welfare, the provisions for development finance and colonial independence.

I wish to express my sincere gratitude to those persons and institutions who made this book a reality. I am particularly grateful to Professor Barry Higman for his support, encouragement and the time he spent reading, rereading and commenting on my drafts. This book would not have been possible without his assistance.

I must also thank the University of the West Indies for financial assistance to conduct my research and prepare my manuscript for publication; Frank Cass Limited, publishers of the *Journal of Imperial and Commonwealth History*, for permission to reproduce two articles which I contributed to it; Dr. Brian Moore, for reading and commenting on my drafts; Dr. Veront Satchell, for assistance with interpreting my data; Professor Roy Augier, for comments, guidance and support; Ms. Noreen

Greenwood, for typing my tables; Pete Young, for helping me to understand the mysteries of the London money market; Cecille Maye-Hemmings for the mechanics of the book's production; and Dr. Satnarine Maharaj, for providing a place of refuge with beverages. Finally, I must thank my wife Norma and son Akeem for allowing me the freedom to write.

Introduction

This book uses primarily the records of the Colonial Office and the Treasury to examine British economic policies at home and in the colonies and their effect on decolonization. It focuses on the relationship between the strategies and mechanisms that Britain employed to maintain its economic stability, to preserve sterling's position in the international economy and to secure its return to free convertibility and colonial policy. After Britain left the Gold Standard in 1931 the Sterling Area[1] was established to facilitate protectionism in trade and commerce between Britain, its dependent territories and other countries that maintained the external value of their currencies in a fixed relationship to sterling. As a result of the impact of the preparations for World War II on the British economy, by 1939 sterling was no longer automatically convertible into other currencies. Its status as a global currency was safeguarded within a system of exchange controls and other restrictions, which applied especially to commercial transactions between the Sterling Area and the Dollar Area.[2] The demands of war on the British economy led to a reinforcement of these measures. The war itself disrupted the leading economic sectors in Britain and other European countries and exacerbated social, political and economic conditions in the British empire. In contrast, countries where there had been no combat at home emerged from the war with an expanded industrial capacity.

At the end of World War II there was a heavy demand for goods and services from countries in the Dollar Area, particularly the United States and Canada. Thus, there was a worldwide shortage of U.S. dollars and Britain had to maintain wartime controls over trade between the Dollar Area and the Sterling Area in order to protect sterling and British gold and dollar reserves. Britain's postwar economic recovery was affected by its commitment first to the Americans, and after 1948 to members of the Organization for European Economic Co-operation (O.E.E.C.), to liberalize its trade practices and restore sterling to international convertibility. The first attempt to make sterling freely convertible in July 1947 was abandoned after six weeks because it destabilized the British economy. The stability of the British economy was also affected by economic crises between 1949 and 1952. Thereafter, there was a gradual improvement in Britain's economic performance. Thus, toward the end of the 1950s the British government was able to honor its commitments to liberalize trade with Western Europe and in 1958 sterling was restored to international convertibility. During the postwar era colonial economic policy was further integrated into Britain's sterling policy and its strategy for economic recovery. Britain also assumed that it could contain the forces demanding political reform, despite the political concessions it was obliged to make in India, Burma and Sri Lanka. However, large-scale civil disturbances throughout the empire in 1948 led to significant changes in Britain's policy toward decolonization.

This book discusses the main factors that determined the nature of economic and political relations between Britain and its colonies between 1939 and 1958. These include: Britain's sterling policy and the state of the British economy; the pressure that was applied by the United States and Western European countries for multilateralism in Britain's trade and commercial policy; the movement toward independence in colonial territories; and the cost of financing colonial development and welfare in the British empire. This study is divided into seven chapters. The first concentrates on the period 1939–1945. It begins with an overview of the decline in Britain's dominance of world trade and the concomitant transformation in the international status of sterling. It addresses the repercussions of British restrictions on the conversion of sterling into dollars on Anglo-American relations and the consequences for imperial policy. It also looks at the effects of the growth of the sterling balances accumulated by colonial territories and the measures used by Britain to commandeer colonial resources and integrate fiscal and monetary policy in the colonies into a broader economic strategy geared to protect sterling and stabilize British balance of payments. The ensuing changes in Britain's economic relations with its colonies are examined against the background of the politicizing of the provisions for colonial development finance following the widespread unrest in the British empire in the 1930s.

Chapter Two considers the period between 1945 and 1949. The disruptions caused by World War II, in Britain as well as its colonies, made it necessary for British governments to introduce measures and programs to reconstruct their economies, to promote economic development and to alleviate the social conditions inhibiting growth. During World War II there was a significant reduction, and in some instances a total cessation, in the production of goods and services in Britain and Europe. In the postwar reconstruction era most of the capital goods and other supplies needed by Britain and European countries were available in the Dollar Area. The large demand for goods and services from the Dollar Area made it difficult for Britain to countenance trade liberalization. However, the independent members of the Sterling Area wanted their reconstruction and development needs to take priority over those of Britain, and therefore were unwilling to support the British government in its attempt to extend into the postwar era the wartime restrictions regulating expenditure by members of the Sterling Area in the Dollar Area. These factors combined to make it difficult for Britain to honor its commitment to the United States on sterling convertibility, and played a major part in the crisis that developed in the British economy in 1947. In 1948 the first in a series of accords to facilitate multilateralism in commercial and monetary transactions in Western Europe was implemented. The British government also initiated steps for the constitutional changes that led to independence in Britain's most important dollar-earning colonies, the Gold Coast, Nigeria and Malaya. This chapter analyzes the extent to which the constraints on the British economy, the collapse of sterling convertibility in 1947 and constitutional reform in the British empire determined colonial economic policy.

The period between the devaluation of the pound sterling in 1949 and the crisis in the British economy in 1952 is the subject of chapter three. The creation of the European Payments Union in 1950 made progress towards multilateralism in European trade possible. However, the outbreak of war in Korea and the seizure of the Abadan oilfields by Iran created problems for the British economy. By 1950 many colonies had established organizations to facilitate economic diversification through industrialization, and some had made important strides toward industrial expansion. The postwar growth in commodity prices together with the restrictions imposed on colonial expenditure in the Dollar Area resulted in significant increases in the size of the colonial sterling balances by 1951. The Gold Coast, Nigeria and Malaya, where constitutional change was gathering momentum, accounted for a significant proportion of the total balances, but the majority of the colonies were not able to maintain or increase their development expenditure without assistance from Britain or other external sources. This chapter looks at the effects of economic conditions in Britain, and developments in Western Europe and the colonies on British imperial policy.

The most critical years for the mobilization of colonial resources by the

British government were the period 1945–1951. Chapter Four examines in detail how the British government earned dollars by expanding colonial exports to the Dollar Area or saved dollars by increasing the colonial output of goods and services which would otherwise have been imported from the Dollar Area. Chapter Five examines the British government's policy toward financing colonial development between 1945 and 1951. The allocations for colonial development and welfare from the British Treasury were without exception inadequate, although Britain claimed that the economic development of its colonies was one of the most important preconditions for granting self-government and independence to colonial territories. Consequently, the amounts allocated were always a source of dispute between the Colonial Office and the Treasury. The British government's attempts to promote economic development by financing large-scale agricultural projects failed. In practice, colonies had difficulty in drawing on the funds allocated by the United Kingdom for colonial development and welfare or spending what they themselves had earned from their trade with the Dollar Area between the Colonial Office and the Treasury.

Between 1952 and 1958 the recovery in the British economy coincided with the advance to independence in the Gold Coast, Nigeria and the Federation of Malaya. Chapter Six examines the impact of the political developments in these colonies on Britain's colonial policy. The subject of Chapter Seven is the relation between the cost to Britain of underwriting economic development in the colonies and decolonization.

NOTES

1.   This was a trading bloc comprising the dominions (except Canada and, for a brief period, South Africa), Ireland, Iceland, the Sudan, Egypt, Iraq, Portugal and Britain. Members were bound by an informal agreement to endeavor to keep the external value of their currencies in a fixed relationship to the pound sterling, and they kept their external reserves largely in sterling balances which were held in London.

2.   The Dollar Area was an informal trading bloc in which market transactions were settled primarily, but not solely, in U.S. dollars and other scarce currencies such as Swiss and Belgian francs. The countries forming a part of this bloc included the United States, Canada, Argentina, Brazil, Switzerland and Belgium. To some extent the term Dollar Area was a misnomer, because it was a bloc in which other scarce currencies apart from the U.S. dollar were used in the settlement of commercial transactions.

1

Sterling and Imperial Policy, 1939–1945

THE PRE–WORLD WAR I ERA: A HISTORICAL OVERVIEW

The evolution of sterling as a major international currency dates back to the Napoleonic Wars of the late eighteenth and early nineteenth centuries. This conflict finished off Amsterdam as London's chief financial rival,[1] and helped in establishing the foundations for the domination of international finance by Britain, the only European country in the alliance against Napoleon to avoid conquest and serious monetary disruption. For the most part, Britain was also largely unaffected by the European revolutions of 1830 and 1848 and the continental wars of 1860, 1864 and 1870. The combined effects of these developments were to strengthen confidence in the stability of sterling as an international medium of exchange.[2]

In the nineteenth century the use of sterling internationally was enhanced by Britain's naval and technological supremacy. This enabled it to procure a large empire and protect its trade and investments in countries and territories spanning the globe.[3] Until at least the 1890s, therefore, Britain was the richest country in the world. For over a century before the outbreak of World War I, the pound was by far the most important international currency in circulation, and London, the most important financial center. During this period the convertibility of sterling was unquestioned and Britain was the world's premier creditor-nation and the greatest exporter of new capital. By 1914 it accounted for 43 percent of the £9,500 million invested internationally. This was 10 percent more than the £3,100 invested by its main rivals, France and Germany.[4] In addition, "the largest proportion of official reserves apart from gold was held in sterling."[5]

However, at the commencement of World War I in 1914, it was becoming increasingly evident that Britain was losing its competitiveness in international trade. Its share of the world market was on par with Germany, marginally more than that of the United States, and the potential for competition from France was increasing rapidly. Alford argues "the balance of evidence points strongly to Britain's weakening performance in world trade stemming from growing weaknesses in industry at home."[6] Other scholars contend that because of its international pre-eminence foreign holdings of sterling grew, and thus British industry had to export less to buy imports than if sterling had not been a reserve currency. Further, the United Kingdom was not forced to adjust prices or its industrial structure to maintain an equilibrium in its balance of payments.[7] By the end of World War I in 1918 Britain's economic position was undermined even further, and sterling's status within international trade and financial circles had also declined steadily.

During the war Britain and the Allied forces depended heavily on the United States for financial assistance and supplies of vital war materials. The deficits incurred by the British in acquiring foodstuffs, raw materials and munitions were financed by selling off American assets and borrowing from the United States and the British dominions to a net amount of £1,290 million.[8] By the cessation of hostilities, the floating of loans and the liquidation of assets by Britain and the Allied countries transformed the United States from a net debtor to a large-scale creditor.[9] This development had major implications for the position of sterling in the international economy. As Cain and Hopkins put it, "the time-honoured financial relationship between Britain and the United States had been turned upside down . . . Britain was now a permanent debtor thus making it impossible for London alone to continue as the principal effective financial center of the world."[10] This transformation meant that internationally sterling no longer commanded the level of confidence that it did in the prewar years.

World War I highlighted the significant degree to which Britain was reliant upon the resources of the colonial empire. It also bolstered Britain's view of itself as an industrialized nation, in a dependent relationship with colonies that produced primary products for the British market. This philosophy was evident in the early 1920s in the British government's contention that with imperial assistance, colonial resources could play a useful role in resolving the industrial dislocation and high levels of unemployment which existed in Britain at this time. These sentiments were epitomized by Winston Churchill, the colonial secretary, who stated that with generous imperial government assistance:

a large amount of work would be provided in this country [Britain] without delay, for it would, of course be a condition of imperial assistance that any plant or materials required should be ordered in this country. The works would benefit the colony, develop markets for British goods, and enhance the purchasing power of the inhabitants in the colonies, with future benefits to British trade.[11]

This view of colonial and metropolitan economic relations persisted throughout the 1920s and was evident in the Colonial Development Act which was passed in 1929. The latter was intended to reduce unemployment levels in Britain, by developing the resources of the empire. By the end of the 1920s, therefore, the philosophy that had guided Britain's economic relations with its colonies after World War I was legitimized as government policy.

STERLING AND THE GOLD STANDARD, 1919–1931

The Gold Standard was the mechanism of international finance which contemporaries judged to be a fundamental part of natural economic law.[12] It was the means through which both the international exchange rate and a country's unit of currency were valued. According to the rules of the standard there had to be free movement of gold, and a country's domestic money supply had to vary in direct relation to its gold reserve. A balance of payments deficit would cause an outflow of gold, this in turn would reduce the money base and the domestic money supply and cause prices to fall and interest rates to rise, and the economy would become more competitive internationally. In the case of a trade surplus the opposite occurred.[13] Although the British government recognized the importance of restoring order to the international financial system in the postwar period, at the end of World War I its economic predicament was such that it could not return to the prewar sterling exchange rate or abide by the rules of the Gold Standard. Therefore, in March 1919 it decided to leave the gold standard and allow the pound sterling to float. The result was that the value of the pound fell rapidly from the official wartime sterling dollar/exchange rate of US\$4.76 to US\$3.40 in February 1920. Between the end of 1922 and 1925 it fluctuated around US\$4.50.[14] Together with the disruption to international finance arising from postwar debts and reparations, the abandonment of the Gold Standard further weakened the international position of sterling. Thus, in the early post-World War I years the pound did not always provide investors with the level of confidence required for international currencies.

The reestablishment of a fully functioning international economic system was one of Britain's principal economic objectives at the end of World War I. This was particularly important because Britain was dependent on international transactions for about one-third of its national income.[15] It was also still the center of a large imperial trading network which needed a reliable exchange rate. In March 1925 Britain returned to the Gold Standard at pre-World War I parity of US$4.86 = £1.00. According to Skidelsky, the choice of prewar parity reflected the special interest of the City of London. To devalue would have been to write down Britain's sterling assets and suggest to foreigners that London was not a good place to hold theirs.[16] The government also eschewed devaluation because it wanted to deter future governments from choosing it as an alternative to balancing their accounts. The British government justified its return to the Gold Standard on the grounds that this would force it to live within its means, establish general international monetary order and promote trade liberalization for its languishing industries.[17] Although it recognized that British industry may have been hurt by the high interest rates, and the revaluation necessary to attract investors in sterling, the British government believed that the benefits of restoration at prewar parity outweighed the costs.

Britain's expectations did not materialize. At prewar parity the pound was overvalued, while the currencies that posed the most serious challenge to sterling, the dollar and the franc, were undervalued, the former slightly, the latter excessively.[18] Britain's other major international competitor, Germany, had also returned the German mark to the Gold Standard at a devalued rate. With New York and Paris as alternative financial centers where funds could be lodged or trade financed, Britain was forced to keep interest rates high to maintain London's status as an international financial center. The result was high levels of unemployment, economic growth below the world average and sluggish exports.[19] Between 1925 and 1929 Britain's trade declined both in proportion to world trade and in absolute terms, and its balance of payments surpluses did likewise. These difficulties were made worse by the Great Depression of 1929 and the slump in commodity prices and the exchange crises that followed. Between 1929 and 1931 production in Britain fell and unemployment increased from 10.4 percent to 16.1 percent of the labor force.[20]

The depression forced creditor countries in Europe to cease lending and demand repayment of loans. Debtor countries, on the other hand, were compelled to pursue deflationary policies and/or repudiate their international obligations, which, being denominated in gold, had become vastly burdensome by 1930–1931[21]. By the summer of 1931 many countries abandoned the Gold Standard and devalued their currencies. In addition, to protect their economies from the external influences, they employed a wide range of protective restrictions "including tariffs, import quotas, exchange controls and special devices to iron out fluctuations in the exchanges."[22] These measures undermined any hope for a multilateral approach to stabilizing the international economy. Britain therefore abandoned the Gold Standard and devalued the pound sterling in September 1931. By the end of 1932 more than half of the countries of the world were no longer on the Gold Standard, and when the United States left the Gold Standard in 1933, "only a handful of countries— France, Switzerland, the Netherlands, Belgium, Italy and Poland— continued to adhere to it."[23]

The abandonment of the Gold Standard and devaluation of the pound sterling were followed by a concerted shift toward protectionism in Britain's trade and commercial policy. This move was not only a reflection of the failure of international efforts to reconstruct a monetary system based upon the free convertibility of national currencies into gold at a fixed rate of exchange, but also a manifestation of sterling's decline as a major international currency.[24] Protectionism in trade and commercial policy in Britain was initiated with the Tariff Act of 1931 which allowed for ad valorem duties of up to 100 percent, and the Import Duties Act of March 1932. This imposed a 10 percent levy on imports, special taxes and exemptions on selected imports and retaliatory duties. Later at the Ottawa Conference of member states of the British Common-wealth in the summer of 1932, a system of imperial preferences was created. Under this system all goods from the empire were guaranteed free entry into the British market, and extra duties were imposed on non-empire goods, which were perceived as competing with imperial goods.[25] With regard to the colonies, the measures adopted at the Ottawa Conference were clearly an elaboration of the thinking that underpinned the Colonial Development Act of 1929.[26] The reliance on colonial resources to preserve sterling's role as an international currency and correct trade imbalances in the United Kingdom was now established as an integral part of Britain's economic policy. However, the potential benefits to the colonial empire of enhanced economic relations with the metropole were reduced significantly because less than 20 percent of colonial primary products was dependent on imperial preferences for survival and prosperity. Moreover, because of international treaty obligations, the biggest producers of colonial primary products in Britain's West African and Far Eastern colonies were hardly affected at all by the Ottawa Agreement.[27]

FROM DEVALUATION TO WAR: 1931-1939

Before the devaluation in September 1931, sterling was used to back local currencies in Britain's colonial dependencies, its dominions (except Canada) and various non-empire countries such as Argentina, Iraq, Iran, Japan, Thailand, Ireland and Portugal.[28] Because of their trading links and banking connections with Britain, most of these countries used the pound sterling for all their international monetary transactions.[29] After

Britain left the Gold Standard, sterling "was used instead of gold as the monetary standard on which the international value of various currencies was based."[30] On the other hand, the pound was devalued against the U.S. dollar and other international currencies and the British government was determined to maintain it as a stable currency. The latter was critical to Britain's international status and the security of its invisible earnings. The British government also wanted to avoid the wage-price spiral and runaway inflation which would have accompanied a continuous depreciation in the value of sterling.[31] The defense of sterling was therefore the centerpiece of Britain's economic policy.

When Britain left the Gold Standard its dependencies, the British dominions (except Canada and, for a brief period, South Africa), Ireland, Iceland, the Sudan, Egypt, Iraq and Portugal followed suit. Together with Britain these countries formed the "sterling bloc" or the Sterling Area.[32] For Britain and its dependencies the Sterling Area was a mechanism through which they could preserve their access to overseas markets and sources of supplies, and to profitable investment outlets for surplus domestic savings. The British dominions and the non-empire countries joined the Sterling Area principally because they were heavily dependent on the British market and/or did most of their trade in sterling. The creation of the "sterling bloc" therefore enabled them to "safeguard their competitive position in the British market [and] maintain the local currency value of their external assets."[33] The dominions also believed in the stated objectives and policies of the Sterling Area, "particularly the raising of commodity prices from the uneconomic levels to which they had sunk because of the depression."[34] Overall because of the economic uncertainty prevailing at this time, "the system of ad hoc sterling arrangements offered its adherents the continuing benefits of substantial exchange stability and reasonably free trade and capital movements."[35] By 1933 there were three monetary blocs in the world economy: the Sterling Area, centered on the United Kingdom; the Dollar Area, centered on the United States; and a rump of countries that still adhered to the Gold Standard (these included countries such as France, Italy, Switzerland, Belgium, the Netherlands and Poland). The birth of the "sterling bloc" enhanced the need for Britain to protect sterling. As the center of the sterling system Britain was obliged to maintain a stable currency in order to retain the confidence of the members of the Sterling Area in the sterling exchange system.[36]

In the months immediately before the commencement of the war in September 1939, Britain's defense preparations together with the threat of impending conflict imposed severe strains on the British economy. To make matters worse, sterling was devalued, and in the climate of instability which ensued many non Commonwealth countries severed their links with sterling. A general flight of capital from Europe to the United States followed as investors and nations sought a safe haven to store their cash reserves. Consequently, the international demand for U.S. dollars expanded vastly.[37] In order to protect the Sterling Area and its own reserves of gold and dollars, and by extension the value of the pound sterling, the British government in consultation with the governments of member states of the Sterling Area worked out a system of exchange restrictions. Moreover, the central banks of independent members of the Sterling Area "which were to have formulated and executed an autonomous policy, had now become in large measure the instruments of a common exchange centered in London."[38] Therefore, Britain had complete control over transactions between members of the Sterling Area and the rest of the world, while simultaneously allowing the free transfer of sterling within the Sterling Area. Britain's colonial dependencies did not escape unscathed. As members of the Sterling Area they were subjected to the general exchange guidelines that governed relations with nonsterling countries. One of the principal features of these regulations was the emphasis placed on limiting colonial govern-ment expenditure in the Dollar Area. Nevertheless, even though they were required to control their spending, the nature of the controls to be imposed on imports from the Dollar Area was left up to the discretion of the colonial governments.[39]

Discrimination against the Dollar Area by members of the Sterling Area was effected through the creation of a "dollar pool." Participants in this pool agreed to sell their surplus gold and dollar reserves to the Bank of England for sterling and to exercise restraint in converting sterling into dollars. They also agreed to import goods from the Dollar Area only when these goods were not available within the Sterling Area. In addition, drawings from the dollar pool were to be made available in accordance with the "need of individual countries, and not according to the gold and dollar contributions of the country concerned."[40] The exigencies of war and international trade therefore led to a gradual strengthening of imperial control over both the independent and dependent members of the Sterling Area. Consequently, at the start of hostilities, the Sterling Area was formally transformed into a bloc of states, organized by Britain, to protect the value of the pound sterling by maintaining common exchange controls against the rest of the world. In the process colonial fiscal and monetary policy became aligned to the United Kingdom's sterling policy and the colonies were vulnerable to the vicissitudes in the fortunes of the British economy and, inevitably, those of the pound sterling.

COLONIAL POLICY AND THE ANGLO-AMERICAN STRUGGLES: 1939–1945

Colonial economic policy became further entwined in the United Kingdom's strategy to defend sterling as a result of settlements reached following Anglo-American negotiations during the war. One of the main problems facing the international trading community at this juncture was the conversion of sterling into gold or dollars. This was restricted by the discriminatory exchange controls that guided the operations of the "dollar pool." The effect of these controls was a very contentious issue in the Anglo-American negotiations that occurred during the war.[41] The American government's main complaint was that the "dollar pool" was inimical to American business in the Sterling Area market. As a result, between 1939 and 1945 the United States was determined to undermine Britain's protectionist policies.

The United States' continuing endeavor to alter imperial economic policy was evident in the dispute over the interpretation of the charter that was signed after the Anglo-American Atlantic Conference in August 1941. American spokesmen claimed "the Atlantic Charter declaration meant that every nation has a right to expect that its legitimate trade will not be diverted and throttled away by lower tariffs, preferences, discrimination or narrow bilateral trade practices."[42] Determined to maintain their policy, the British pointed to the caveat in Clause IV of the declaration "with due respect to their existing obligations."[43] Prime Minister Churchill explained later that these words were inserted for the express purpose of retaining in the House of Commons and in the dominion parliaments the greatest possible rights and principles over the question of imperial preferences.[44] Sumner Welles, the United States under secretary, captured the general sense of frustration felt by American negotiators with his comment that "the 'saving clause' deprived the article concerned of virtually all significance and provided for the retention of the system."[45] Although Britain successfully repulsed this attack on its imperial preferences policy, its increasing dependence on the United States militated against forthright public declarations of British opposition to multilateralism.

When Britain and the United States met to negotiate the Mutual Aid Agreement in February 1942, their main purpose was to establish the guidelines governing American supplies to Britain under the Lend-Lease Act which was passed in the United States in March 1941. Amery contends that while the preamble to the agreement "was a broad and generous acceptance of the principle that we were engaged all out in a common venture for our common civilization . . . it is not true that it took the dollar sign out of co-operation."[46] There is general consensus among scholars that Article VII of the Mutual Aid Agreement encapsulated American attempts to force Britain to commit itself to more liberal trade and monetary practices.[47] Although this article stated that the terms and conditions of Lend-Lease should not burden commerce between the United States and Britain, it called for action to be taken toward the "elimination of all forms of discriminatory treatment in international commerce, and to the reduction of tariffs and other trade barriers."[48] Both countries also agreed to early discussions about the attainment of these objectives. The American fixation with the abolition of discriminatory trade practices in international trade was a continuation of an objective the United States had pursued with Britain without success for much of the 1930s.

When the Mutual Aid Agreement was being negotiated with the British, the Americans were in a good position to extract concessions which had thus far eluded them. Britain's external debt burden had increased greatly, because France had fallen and it had taken over the financing of French orders for military supplies from the United States. Its gold and dollar reserves had fallen from £605 million at the beginning of 1940 to £74 million at the end of 1940 and by the time the Mutual Aid Agreement was signed, they were virtually exhausted.[49] Britain's heavy dependence on imports from the United States during the war was likely to continue at least into the early period of postwar reconstruction. Dollars were in short supply, and it was extremely difficult for Britain to pay for purchases from the United States, because the diversion of manpower to wartime industries had led to a drastic reduction in exports and an increase in Britain's balance of payments deficit.[50] These problems cast a shadow of gloom over Britain's trade prospects in the early postwar era. Their existence meant that Britain could not afford to abandon any device that might have enabled it to regain lost ground or expand its share of world trade. Thus, while the Americans clearly held the upper hand in the negotiations, the British were determined to avoid concessions that they saw as detrimental to their economic well-being.

Three-quarters of Churchill's cabinet was opposed any reference to trade preferences in the Mutual Aid Agreement. "To them it seemed to make the dismantling of the Commonwealth the price of Lend-Lease."[51] In addition these cabinet members believed "it would clearly be quite wrong to suppose she [Britain] retained as great a freedom to determine her own economic policy as she would have if the article had not been signed."[52] According to Amery the agreement was eventually signed only after Churchill secured, in private correspondence, an assurance from U.S. President Roosevelt "that we [the British] were no more committed to the abolition of imperial preferences than the Americans were committed to the abolition of their high protective tariffs."[53]

Anglo-American financial negotiations continued in Washington in 1943. In addition to resolving the monetary problems caused by the disruptions in international trade, these deliberations were also intended to establish a new international economic order. The discussions culminated in "The Joint Statement of Experts on the Establishment of an International Monetary Fund (I.M.F.)" which was publicized in April 1944. The provisions of this document "were embodied, with only minor changes in the Articles of Agreement of the I.M.F."[54] which were adopted at Bretton Woods in July 1944. In the House of Lords debate on 23 May 1944 Lord Keynes, an adviser to the British Treasury, alluded to what he perceived as the five advantages of the monetary proposals that were eventually adopted at Bretton Woods. First, Britain was entitled to retain its system of Imperial Preferences and other restrictions for an unspecified postwar transitional period. Second, the free convertibility of the pound sterling would be established when the British economy had recovered sufficiently. Third, a stock of monetary reserves would be used to restore equilibrium in world trade. Fourth, a proper share of the responsibility for maintaining equilibrium in the balance of payments was placed on the creditor countries. Fifth, the plan set up an international institution with substantial rights and duties to preserve orderly arrangements in matters such as exchange rates.[55]

In terms of imperial economic policy, the wartime Anglo-American financial negotiations and agreements had two important consequences. First of all, by the end of World War II Britain's need to retain imperial preferences for an unspecified period in the postwar era was no longer in dispute. As a result, the defense of sterling continued to be a feature of Britain's postwar imperial economic policy. Second, Britain had committed itself to the unrestricted conversion of the pound sterling into the leading international currencies. This move was always fraught with danger because of the devastating effect of World War II on Britain's balance of payments. Mobilization for war had disrupted production for export in Britain so severely that by 1944 export levels had fallen to one-third of the level of 1938. Moreover, Britain lost a quarter of its national wealth which stood at £30,000 million before the war and a considerable portion of her merchant shipping.[56] When these facts are placed alongside external disinvestment, the repatriation of loans to overseas debtors, and, of course, the huge sterling debts, the British economy was clearly in a very unhealthy state. In these circumstances, therefore, in the postwar era Britain could not afford to alter the policies that it employed during the war to channel colonial resources into the defense of sterling.

In September 1945 following the U.S. sudden abrogation of the Lend-Lease Agreement, the first formal session on Anglo-American loan negotiations was held in Washington. In terms of colonial economic policy, these negotiations are significant because of their profound impact on the restoration of sterling to full international convertibility. At the start of loan negotiations the optimism of Lord Keynes, Britain's chief negotiator, evaporated when it was evident that the British objective of grants-in-aid was unattainable. Harrod claims that the loss of life during the war, uncertainty about the future, the danger of inflation, and labor disputes eroded America's predilection to become too deeply involved in the financial problems of its allies.[57] After three months of negotiations an agreement was finally signed in December 1945. From the provisions of this agreement it is clear that "the American government carried out its plan to exact a British pledge of co-operation in multilateral projects as a condition for a generous Lend-Lease settlement."[58] To a large extent the conditions "attached to the Loan consisted of nothing more than the reaffirmation and application of the policy to which Britain had pledged itself by the signature of Article VII of the Mutual Aid Agreement."[59]

The most significant diversion from the latter agreement was the proviso that the pound sterling was to be freely convertible from 12 July 1947. This proviso meant that the "dollar pool," which was a major source of discrimination against American goods, had to be dissolved; and with it, Britain's only guarantee of ensuring economy in the use of scarce currencies and the control of the Sterling Area and colonial economies. Therefore, as a result of the Loan Agreement of 1945, Britain entered the postwar era with a commitment to abolish a vital element in the system of protection that had developed within the Sterling Area during the war. Britain's efforts to honor this commitment had a decisive impact on postwar colonial economic policy, especially the colonial role in Britain's strategy for postwar economic recovery and the restoration of sterling to full international convertibility.

THE DISPOSAL OF THE ACCUMULATED STERLING BALANCES, 1939–1945

The Anglo-American agreement on sterling convertibility was not the only factor that helped to determine the character of metropolitan/ colonial economic relations in the postwar period. The growth of accumulated sterling balances was also very important. During World War II Britain operated a system of deferred payments to pay troops, obtain vitally needed supplies, establish military installations and construct roads, railways, harbors and airfields.[60] Expenses were charged to accounts held by the creditors in London. By the end of 1945 there was a massive accumulation of sterling balances in these accounts. Overall, externally held sterling balances totaled approximately £3,688 million. About £2,605 million was held by creditors within the Sterling Area, the largest being India, to whom about £1,177 million was due.[61]

These balances represented a claim on the United Kingdom's resources itself, because they were a part of its total sterling liabilities. Thus, their disposal was a conundrum for Britain, in terms of both its domestic and foreign policy in the postwar period. While the members of the Sterling Area were in dire need of their balances, the unregulated release of sterling was potentially dangerous. The danger was underscored by the general lack of confidence in the pound sterling, the buoyancy of the American economy and the inability of British production to expand quickly enough, to absorb the inevitable escalation in demand which such a move would have produced. Because of the threat they posed to the stability of the U.K. economy and the value of sterling, therefore, in 1945 the overall size of its accumulated sterling balances was a matter of great anxiety to the British government.

The contingencies of war had made it impossible for the British government to grant its colonies unrestricted access to their sterling reserves. Thus, it allowed them to accumulate sterling assets (Table 1.1).

Table 1.1
The Sterling Assets of the U.K. Colonies, 1941–1945

End of Year	Colonial Sterling Assets (£M)
1941	205
1942	258
1943	326
1944	326
1945	454

Source: P.R.O. T 236/3562. A. M. Kamark, "The Sterling Balances," p. 5. This paper was prepared for the Bank of England in 1954.

By 1945 Britain's colonial dependencies were its second largest sterling creditors, with an accumulated sterling balance of £454 million.[62] They were composed of a variety of monetary reserves (stocks, bonds, securities and cash) and sums held on deposit in the United Kingdom on behalf of the colonies. The principal components of the colonial sterling balances were Colonial Government Funds, Currency Funds, Marketing Board Reserves and the reserves of commercial banks that were operating in the colonies but not investing locally.[63] These were theoretically assets that could have been withdrawn by the colonies without restrictions.[64] However, because of the statutory regulations governing budgetary and currency policy in the colonies, in reality only a portion of these funds was immediately available to colonial governments. In the case of the

Government Funds, for example, a percentage of the annual budgetary expenditure was retained as a reserve against budget deficits in times of falling trade. The Currency Fund was inaccessible because currency in circulation in the colonies had to be backed by sterling 100 percent. The most accessible funds were the Marketing Board reserves. It was therefore the growth in the size of individual funds with balances immediately available to colonial governments, which were a potential danger to Britain's economic stability. However, as long as colonial rule was maintained a simultaneous withdrawal of these balances by individual colonies was extremely unlikely.

Nevertheless, some government officials thought it was prudent to consider ways in which the funds or reserves that comprised the balances could be utilized. As early as June 1941 Lord Moyne, the colonial secretary, recognized that the policies pursued by the imperial government would have led to an increase in the surpluses available to some governments and "the question will then inevitably arise of what is to be done with such surpluses."[65] After considering all the options Moyne concluded:

It seems to me definitely preferable that the colonial governments, if they are able to do so, should accumulate surplus balances now which they can use for purposes of reconstruction and development after the war, without having recourse to assistance under the Colonial Development and Welfare Act, rather than that such balances should be surrendered now and applications for assistance made at a later date. . . . Where, however, it is thought preferable to accumulate reserves for postwar needs I would suggest that it would be reasonable to take the view that the holding of such reserves should not be a source of profit to the government concerned. . . . In the present conditions, I suggest that reserves accumulated during the war might very well be lent to Her Majesty's Government, free of interest, on condition that repayment will be made at the end of the war, i.e., on substantially the same terms as interest-free loans are accepted from private individuals. Such a policy would have the advantage of placing the reserves at the disposal of His Majesty's Government, without charge, during the period in which they are required, while permitting the Dependencies to resume the use of them when they are required for post-war purposes.[66]

As far as Moyne was concerned, therefore, the underlying principle governing the accumulation of colonial sterling balances was that they be used for postwar colonial development finance. Moyne's ideas were never developed into policy. Moreover, it is clear that he did not anticipate the dismal economic conditions that Britain faced in the postwar years.

The feasibility of using a portion of the colonial sterling balances to finance colonial development was also considered by government officials in May 1943.[67] This led Sydney Caine, the Colonial Office financial adviser, to solicit Lord Keynes' view on the imperial government's policy at this time, that is, of investing the increments to the colonial currency fund in London, instead of spending it on current expenses or on capital development in the colonies.[68] Caine pointed to some of the benefits that may have accrued to the government if it adopted an alternative strategy and allowed the colonial governments to spend a portion of their reserves on colonial development projects. He contended that this "would have precisely the same effect on the government's finances as if it raised a loan, i.e. the government would be drawing funds from the London market, and its net income would be lower by the interest on those funds."[69] He juxtaposed this with the government's policy of allowing colonial governments to raise loans for colonial development on the London market, while simultaneously investing funds for future income in London, through their currency accounts.[70] "At first sight," he argued, "it looks as if it might be better to simplify the business by using the currency funds directly for the kind of expenditure which might otherwise be financed from loans."[71]

Caine felt that it may be possible to make some kind of special arrangement with the currency authorities which would facilitate the short-term issue of Treasury bills, and thus allow colonial governments to raise loans locally. Nevertheless, he did not see any "great advantage in a change in the current practice,"[72] and was opposed to radical reforms of the existing system, because to him, the colonies were an integral part of a much wider British financial system. Caine's analysis was endorsed by Keynes.[73] Keynes noted that the existing practice for dealing with the colonial currency reserve funds "was designed, probably on purpose, to promote a high degree of conservatism in development,"[74] because a colony would have been more reluctant to spend money on development if it felt that it had to borrow rather than use its own funds. Moreover, the policy of holding a 100 percent currency reserve, when the reserve was increasing, "in a form equivalent to gold (i.e. external liquid assets) instead of having a proportionate fiduciary issue,"[75] led to an underestimation of the financial strength of the colony. Keynes thought that there were alternatives to what he termed "the excessive conservatism of the present system", but he did not elaborate.

This exchange between Caine and Keynes set the stage for an ongoing debate on imperial policy toward the management of the colonial sterling balances which continued for most of the period under review. The main contributors to this debate were officials from the Treasury, the Colonial Office and the Bank of England. Discussions focused on what many officials believed was, ultimately, the principal contradiction in the imperial government's strategy relative to the colonial sterling balances. Colonial development was being financed out of scarce U.K. funds, while the colonies went on accumulating sterling balances in the metropole. Between 1943 and 1945 the need for an alternative to the imperial government's policy of simply allowing colonial balances to accumulate in London was supported by most Treasury officials. Notable among these was Ernest Rowe-Dutton, the principal assistant secretary. He felt that a fiduciary issue was needed to correct the conservatism that prevailed in the existing arrangement.[76] On the other hand, officials such as N. E. Young, assistant secretary, opposed the suggestion on the grounds that there would have been practical difficulties in resisting further encroachments once the principle of 100 percent cover for colonial currencies was breached. Moreover, Young did not believe that the colonies were equipped to deal with the step being proposed.[77] The extent to which the state of the imperial economy influenced the debate within government circles at this time remains problematical. However, the importance of this factor cannot be ruled out. To begin with, British experts were worried about the implications of Britain's sterling debtor status since 1942.[78] In addition, it seems highly likely that concerns for the knock-on effects on the British economy, not least in light of the explosive growth in sterling liabilities after 1942–1943, increased official sensitivity to the potential problem posed by the size of the rest of the other colonial balances.

The most strident criticism of the imperial government's policy toward the colonial sterling balances during the war years came from the Colonial Office.[79] It claimed that the policy governing colonial currency funds was incapable of adjustments to deal with local conditions. The Colonial Office pointed out that local credit policy followed that of the United Kingdom whose interests were not always the same as those of the primary producing colonies. Further, the practice of holding a minimum sterling balance of 100 percent entailed an export of capital which should have been available for local development.[80] The position of the Colonial Office was therefore that the British government's policy was not in the best interest of the colonies.

The Bank of England rejected the Colonial Office's contentions on the question of the 100 percent colonial currency cover as misconceived. It claimed that there was no export of sterling involved in holding a 100 percent reserve in sterling.[81] However, the Bank conceded that "there may be a case for the creation of a fiduciary issue."[82] It added that the sterling reserves that would have been released "could be put at the disposal of local governments and could be used for capital development, for the repayment of sterling debt, or simply held as a reserve for unforeseen contingencies—but held at the local government's discretion and not in the form of Currency Board funds."[83] However, the Bank warned that there were "dangers that pressure may be applied for a greater margin of fiduciary issue than we should think wise."[84] In addition, it felt since money was being made available from various sources for colonial development the time was not right to raise the fiduciary issue.[85]

In 1945, the Bank of England, the Colonial Office and Treasury all supported the need for the introduction of measures that would have allowed the colonies to use a portion of their accumulated colonial sterling balances for development purposes. However, most of them had reservations about the wisdom of the immediate implementation of changes in policy. These were couched, for the most part, within the context of the uncertainties that were likely to confront the colonies in the postwar period. They should also be seen in the general framework of developments in the metropolitan economy at this time. This was a period in which it was realized that the United Kingdom's accumulated sterling liabilities were potentially the most intractable claimants on exports and on its gold and dollar reserves.[86] The United Kingdom's sterling liabilities were acknowledged as a great potential constraint on its adoption of new international arrangements, especially those involving its relations with the United States.[87] These circumstances were not conducive to action on the colonial sterling balances which would have involved increasing spending power in the colonies.

The debate over the policy which the imperial government should adopt toward the colonial sterling balances represented only one aspect of the discussions within British government circles at this time. Toward the end of the war the Americans were adamant in their resolve to make Britain reduce the accumulated sterling balances, because to them it was an obstacle to their postwar economic policies. Their position was clarified by F. M. Vinson, director of War Mobilization and Reconversion, in April 1945. Vinson stated:

Our postwar objective of a high level of prosperity and full employment will necessitate exports of at least 10,000,000 dollars. It will be difficult to maintain markets for such a volume of trade if the nations of this world revert to restrictive trade practices. The current pent up foreign demand for consumer durable goods alone has been estimated at approximately 2,500,000,000 dollars and will become effective as soon as export controls are relaxed making it possible for these countries to utilize their accumulated dollar balances.[88]

Considering the needs of its creditors, that of its own economy and the intentions of the Americans, the release of accumulated balances was indeed an enigma for the British government.

Harrod's solution to this dilemma "was to take the major part of the balances right out of the banking system,"[89] leaving working balances in the names of the various creditors. He argued that while "there is no doubt the removal of these balances would have given a great shock to the creditors . . . they were living in a dream world if they supposed that £3,700 million could be immediately encashed in a few years in either gold or goods."[90] The latter was seen as a permanent solution to the problem. Sterling thereafter would have been rendered a healthy desired currency.[91] Harrod claims that Lord Keynes was of the opinion that the accumulated balances should not have been allowed to stand in the way of convertibility and "in the last resort it would have been better to handle our creditors drastically, as for instance by freezing the balances than to forgo convertibility."[92] While this may have been the case it is equally true that Keynes favored a solution that would have safeguarded Britain's financial credibility and acknowledged the contribution of its sterling creditors to the war. Keynes stated:

Having set up a pooling system when it suited us and having taken more than £2,000 million out of the pool, we cannot suddenly and forthwith freeze it when the current turns the other way. We have persuaded the other countries concerned to entrust us with virtually the whole of their accruing external reserves, and we cannot refuse to make at least part of these available in so far as they are required for immediate needs. . . . The continuance during the interim period of a modified sterling area system, revised to suit the new circumstances, would be very much the easiest and most honorable and least disturbing way of meeting an inescapable obligation.[93]

Despite this and other acknowledgments of the existing dilemma, the provisions of the Loan Agreement inevitably did not provide a clear solution. Under the terms of the agreement, Britain pledged to make an early settlement with the countries concerned by dividing the sterling balances into three categories: "those to be released at once; those to be released by installments over a period of years beginning in 1951"; and "balances to be adjusted as a contribution to the settlement of the war and post-war indebtedness."[94] The prolonged character of the debate on imperial policy toward the colonial sterling balances testified to the complexity and, at times, seemingly irreconcilable nature of the variables being considered. From the solution, it is clear that Britain attempted to appease all parties concerned. However, as was the case with its agreement to restore sterling to international convertibility, by agreeing to reduce the accumulated sterling balances, it had committed itself to dismantling another of the pillars that had protected the pound sterling during the war years.

STERLING AND COLONIAL DEVELOPMENT POLICY, 1940–1945

The desire to preserve the value of sterling had a significant impact on colonial development policy. Britain entered World War II with a commitment to resolve the socioeconomic problems in the empire. These were highlighted in the 1938 report of the West India Commission which investigated the riots in the West Indies in the late 1930s, and Lord Hailey's *African Survey*[95] which was also published in 1938. These publications exposed the alarming levels of poverty and underdevelopment that were prevalent in Britain's dependencies in Africa and the West Indies. However, it was generally believed in official circles that the situation was the same elsewhere in the British empire.

At the beginning of World War II inadequacies in the provisions for potable water, health care and sanitation agriculture were cited as the major contributory factors in the prevalence of tuberculosis, malaria, leprosy, yellow fever and the helminthic diseases in Africa. Malaria was so widespread that it was often credited with retarding the development of the native populations, and more than any other factor, with responsibility for the high rate of infant mortality. In Central and East Africa and the forested regions of West Africa, socioeconomic progress was stymied because sleeping sickness had rendered large areas unsuitable for livestock. To Hailey the financial provisions for health care were derisory considering the magnitude of the problem and the scope of the operations required to rectify it.[96] The social problems in Britain's African colonies were made worse by the inequity in the colonial distribution of development capital. In 1934, for example, territories rich in mineral resources such as the Rhodesias attracted £38.4 per capita in foreign investment, while British dependencies in East Africa received about £8.1 per capita and those in West Africa about £4.8 per capita. The imbalance in the allocation of development capital in the British territories was evident in the fact that in 1934 more money was spent on railway construction in the Rhodesias, Kenya, Uganda and the Sudan than in the Gold Coast and Nigeria.[97]

Social and economic conditions in the British West Indian territories were in some ways akin to those in Africa. At the onset of the Second World War agriculture was the principal economic activity, the supply of potable water was inadequate and diseases such as malaria and hookworm were common. In addition, provisions for housing were unsatisfactory and in most rural areas sanitation was often considered primitive. The scarcity of funds for medical work was one of the main reasons for the continuation of the unhealthy social conditions. The social problems existing in the British West Indies were aggravated by low wages and high unemployment.[98]

In an attempt to remedy the socioeconomic problems identified by Lord Hailey and the West India Commission, Britain passed the Colonial Development and Welfare Act in June 1940. It provided for the expenditure of a maximum of £5,000,000 per year on colonial development and welfare for a period of ten years. In its statement of policy governing this act "the [British] government insisted on planned development and called for proper machinery and adequate personnel both for planning and for carrying out plans."[99] It also urged colonial governments "to prepare development programmes for a period of years ahead as a condition for assistance under the Act."[100] The Colonial Development and Welfare Act of 1940 represented a major shift in the British government's attitude toward colonial development and welfare. In response to the growing criticism of its policies and the need to ensure colonial support for its war effort, Britain accepted responsibility for the social and economic development of its colonies. By so doing the foundation for the postwar economic relationship between the United Kingdom and its colonial territories was completed. It rested upon two major tenets. First, colonial territories were expected to contribute to the preservation of sterling as an international currency and the correction of Britain's trade imbalance with the Dollar Area and other sources of hard currency. Thus, the value of the colonies was tied to the nature of their contribution to the British economy. Second, the British government undertook to provide funds for colonial development and welfare.

The nature and impact of colonial development policy were inevitably influenced by events during the course of the war. As the war progressed Britain's predicament worsened. Thus, in September 1940 the colonial secretary, Lord Lloyd, established three conditions for the approval of development and welfare schemes. First, schemes had to be implemented without jeopardizing the war effort. Second, they had to be urgent enough to warrant funds from the United Kingdom, and finally, they could not involve expenditure outside the Sterling Area.[101] These guidelines had important implications for colonial development and welfare because the progress of development and welfare schemes was linked not only to the requirements for the war, but also to the defense of sterling. Because of the latter, the Dollar Area was to be avoided at all costs, and the burden for satisfying the capital and consumer needs of the colonies was placed upon the limited resources of the United Kingdom and the Sterling Area. The desire to conserve dollars not only constrained expenditure under the Colonial Development and Welfare Act, it also accentuated shortages in the colonial supply of capital and consumer goods, added to inflationary pressures and exacerbated the living conditions of colonial peoples.

The stipulations governing the release of colonial development funds were reviewed in a circular dispatch to the colonial governors by the new secretary of state, Lord Moyne, on 5 June 1941. According to Moyne the British government wanted to divert colonial resources to its war effort, but it did not want colonial development to be totally disrupted. Further,

Moyne acknowledged that the pressure on the United Kingdom and the empire's productive capacity was such that "goods supplied from sterling sources will ultimately have to be replaced from dollar sources."[102] However, the United Kingdom was only prepared to arrange for the supply of material from non-Sterling Area sources if the scheme was urgently needed and the material required formed only a relatively small part of the total costs. Ultimately, regardless of the source of colonial development finance, in initiating development and welfare schemes colonial authorities had to weigh the need to improve colonial living standards against the diversion of resources from the war effort. The bottom line was that schemes had to be urgent and important enough to justify the expenditure of funds by the United Kingdom.[103] There were a few exceptions to Moyne's general guidelines. Sympathetic consideration was given to requests for financial assistance for the preservation of resources (especially soil conservation); schemes that produced commodities or materials of special wartime value; and technical training for local personnel such as rural teachers, health workers and agricultural demonstrators.

Moyne's circular testifies to the difficulties involved in both financing colonial development and addressing the social and economic problems that were identified in British dependencies in the late 1930s during the war years.[104] Thus, it is hardly surprising, as Wicker shows, that between 1940 and 1943 expenditure under the Colonial Development and Welfare Act amounted to just under £1 million. It increased to £1.6 million in 1944 and reached £3 million in 1945.[105] The large disparity between the £5 million allocated annually and the actual expenditure indicated "that the 1940 Act was in retrospect little more than a premature statement of postwar aims and policy."[106] The shortfall in expenditure under the act led to "a cynical belief in many of the colonies and even within some parts of the Colonial Service, that the gesture was never meant to be more than a gesture."[107] To reestablish credibility in the British government's commit-ment to colonial development and welfare, therefore, in November 1944 Oliver Stanley, the colonial secretary, made a submission to cabinet requesting a substantial increase in funding to meet the ongoing increase in the needs for economic and social development in the colonies.[108]

In 1945 the need for coordination between the planning activities of the colonial governments and the Colonial Office was acknowledged with the appointment of an Adviser on Development at the Colonial Office, and the passage of a new Colonial Development and Welfare Act. This made provisions for funding amounting to £120 million over a ten-year period beginning in April 1946. It stipulated that no more than £17.5 million could be spent annually on development and welfare projects and £1 million on research. When the act was passed two alternative methods of allocating funds were considered. The first favored keeping the entire sum under the direct control of the secretary of state and disbursing it only in accordance with directives from Whitehall. The other called for the allocation of the major part of the £120 million to different colonial governments, leaving them to formulate programs for its use. In the end the second option was adopted, because Britain wanted to avoid accusations of exploitation and it was felt that overcentralization would lead to chaos.[109]

By 1940 the basis for postwar economic relations between Britain and its colonial territories was firmly established. However, during the war years it is not always possible to disentangle the policies initiated by the British government to facilitate the war from the ones geared primarily to the defense of sterling. Nevertheless, expenditure under the Colonial Development and Welfare Act of 1940 was partially influenced by the need to defend sterling and stabilize the British economy. Together with the problems created by the war, Britain's sterling policy made it impossible for colonial governments to undertake programs for economic expansion or to improve the welfare of colonial peoples.

COLONIAL RESOURCE MOBILIZATION AND COLONIAL REFORM: 1939–1945

During World War II Britain implemented a number of measures to strengthen its control over colonial expenditure and the production and marketing of colonial produce. In December 1939 the question of colonial payments to hard currency areas such as the Dollar Area was the subject of much discussion. The Bank of England was dissatisfied with the effectiveness of the measures implemented by colonial governments to regulate payments to hard currency areas at the beginning of the war. Therefore it called for them to be strengthened through the adoption of compulsion in the collection of the hard currency proceeds from colonial exports to the United States and some parts of Europe.[110] The bank advised the British government to begin with the dollar earnings of a few easily recognizable commodities which were good dollar earners.

This led to an Order-in-Council in 1940, in which the British government tightened its control over the transfer of sterling securities by British residents to nonresidents. Colonial governments were also required to submit an analysis of their sales of foreign exchange to Britain. This involved a detailed breakdown specifying items sold and the currency in which the transaction was conducted. Together with the system of bulk purchasing and guaranteed markets, the strengthening of exchange controls in 1940 gave the British government an unprecedented amount of leverage over colonial economic policy during World War II. Moreover, it had at its disposal mechanisms that could have been used to mobilize colonial resources and direct colonial economic policy toward initiatives to facilitate postwar economic recovery and preserve the stability of sterling.

Britain's mobilization and control of colonial resources during World War II was in part an inevitable consequence of the interdependent nature of metropolitan/colonial economic relations. In 1938, for example, 11.2 percent of all U.K. exports went to the colonial empire while the U.K. market accounted for 25 percent of colonial imports and 27 percent of colonial exports.[111] Their links to the British market notwithstanding, British colonial territories were also among the major suppliers for a number of commodities traded internationally. In 1939 British dependencies accounted for 39 percent of all copra exports, 58 percent of palm kernels, 39 percent of palm oil, between 40 and 50 percent of cocoa,[112] and 40 percent of the rubber on the world market.[113] The mobilization and control of some colonial resources, therefore, was an important means through which the British government could obtain hard currency. Forty percent of Malayan rubber exports, for example, went to the United States. The United States was also the world's leading importer of Malayan tin. Malaya was thus regarded as a British "dollar arsenal."[114] Other commodities such as oilseeds and vegetable oils also had good dollar-earning potential. They were essential to food consumption and industrial production and the international demand for them was destined to increase as the supply of other fats, especially butter and marine oils, dwindled. Therefore, it was important for Britain to control their production and export.[115]

When war broke out in 1939 most of the resources of the empire were brought under centralized control.[116] Foodstuffs were managed by the Ministry of Food, raw material (except mineral oils) by the Ministry of Supply, tobacco by the Board of Trade, and mineral oils by the Ministry of Fuel and Power. In addition, a system of bulk purchasing and guaranteed markets was introduced to ensure that Britain and its allies received adequate supplies and also to cushion colonial producers against the effects of market disruptions. Bulk purchasing agreements and guaranteed markets were particularly important to the producers of cocoa, which was the first crop to be controlled when the system began in 1939. Cocoa was primarily an export crop, and the outbreak of war cut off important overseas markets. As a result of this and "having regard to the importance of cocoa in the economies of the Gold Coast and Nigeria and the disastrous consequences likely to accompany a cessation of local buying,"[117] the British government decided to purchase the entire crop. It undertook "on the one hand to bear any eventual loss on resale and on the other to invite Parliament to vote a sum equivalent to any eventual profit realized for payment directly to the producers . . . or for expenditure on objects of benefit to them."[118] In January 1940 the British government's system of bulk purchasing and guaranteed markets was extended to include groundnuts from Nigeria and Gambia, bananas from Jamaica, citrus fruits from Palestine, copra from the South Sea and rubber from the Far East. These marketing arrangements were a clear indication of the impact of the war on imperial attitudes toward the production and marketing of colonial resources and the growing significance that was being attached to colonial products. However, there is no evidence that existing arrangements were influenced by factors exogenous to the immediate needs of the war. Thus, one can agree with Bowden's conclusions that state marketing "was introduced for political reasons to soften the blow to the colonial producers as a result of the collapse of export markets."[119]

Despite the scope of the effort which was made to mobilize colonial resources at the commencement of the war, the problem for Britain was that before the outbreak of World War II, colonial resource mobilization was limited in scale. As a result, the economic potential of some parts of its empire, especially its African dependencies, was never fully tapped. Governor Bourdillon of Nigeria aptly summarized the situation in April 1939 when he pointed out, "we [the British] have fallen short in our duty to the world by allowing natural resources to deteriorate, and in our duty to the British taxpayer by failing to expand with sufficient rapidity the market for British goods, we have also failed in our duty to promote the economic welfare of the people."[120] Consequently, in the short run it was going to be difficult for Britain to optimize the use of the resources of its African dependencies without increasing spending on development.

Cowen and Westcott caution that the colonial capacity to supply materials should not be overemphasized.[121] They note that while British colonial products such as cocoa, rubber and tin separately accounted for more than 40 percent of world production, cotton, coffee, tobacco, sugar and copper accounted for 1, 2, 1, 6 and 12 percent, respectively, of world output.[122] Also, in 1936 "nominal British investment, of all forms in East and West Africa accounted for 2 percent of total British overseas investment."[123] This was indeed almost insignificant compared with the 22 percent for India or 33 percent in Australia and New Zealand. Apart from India and the dominions, British investors were generally apathetic toward investing in other parts of the empire, particularly in the African colonies. Their attitude was consistent with that of the imperial government. The latter vigorously opposed the use of its own funds to finance schemes for colonial development until the eve of the war. In light of its failure to develop the full potential of its colonial resources in the prewar years, therefore, during the early years of World War II Britain did not attach much importance to the role that the colonies could play in its postwar economic recovery.

The Japanese victory over the Allied forces and the consequent collapse of Britain's colonies in the Far East in February of 1942 marked a watershed in imperial policy toward the resources of its African colonies. The Japanese success eliminated a major source of supply for ground-nuts, palm oil, rubber, tin and several other commodities. In the preceding two years there had been no demand for maximum production for export; indeed there had been some restrictions of exports. But in 1942 an entirely different position arose and Nigeria's produce became vitally important to the prosecution of the war.[124] Britain also focused more intensely on its West African colonies as a source for essential raw material needed to prosecute the war. As a result campaigns were launched to maximize the production of groundnuts, palm oil and palm kernels, cotton and other commodities produced in British West Africa. Initially this expansion in commodity production was not part of a general strategy to facilitate postwar recovery in Britain. It was intended to alleviate the shortages that stemmed from the disruption of supplies from the Far East. To facilitate the mobilization of produce for export, the functions of the West African Cocoa Control Board were enlarged to incorporate the purchase and distribution of the surplus oil and oilseeds from the West African territory. The board was renamed the West African Produce Control Board and the functions of the Colonial Office were extended to cover its operations. The secretary of state for the colonies thus had ultimate responsibility for the purchase and sale of colonial produce.

The disaster in the Far East also led to an acceleration in the pace of colonial economic reform.[125] The easy conquest of Britain's Far Eastern colonies by the Japanese shocked Britain and its allies.[126] The indifference of the indigenous people toward conquest and the incompetence of the local officials in the Far East undermined faith in the quality of Britain's colonial administration. It also provoked criticism from the United States. From this point onward the British government was under growing pressure to produce the kind of declaration that would seize the imagination of officials in the Colonial Service and inspire confidence about the future.[127] The defeat also highlighted the need for a more organized approach to colonial planning, and despite the contingencies of the existing situation the imperial government felt compelled to take remedial action. In the early months of 1942 two new posts of under secretary were created in the Colonial Office. In addition the Economic Division at the Office was expanded and a Production Department was established. Caine, the Colonial Office's financial adviser, was given the task of supervising colonial development and welfare policy. In August 1943 he presented his colleagues with a memorandum on the fundamental problems involved in development planning.

He stressed the importance of state participation in development planning. He was convinced also that the future social and economic development of the colonial empire lay in "a strong central organization for general supervision and assistance . . . with a much greater development of initiatory power at the center."[128] Caine's memorandum was discussed at a meeting between Colonial Office officials on 20 August 1943. The whole subject of development planning in the colonies was evaluated and Caine's main recommendations were accepted. By the middle of 1943, therefore, the concept of planning became established as an important feature of colonial development policy. Petter and Lee claim that "neither constitutional policy nor international affairs received anything like the same investment of time and manpower for forward planning that was devoted by the office of development and welfare."[129] This was primarily because the devolution of political power was seen as being dependent on the rate of social and economic progress.

The emphasis on development planning in colonial affairs, which was increasingly evident in 1943, was also noted by Bowden. She claims that Stanley, the secretary of state for the colonies, visited West Africa in September 1943 "in order to gain support for the planning drive and to offer advice on certain political issues that were posing special problems for colonial governments."[130] She points out that by this time Britain's four West African colonies had established committees to promote and coordinate economic and social welfare plans. The debacle in the Far East led to a fundamental revision in the Colonial Office's approach to colonial development. When the Colonial Office solicited an extension of the funds provided under the Colonial Development and Welfare Act (CDWA) of 1940 from the Treasury in July 1944, the concept of "planned development" was firmly established as an important feature of colonial economic policy. Henceforth, a lot of emphasis was placed on the improvement of economic infrastructure and the provision of social welfare amenities in the colonies.

CONCLUSION

By the 1930s the declining role of sterling as an international currency and turmoil in the British economy engineered the start of what was to develop into a profound transformation of Britain's colonial economic policy. The dominant feature of this process was Britain's increasing reliance on colonial resources to stabilize its balance of payments and safeguard the position of sterling as an international currency. These two factors also influenced the United Kingdom's response to the interwar changes in the international economy, particularly the adoption of discriminatory trade practices, the creation of the system of imperial preferences and organization of the Sterling Area. On the other hand, with the passage of the Colonial Development and Welfare Act of 1940, indications were that Britain was going to play a more important role in colonial development and welfare.

Between 1939 and 1945 the desire to protect sterling and the stability of the British economy, together with the contingencies of war, underpinned almost every aspect of colonial economic policy. Together they were responsible for the harmonization of colonial fiscal and monetary policy with that of the metropole, and the adoption or consolidation of measures that gave Britain an unprecedented level of control over the resources of the Sterling Area and its colonial empire. On the other hand, as Britain's economic fortunes declined and its balance of payments' position deteriorated, it was forced to submit to American pressure to liberalize its trade practices, end discrimination against the Dollar Area, reduce its holdings of accumulated sterling balances and restore sterling to full international convertibility by July 1947. Therefore, Britain entered the postwar era committed to the implementation of a series of measures that had major implications for the nature and character of its colonial policy.

NOTES

1. S. Strange, *Sterling and British Policy: A Political Study of an International Currency in Decline* (London: Oxford University Press, 1971) p. 42. Chapter 2 of this study gives an excellent account of the evolution of sterling as an international currency. See also A. C. Day, *The Future of Sterling* (London: Oxford University Press, 1954) and J. Polk, *Sterling: Its Meaning in World Finance* (New York: New Harper and Bros., 1956).

2. Ibid., p. 43.

3. Ibid., p. 43

4. A. G. Kenwood and A. L. Lougheed, *The Growth of the International Economy 1820–1990*, 3rd ed. (London: Routledge, 1992) pp. 26–27.

5. B. J. Cohen, *The Future of Sterling as an International Currency* (London: Macmillan, 1971) p. 59.

6. B.W.E. Alford, *Britain in the World Economy since 1880* (London: Longman, 1996) p. 71. This chapter gives a very interesting interpretation of the performance of British industry during this period.

7. J. Foreman-Peck, *A History of the World Economy* (New Jersey: Barnes and Noble, 1983) p. 170. See also R. J. A. Skidelsky, "Retreat from Leadership: The Evolution of British Economic Foreign Policy, 1870–1939", in B. M. Rowland, ed., *Balance of Power or Hegemony: The Interwar Monetary System* (New York: New York University Press, 1976).

8. Skidelsky, "Retreat from Leadership," p. 165.

9. D. H. Aldcroft, *The European Economy 1914–1990*, 3rd ed. (London: Routledge, 1990) p. 13.

10. P. J. Cain and A. G. Hopkins, *British Imperialism: Crisis and Deconstruction 1914–1990* (London and New York: Longman, 1993) p. 59.

11. M. Havinden and D. Meredith, *Colonialism and Development: Britain and Its Tropical Colonies, 1850–1960* (London and New York: Routledge, 1993), p. 141.

12. Alford, *Britain in the World Economy*, pp. 72–80.

13. Ibid., p. 72. See also B. J. Eichengreen, *Golden Fetters: The Gold Standard and the Great Depression, 1919–1939* (Oxford: Oxford University Press, 1992).

14. Skidelsky, "Retreat from Leadership," p. 169.

15. Alford, *Britain in the World Economy* p. 128.

16. Skidelsky, "Retreat from Leadership," p. 170.

17. Ibid., p. 170.

18. Cohen, *The Future of Sterling*, p. 64.

19. See Cain and Hopkins, *British Imperialism*, pp. 63–72; Alford, *Britain in the World Economy*, pp. 128–135; and Skidelsky, "Retreat from Leadership," pp. 169–173.

20. Alford, *Britain in the World Economy*, ch. 4. This chapter provides a useful analysis of Britain's predicament in the context of developments in the international economy. See also A. Cairncross and B. Eichengreen, *Sterling in Decline: The Devaluations of Sterling 1931, 1949 and 1967* (Oxford: Basil Blackwell, 1983).

21. Aldcroft, *The European Economy 1914–1990*, pp. 72–73.

22. Ibid., p. 72.

23. Alford, *Britain in the World Economy since 1880*, p. 144.

24. Ibid., p. 1.

25. Ibid., p. 19.

26. D. J. Morgan, *The Official History of Colonial Development. Vol. 1: The Origins of British Aid Policy 1924–1945* (London: Macmillan, 1980), p. 7.

27. Ibid., p. 9. See also S. R. Ashton and S. E Stockwell, *Imperial Policy and Colonial Practice* (London: HMSO, 1996), Vol. 2, Doc. no. 82, pp. 21–22.

28. Cohen, *The Future of Sterling*, pp. 65–70.

29. Ibid., p. 76.

30. *The Sterling Area: An American Analysis* (London: The United States Economic Cooperation Administration Special Mission to the United Kingdom, 1951), p. 25. For further details on the problems of the pound sterling at this time, see also A. Feavearyear, *The Pound Sterling: A History of English Money* (Oxford: Clarendon Press, 1963), pp. 337–385; and S. Strange, *Sterling and British Policy: A Political Study of an International Currency in Decline* (London: Oxford University Press, 1971), pp. 41–74.

31. Cain and Hopkins, *British Imperialism*, pp. 76–79.

32. Ibid., p. 68. See also Cairncross and Eichengreen, *Sterling in Decline*, pp. 23–24 and *The Sterling Area: An American Analysis*, p. 26. Cairncross and Eichengreen point out that initially the Scandinavian countries allowed rates to move by half the change in the sterling/dollar rate, but once the dollar began to fluctuate in 1933 they effectively joined the "sterling bloc". Also, countries such as Japan, Argentina, Greece and Yugoslavia pegged their currencies to sterling for extended periods of time but because they maintained exchange control or

multiple exchange rates, they were not considered to be members of the "sterling bloc" (p. 24).

33. Cohen, *The Future of Sterling*, p. 80.

34. *The Sterling Area: An American Analysis*, p. 26.

35. Cohen, *The Future of Sterling*, p. 81.

36. Ibid., pp. 79–82.

37. *P.R.O.* CO 537/3047. Desirable and less desirable markets. Undated.

38. A. R. Conan, *The Sterling Area* (London: Macmillan, 1953), p. 153.

39. P. W. Bell, *The Sterling Area in the Postwar World: Internal Mechanism and Cohesion 1946–1952* (Oxford: Clarendon Press, 1956), pp. 51–52. See also Ashton and Stockwell, *Imperial Policy and Colonial Practice*, Vol. 2, Doc. 98.

40. K. Wright, "Dollar Pooling in the Sterling Area, 1939–1952", *American Economic Review*, Vol. 44, pt. 1 (1954), pp. 560–563. The actual dollar pool was deemed to be the reserves of gold and dollars held in the exchange Equalisation Account in London, which were mobilized through the exchange control measures that were enforced at the start of World War II.

41. The creation of a "dollar pool" intensified the tension in AngloAmerican trade relations. Gardner points out that "American producers, beset by the Great Depression, were anxiously looking to foreign markets. In the midst of their difficulties they were met with the Ottawa Agreement." The American secretary of state at the time sympathized with the complaints of domestic exporters and described the agreement as "the greatest injury, in a commercial way, that has been inflicted on this country since I have been in public life." R. N. Gardner, *Sterling Dollar Diplomacy in Current Perspective* (New York: Columbia University Press, 1980), p 19.

42. A. P. Dobson, *The Politics of the Anglo-American Economic Special Relationship 1940–1987* (New York: St. Martin's Press, 1988), ch. 2.

43. L. S. Amery, *The Washington Loan Agreements: A Critical Study of American Economic Foreign Policy* (London: MacDonald and Co. Ltd., 1946), p. 95. Amery was a member of the British War Cabinet during World War II. He claims that this provision repulsed the direct attack on Imperial Preferences. He contends further that "a clear cut and public declaration that Imperial Preferences was not a matter which we were prepared to discuss would, no doubt, have been much better. But at the moment, with America not yet in the war, Mr. Churchill did the best that could be done" p. 95.

44. Ibid., p. 95.

45. Gardner, *Sterling Dollar Diplomacy in Current Perspective*, p. 51.

46. Amery, *The Washington Loan Agreements*, p. 96.

47. The article in question included provisions for "agreed action by the United States of America and the United Kingdom, open to participation by all other countries of like mind, directed to the expansion, by appropriate international and domestic measures, of production, employment, and the exchange and consumption of goods, which are the material foundations of the liberty and welfare of all peoples; to the elimination of all forms of discriminatory treatment in international commerce, and to the reduction of tariffs and other trade barriers." See Amery, *The Washington Loan Agreements*, pp. 162–163. Some of the most useful studies dealing with this issue include: R. F. Harrod, *The Life of John Maynard Keynes* (London: Macmillan, 1951); Gardner, *Sterling Dollar Diplomacy in*

Current Perspective; D. Moggridge, ed., *The Collected Writings of John Maynard Keynes,* Vol. XXVI, London: Macmillan, 1980); and Strange, *Sterling and British Policy.*

48. L. S. Pressnell, *External Economic Policy since the War: Vol.1 The Post-War Financial Settlement* (London: HMSO, 1987), pp. 4–5. See also chs. 1 and 4.

49. *Parliamentary Papers 1945–1946,* XIX (Cmd. 6707). "Statistical Material Used during the Washington Negotiations."

50. For details see S. Pollard, *The Development of the British Economy 1914–1967* (London: Edwin Arnold, 1979), ch. 6, Feavearyear, *The Pound Sterling,* p. 392, and R. F. Harrod, "The Pound Sterling" in *Essays in International Finance,* No. 13 (February 1952), p. 10.

51. Gardner, *Sterling Dollar Diplomacy in Current Perspective,* p. 61.

52. Harrod, *The Life of John Maynard Keynes,* p. 517.

53. Amery, *The Washington Loan Agreements,* p. 97.

54. Gardner, *Sterling Dollar Diplomacy in Current Perspective,* p. 110.

55. Keynes' address to the House of Lords on 24 May 1944. This is reproduced in D. Moggridge, *The Collected Writings of John Maynard Keynes: Activities 1941–1946. Shaping the Post-War World Bretton Woods and Reparations,* Vol. XXVI (London: Macmillan, 1980), p. 11.

56. *Parliamentary Papers 1945–1946,* XIX (Cmd. 6707), "Statistical Material Used during the Washington Negotiations."

57. It is possible also that President Roosevelt's death undermined Britain's chances of achieving its objective. Throughout earlier crises Churchill's personal relationship with Roosevelt made the winning of the war the main item on all agendas for AngloAmerican negotiations. Moreover, Churchill was able to get Roosevelt to restrain U.S. officials who wanted to extract the maximum price for U.S. help. With Roosevelt's death, Britain lost its most influential lobbyist in the United States.

58. Gardner, *Sterling Dollar Diplomacy in Current Perspective,* p. 209. See also C. S. Newton, "The Sterling Crises of 1947 and the British Response to the Marshall Plan," *Economic History Review,* Vol. 37 (1984), pp. 392–393.

59. Harrod, *The Life and Times of John Maynard Keynes,* p. 605.

60. *The Sterling Area: An American Analysis,* p. 27.

61. Ibid., p. 195. Table 69. Apart from India, Britain's other main creditors were Egypt (£400 million) and the British dependent territories (£447 million).

62. *P.R.O.* T 236/3562. A. M Kamark, "The Sterling Balances," p. 5.

63. The Government Funds consisted of the various central and local government reserves and funds for which colonial governments acted as bankers. The Currency Funds were made up of sterling or sterling securities, equivalent to at least 100 percent of the value of the local currency issued. It also included the profits from commission charges and the interest on investments made by the colonial currency authorities. The Marketing Board Reserves consisted of the surplus funds that the various marketing boards had set aside for price stabilization, research and development. The percentage of the total colonial sterling balance represented by each of its main components varied according to the economic earnings and the level of economic activities in the colonies. For more details on the nature and the structure of the colonial sterling balances see *P.R.O.* T 236/3562. Memorandum on the Sterling Assets of the British Colonies. (Col. no.

298) 18 December 1953. *P.R.O.* CO 852/388/5. Lord Moyne circular dispatch 5 June 1941.
    64. Ibid., *P.R.O.* T 236/3562. Memorandum on the Sterling of the British Colonies, pp. 2–9.
    65. *P.R.O.* CO 852/388/5. Lord Moyne circular dispatch 5 June 1941.
    66. Ibid.
    67. *P.R.O.* T 236/4090. C.H.M. Wilcox to N. E. Young 1/7/43.
    68. *P.R.O.* T 236/4090. S. Caine to Keynes 14/5/43.
    69. Ibid.
    70. Ibid.
    71. Ibid.
    72. Ibid.
    73. *P.R.O.* T 236/4090. Keynes to Caine 18/5/43.
    74. Ibid.
    75. *P.R.O.* T 236/4090. Keynes to Caine 18/5/43.
    76. *P.R.O.* T 236/4090. E. Rowe-Dutton to Sir David Waley 13/4/45. In this context a fiduciary issue refers to an issue of colonial currency which was not backed by its equivalent in sterling or sterling securities.
    77. *P.R.O.* T 236/4090. Minute by N. E. Young 5/7/43. Although 100 percent was the minimum sterling reserve requirement governing the issue of colonial currencies, sometimes 110 percent or 115 percent was held in reserve. According to the Bank of England this occurred when surplus income accumulated by currency boards was reinvested in sterling rather than redistributed to colonial governments. See *P.R.O.* T 236/4090. Questions of Policy in the Management of Colonial Currencies (comments on memorandum for Finance SubCommittee of the Colonial Economic Advisory Council) 7/5/45.
    78. B. R. Tomlinson, "Indo-British Relations in the Post-Colonial Era: The Sterling Balances Negotiations 1947–49," *Journal of Imperial and Commonwealth History*, Vol. 13, No. 3 (May 1985), p. 143. See also p. 159 endnote no. 4.
    79. *P.R.O.* CO 852/535/7. "Questions of Policy in the Management of Colonial Currencies." Draft memorandum CEAC (Finance) (45)10 Colonial Economic Advisory Committee Finance SubCommittee 13/2/45.
    80. *P.R.O.* T 236/4090. "Questions of Policy in the Management of Colonial Currencies" (comments on the memorandum for the Colonial Economic Advisory Committee) 7/5/45.
    81. *P.R.O.* T 236/4090. "Questions of Policy in the Management of Colonial Currencies" (comments on the memorandum for the Colonial Economic Advisory Committee) 7/5/45.
    82. Ibid.
    83. Ibid.
    84. Ibid.
    85. Ibid.
    86. Pressnell, *External Economic Policy since the War*, p. 216. See also A. Cairncross, *Years of Recovery, British Economic Policy, 1945–1951* (London: Methuen, 1985).
    87. Ibid., p. 225.
    88. *P.R.O.* CO 852/584/1/19037/16. Washington to Joint American Secretariat. Sever no.702 26 April 1945. This quote is an excerpt from Vinson's

testimony to the U.S. House of Representatives Ways and Means Committee on the Reciprocal Trade Agreements Bill.

89. Harrod, *The Life and Times of John Maynard Keynes*, p. 11.

90. Ibid.

91. Ibid., p. 13.

92. Ibid., p. 394.

93. "Notes on External Finance in the Post-Japanese Transitional Period," reproduced in D. Moggridge, *The Collected Writings of John Maynard Keynes: Activities 19441–946: The Transition to Peace.* Vol. XXIV, (London: Macmillan, 1980), p. 8.

94. Amery, *The Washington Loan Agreements*, p. 121.

95. J. H. Bowden, "Development and Control in British Colonial Policy, with Special Reference to Nigeria and the Gold Coast 1935–1948" Ph.D. thesis, Birmingham, 1980), p. 73. M. Petter and J. M. Lee note the changes that were taking place in colonial policy in the late 1930s. They point out that the idea of a Social Services Department in the Colonial Office first rooted in the spring of 1938 became a reality by March 1939. To them "these arrangements symbolised the office's reappraisal of the situation." See M. Petter and J. M. Lee, *The Colonial Office, War and Development Policy* (London: Maurice Temple Smith, 1982). See also S. Constantine, *The Making of British Colonial Development Policy 1914–1940.* (London: Frank Cass Ltd., 1984), ch. 8. This was followed by the Report of the Committee on Nutrition which was published as a White Paper in July 1939. It was an important landmark because nutrition was the first area of social welfare to be the subject of a major investigation and reflected the general trend in which policy was moving prior to World War II.

96. W. M. Hailey, *An African Survey* (London: Oxford University Press, 1957), pp. 1119–1146.

97. Ibid., pp. 1317–1318.

98. *Parliamentary Papers 1939–1947*, Vol. X (Cmd. 7167), 403. Report on the Colonial Empire 1947–1948, pp. 53–79.

99. E. R. Wicker, "Colonial Development and Welfare, 1929–1957: The Evolution of a Policy." *Social and Economic Studies*, Vol. 7 (1958), p. 182.

100. Ibid.

101. These were quoted by Moyne in P.R.O. CO 852/388/5, Lord Moyne circular dispatch 5 June 1941.

102. P.R.O. CO 852/388/5. Lord Moyne circular dispatch 5 June 1941.

103. Ibid.

104. Colonial development planning was not the only aspect of colonial affairs affected by the war. Petter and Lee point out that by the end of 1940 the Colonial Service Department was regarded as so reduced in status that its assistant secretary was transferred to handle the new department in French relations. Moreover, "although the wartime system of economic controls brought the Colonial Office into closer contact with other departments in Whitehall, there was often considerable difficulty in getting colonial interests represented in the proper forum of debate. . . . The Secretary of State's 'dual role'. . . was not fully appreciated outside the Colonial Office and was particularly vulnerable to being slighted in the bustle of wartime activity." See Petter and Lee, *The Colonial Office, War and Development Policy*, Chapter 2.

105. Wicker, "Colonial Development and Welfare 1929–1957," p. 182.

106. Ibid., p. 183. See also M. Havinden and D. Meredith, *Colonialism and Development: Britain and Its Tropical Colonies, 1850–1960* (London: Routledge, 1993), pp. 225–227. They claim that by March 1945, only £3.8 million of the funds allocated under the Colonial Development and Welfare Act was actually spent.

107. Ibid., p. 226.

108. Ibid.

109. *P.R.O.* CO 852/863/2/19275/95. Draft memorandum for submission by the S/S to the Economic Policy Committee: Allocation of funds provided under the Colonial Development and Welfare Act of 1945.

110. *P.R.O.* CO 852/302/10. Payments for exports to hard currency countries. Minutes of a meeting held in the Treasury Library on 28 December 1939.

111. K. M. Stahl, *The Metropolitan Organisation of British Colonial Trade* (London: Faber and Faber, 1951), pp. 1–2.

112. C. Leubuscher, *Bulk Buying from the Colonies* (Oxford: Oxford University Press, 1956), part 1, pp. 8–66.

113. Stahl, *The Metropolitan Organisation of British Colonial Trade*, p. 99.

114. Ibid., p. 100.

115. Leubuscher, *Bulk Buying from the Colonies*, p. 10.

116. *P.R.O.* CO 852/650/4. British Colonial Exports: Memorandum prepared by F. V. Meyer, August 1946. See also R. Dumett, "Africa's Strategic Minerals during the Second World War," *Journal of African History*, Vol. 26, no. 4 (1985), pp. 381–408 and D. Killingray and R. Rathbone, *Africa and the Second World War* (London and New York: Macmillan, 1986).

117. Ibid.

118. Ibid.

119. Bowden, "Development and Control in British Colonial Policy," p. 123.

120. *N.A.I.* Oyo Province 2/3/c 217. Confidential dispatch Bourdillon to MacDonald 5/4/1939.

121. M. P. Cowen and N. Westcott, "British Imperial Economic Policy During the War," paper presented at the Decolonisation Conference in London, May 1985, p. 6.

122. Ibid.

123. Ibid.

124. *N.A.I.* S/N/P. 16/8/6835. Statement of the Policy Proposed for the Future Marketing of Nigerian Oils, Oilseeds and Cotton. Sessional Paper no. 18 of 1948, p. 3.

125. Ibid., p. 121.

126. F. Furedi, *Colonial Wars and the Politics of Third World Nationalism* (London: I B Publishers, 1994), pp. 57–65.

127. Petter and Lee, *The Colonial Office, War and Colonial Policy*, p.121.

128. Ibid., p. 173.

129. Ibid., p. 193.

130. Bowden, "Development and Control in British Colonial Policy," p. 206.

2

British Economic Trials and Devaluation, 1945–1949

At the end of World War II Britain was in dire financial straits. In order to meet the cost of goods and services supplied by overseas countries during the war, it had sold or mortgaged a lot of its foreign assets and also incurred huge debts overseas. Between 1939 and 1945 the sale of British assets overseas amounted to £1,118 million. Its external debt increased from £500 million in 1938 to £3,355 million (by June 1945) and its reserves of gold and dollars fell from £864 million in 1938 to about £453 million in October 1945.[1] It was estimated that Britain needed to increase its exports by at least 50 percent above the prewar level merely to eliminate its current account deficit.[2] To complicate matters further, the end of the war heralded a period of optimism and national euphoria in which the British government faced tremendous pressures for new domestic programs. These included "an extension of social insurance, a public health service, advances in education, and a guarantee of full employment."[3] These demands effectively ruled out any economic solution that would lower standards of living and increase unemployment.

The outlook for the British economy was in stark contrast to that of the United States. It emerged from the war with an expanded productive capacity and improvements in living standards. In 1945 the index of the volume of total farm production in the United States was 33 points above the base period 1935–1939. Food crops and livestock increased by 29 and 41 points, respectively. For the same period the overall increase in the index of the volume of industrial production was 103 points. The production of durable goods increased by 174 points, nondurable 66 points and minerals 37 points.[4] The United States was also the world's most important source of capital for foreign investment. Consequently, Britain, like most other countries at the time, relied heavily on the United States for urgently needed goods and services.[5] This worldwide demand for foodstuffs, raw materials and other commodities from the Dollar Area made a "dollar shortage" inevitable. Briefly put, at any given set of price levels, exchange rates and levels of real income, there was a persistent tendency for the demand for dollars by the nondollar world as a whole to exceed the supply of dollars that could have been maintained in the course of normal trade and commerce. Considering the precarious state of Britain's finances and its commitments under the Anglo-American Loan Agreement, the impending "dollar shortage" had significant ramifications for postwar colonial economic policy.

FULFILLING THE LOAN AGREEMENT: DECEMBER 1945–JULY/AUGUST 1947

Under the terms of the Loan Agreement, Britain was committed to the convertibility of sterling used in current transactions and receipts with the United States as soon as the agreement became effective, and for the Sterling Area and the rest of the world not later than 15 July 1947; its employment of discrimination in quantitative import restrictions was to be terminated with effect from 31 December1946; and it was to endeavor to secure an overall settlement of all sterling balances as soon as possible.[6] When the Loan Agreement was signed in December 1945, the Bank of England and the Treasury feared that Britain's commitment to the United States on convertibility would lead to disaster. However, the government was in an invidious position. An immediate change in direction on the restoration of sterling to full international convertibility was dangerous because it would have undermined international confidence in sterling and damaged Britain's relations with the United States.[7] Thus, Britain had no choice but to continue without protection along the path to which it was pledged. If it was to avoid economic calamity, Britain would have instead to persuade member countries of the Sterling Area to continue to exercise restraint in their expenditure in the Dollar Area, monitor carefully the release of sterling balances, and develop the resources in the colonial empire that could either earn or save dollars.

Between 1946 and July 1947 Britain attempted to restrict the dollar expenditure of the Sterling Area with the same informal methods it used during the war, that is, "dollar spending" was left largely up to each individual member.[8] This policy was a colossal failure because members of the Sterling Area were unwilling to sacrifice pressing national needs for those of the Sterling Area in general.[9] Their intransigence was evident in the vast increase in imports from the Dollar Area during this period.

While the United Kingdom's imports from the Dollar Area rose by nearly 50 percent, the imports of the rest of the Sterling Area more than doubled.[10] In addition, "in pre-war days the exports of these countries to the Dollar Area had been sufficient to pay for 115 percent of their dollar imports; in 1947 they were sufficient to pay for only half of those imports."[11] Between 1946 and 1947 the value of the dollar imports of the independent members of the Sterling Area increased from US$778 million to US$1,549 million and their withdrawals from the "dollar pool" increased from US$427 million to US$1272 million. Moreover, to complete a dismal picture for Britain, its own withdrawals from the "dollar pool"increased from US$1,211 in 1946 to US$2,059 in 1947.[12] In addition, "it was the misfortune of the Sterling Area to find in the post war period its two most important dollar exports—gold and rubber—had become less valuable in relation to other commodities, than they had been in pre war years."[13] By July 1947, therefore, the demands of national reconstruction and development had made it virtually impossible for both the independent Sterling Area countries and Britain to exercise economy in their transactions with the Dollar Area. This in turn placed an intolerable burden on the "dollar pool"—the symbol of economy in dollar expenditure during the war—and, ultimately, it proved to be an important factor in its collapse.

Prior to the emergence of the "dollar crisis" in 1947, the mobilization of colonial resources was not a significant feature of the British government's overall strategy to equilibrate its dollar account in order to facilitate economic recovery. In the period between the end of the war in 1945 and the first quarter of 1947, the imperial government focus on colonial resource mobilization was mainly the expansion of primary production to alleviate existing worldwide shortages of foodstuffs, especially fats and oils. This emphasis can be traced to the impact of the international shortages in these commodities on the British economy in the early months of 1946. In Nigeria, for example, the minister of food informed the governor in June 1945 that it would remain necessary to obtain the maximum quantity of vegetable oil and oilseeds from West Africa for the next 3 years and "on present showing 1946 appeared likely to be the most difficult year."[14] This was reiterated by the secretary of state for the colonies in September 1945. He was very worried about the recent decline in the export of palm oil from Nigeria and he informed Governor Richards "of the grave concern of cabinet at the reduction of oil and fats imports into the UK."[15] He asked him to make the greatest possible effort to secure the maximum exports, because "the world deficiency in oil and fats is as serious as ever and maximum production is still required."[16]

The world shortage of fats and oils was particularly severe in

European countries because they accounted for about 75 percent of all the imported fats and oils in the prewar era.[17] Britain and Germany, the continent's leading importers, were the countries most affected. Despite overall increases in the world production of fats, oils and oilseeds in the early postwar years, in some categories world production was still below prewar levels. Between 1934–1938 and 1947, for example, the world production of slaughter fats was 5,270 metric tons and 4,750 metric tons, respectively; the figures for butter and ghee were 4,150 metric tons and 3,025 tons; palm oil was 690 metric tons and 430 metric tons; linseed was 1,110 metric tons and 870 metric tons; and cottonseed 1,475 metric tons and 1,155 metric tons. In the case of copra and groundnuts production was marginally above prewar levels. When compared with their prewar levels the quantity of fats, oils and oilseeds exported by the major producers had declined also between 1934–1938 and 1946. The slump was greatest in British Malaya, which exported 148.3 metric tons of oils and oilseeds in 1934–1938 and 10.4 metric tons in 1946, and Indonesia, which averaged 589.3 metric tons in 1934–1938 and 34.1 metric tons 1946. Although the decline was not as dramatic, exports from British East and West Africa fell from 514.6 metric tons in 1934–1938 to 441.3 metric tons in 1946. The figures for French West and Equatorial Africa were 252.6 metric tons and 141 metric tons, respectively.[18]

In April 1946 the British government published a White Paper to show how the crisis developed and the steps it took to resolve it. The paper explained that long before the end of the war, food shortages were anticipated. However, toward the end of 1945, the overall world food situation assumed crisis proportions because of an exceptional succession of droughts in many of the world's main producing areas during the 1945/46 harvest. This aggravated further the already seriously dislocated world agricultural economy.[19] The British government was not optimistic about the prospect for an early alleviation of the crisis. The White Paper noted, "it should be emphasized that the present difficulties are unlikely to disappear with the next harvest. Some increase in production may be expected in the former war zones and a repetition of the season's disastrous drought is improbable, but against this exportable surpluses will fall heavily."[20] In an attempt to remedy the problems caused by the shortage of fats and oils the British government dispatched the Keen Mission to West Africa in August 1946 to investigate and report on the possibilities of increasing, "during the period of the immediate world shortage, the exportable surpluses of vegetable oils and oil seeds in West Africa."[21] It also initiated the East African Groundnut Scheme in November 1946.

Britain's perception of the role to be played by colonial primary production in its strategy for economic reconstruction in the immediate postwar years was evident also in its relatively relaxed attitude toward the control of colonial expenditure in the Dollar Area. For much of 1946 and the early part of 1947, colonial governments were simply advised to limit their spending on imported "dollar" goods and services. The British government did not attempt enforce detailed control from London. Nevertheless, colonial governments were very cooperative. In 1946, whereas Britain and the independent members of the Sterling Area were responsible for the total US$1,638 withdrawn from the "dollar pool", the dependent members of the Sterling Area contributed 26 percent or US$134 million of the US$509 million supplied to the "dollar pool".[22] Although there were misgivings about the possible adverse effects of the restoration of sterling to full convertibility for the British economy within government circles, the magnitude of the problem was clearly underestimated. In part, this can be attributed to the fact that although "the dollar problem had been looming up all through the first half of 1947, it had not arisen acutely in 1946."[23]

The shift in the emphasis from the development of colonial resources to satisfy the world shortages to a reliance on expanding colonial primary production as part of the wider solution to Britain's balance of payment problems can be traced to a minute by C. G. Eastwood, the assistant under secretary of state at the Colonial Office in April 1947.[24] Eastwood agreed with an earlier suggestion by the Colonial Office's agricultural adviser, that colonial produce should be reviewed commodity by commodity taking into account, among other things, Britain's balance of payments difficulties. Eastwood called for the establishment of a committee comprising officials from the Colonial Office, the Ministry of Food, the Ministry of Supply and the Board of Trade to undertake this task. This committee was duly constituted in May1947 as the Colonial Primary Products Committee (CPPC) and Eastwood was appointed as its first chairman. The CPPC's first task was to conduct a comprehensive review of colonial commodity production to determine the possibilities for expanding production. This exercise was to be undertaken with due regard to the interests of the colonial empire, the present and prospective world needs and the desirability of increasing foreign exchange resources.[25] The establishment of the CPPC confirmed the British government's decision to attempt to expand colonial commodity production as a part of its plan for remedying its balance of payments difficulties.

In light of this, at the first meeting of the CPPC in May 1947, some members expressed reservations about the thrust of British imperial policy and were anxious to dispel any notion that Britain intended to exploit the colonies. The chairman reminded members "that colonies were not British estates which could be exploited by the UK for her own advantage."[26] In the mobilization of resources the primary consideration was supposed to be the benefit to the colonies themselves.[27] Nevertheless, he added that "there were of course many possible developments which, while benefitting the colonies would benefit also the UK and the world at large."[28] Sir Frank Stockdale, the Colonial Office development adviser, also warned of the committee of danger of a concealed form of exploitation. "Production," he said, "must not be allowed to drain away the fertility of the colonies."[29] Ultimately, despite the reservations of some members, the general feeling emanating from this CPPC meeting was that the development of colonial resources promised mutual benefits for Britain and the colonies.

The first official statement linking the development of colonial resources to the general imperial strategy to combat Britain's growing dollar deficits was issued on 26 June 1947. In a circular telegram to all colonial governments (except Ceylon), the secretary of state for the colonies explained that the CPPC's review of the empire's primary products was necessary because of the serious food shortages and the need to conserve dollar imports.[30] For most of the period before the deadline for restoring sterling to full international convertibility in July 1947, therefore, colonial economic policy was not fully integrated into a broader British strategy for economic revival. However, by April 1947, there were clear signs that Britain intended to depend heavily on the maximization of export production in its colonial dependencies, in order to achieve a surplus in the Sterling Area's transactions with the Dollar Area.

THE COLONIAL STERLING BALANCES: CHOICES AND DECISIONS, 1945–1947

At the end of World War II the British government could not opt for measures that would have reduced the colonial sterling balances, because it was impossible to find a formula that was acceptable to the colonies. Moreover, the state of the United Kingdom's economy militated against allowing the colonies unbridled access to their reserves. Instead at a meeting of Treasury, Bank of England and Colonial Office officials on 20 February 1946 "it was agreed that for the next five years the problem was basically how to prevent accumulated sterling from being liquidated against imports."[31] In short, the colonial balances were going to be allowed to grow. A number of measures to facilitate the attainment of this objective were discussed, including increased taxation, stricter import controls, and the devaluation of colonial currencies. Ultimately, they were all dismissed as unsatisfactory. The wartime policy of simply allowing increases in the colonial sterling balances thus continued.[32]

Between 1946 and 1947 increases in the direct dollar earnings of the colonies were not matched by an increase in the supplies of urgently needed goods and other commodities to the colonies.[33] The secretary of state for the colonies noted in July 1947 that "nearly two years after the end of the war, the difficulties in fulfilling essential import needs continue to retard progress in the colonies. . . . There is practically no aspect of economic life which is not affected by the basic shortages of imported materials."[34] This discrepancy between colonial earnings and colonial spending power was one of the main contributory factors to the growth in the colonial sterling balances between 1945 and 1947. During this same period the sterling assets of the British colonies increased from £454 million to £510 million. Judging from their definition of the problem confronting the British government, and the continued use of wartime restrictions on colonial expenditure, it is clear that imperial officials were influenced by two major factors, both of which were intimately related to the state of the British economy: first, the inability of the imperial government and the general Sterling Area to satisfy the postwar colonial demand for imported capital goods and other commodities, and second, the need to prevent the colonies from obtaining these supplies from the Dollar Area.

Even though government officials were unable to reach a consensus with regard to Britain's policy toward the management of the colonial sterling balances, this matter received a lot of attention in the early postwar period. At this time officials were primarily concerned with the overall size of the colonial balances. There was no disaggregation of the balances to determine the sums available for colonial development, their distribution among the individual colonies and the nature of the threat they posed to the British economy. In discussing—and after disagreeing about—measures to resolve this problem, the experts in Whitehall kept referring to three major considerations. First, should a part of the colonial sterling balance be cancelled? Second, should colonies be asked to make interest-free loans to the U.K. government? Third, should the colonies be asked to make greater use of their existing sterling balances before being permitted to raise fresh loans on the U.K. market? In 1946 the Colonial Office was of the view that the government of the United Kingdom should have made a full financial settlement of the sterling balances that it owed to the colonies.[35] It questioned the morality of "cancellation", in light of the promises for colonial development that the government had made during the war. It pointed to the contradiction between the U.K. government's giving loans to the colonies while at the same time canceling its sterling debts to them. Moreover, it argued that as trustees for the interests of colonial governments and peoples who were not able to negotiate for themselves, the U.K. government could not have used the same yardstick for treating them as that used for the dominions and independent countries.[36] As far as the Colonial Office was concerned, "cancellation" was an option that should have been seriously considered only if it was demonstrably inescapable.[37]

The Colonial Office's view was vigorously opposed by the Treasury. The Treasury argued that the Colonial Office was prepared to sacrifice the welfare of the United Kingdom to finance colonial development and welfare and repay the accumulated sterling balances. It added that unless the United Kingdom had the colonies accept the principle of "cancellation" it seemed "quite hopeless to expect India, and Egypt etc., whose populations are as poor as those of most of the colonies and whose need for development is as great, to accept cancellation."[38] To solve the problem the Treasury proposed that a portion of the currency fund should be allocated as a contribution to colonial development and welfare, and possibly in addition some, or all, of the interest-free loans made by the colonies during the war should be similarly allocated.[39] The crux of the disagreement between the Treasury and the Colonial Office was therefore the question of the cancellation of part of the colonial balances to facilitate Britain's post war recovery. On the other hand, both government agencies believed that the colonial balances could be used to assist in reducing the cost of colonial development borne by the Britain.

In June 1946 a working party comprising officials from the Treasury, the Colonial Office, the Bank of England and the Board of Trade was established to consider the policy to be followed with respect to the colonial sterling balances. In their initial submissions to the Working Party, the Treasury and the Colonial Office reiterated their previously stated positions, the former tending toward the United Kingdom, the latter instinctively toward the colonies. However, one of the principal underlying factors behind the Treasury's stance on the colonial balances was soon evident. The Chancellor of the Exchequer, Hugh Dalton, explained, "we must not admit—till a very late stage, if at all,—that any sterling creditor can make no 'adjustment'."[40] In short the "cancellation" or adjustment of the colonial sterling balances would have been undertaken only as a last resort. However, so long as the United Kingdom's economic future was threatened the Treasury was unwilling to guarantee that the colonies, or any of its sterling creditors, would not be asked to make a contribution toward Britain's recovery from their sterling balances.

By March 1947 the Colonial Office had modified its opposition to the idea of a colonial contribution to the postwar reconstruction of the United Kingdom. In a second proposal to the Working Party, it suggested that instead of the outright cancellation of any of their accumulated sterling balances, the colonies should be asked to make interest-free loans to the

United Kingdom from their currency reserves and their surplus funds.[41] These loans would be repayable only when they were needed to meet certain specified obligations to the colonial governments.[42] The Colonial Office also proposed that restrictions should be imposed on colonial imports, and taxes increased to restrain colonial spending and to raise funds to defray the cost of colonial development.[43] These suggestions were welcomed by the Treasury. For their part the Treasury's representatives on the Working Party accepted that a special relationship existed between the United Kingdom and the colonies, thus entitling them to more generous treatment relative to the sterling question than could have been expected in the case of India and Egypt.[44]

The spirit of compromise evident in the submissions of the Colonial Office and the Treasury to the Working Party provided a basis for the first alterations in the United Kingdom's policy toward the colonial sterling balances in the postwar period. It was agreed that long-term interest-free loans from the colonies to the imperial government were to be substituted for the outright cancellation of a part of the colonial sterling balances. These loans were to be made from the colonial currency reserves and there was provision for premature repayment "if, but only if, this should have become necessary in order to maintain the convertibility of any currency into sterling."[45] As far as the use of the currency reserves for colonial development was concerned the imperial government felt that action in this regard was unnecessary. It believed that the sums made available under the Colonial Development and Welfare Act, together with loans raised on the London money markets, private investment from the United Kingdom and local revenues, were sufficient to meet colonial demands for finance.[46] The nature of the deliberations and the eventual change that occurred in the imperial government's policy toward the colonial sterling balances were a manifestation of developments within the wider context of the state of the U.K. economy in 1946 and the early months of 1947. Taken in conjunction with the transfer agreements between Britain and some of its sterling creditors, the shift in imperial policy toward colonial sterling balances was clearly part of the overall package of measures that were designed to make the restoration of the free convertibility of the pound sterling a success. As the deadline of 15 July approached, therefore, the colonies were expected to make the United Kingdom's recovery a matter of priority because it was contended that their welfare depended on it. After its initial opposition, in March 1947 the Colonial Office eventually concurred with this view, and modified its position on the use of colonial balances to facilitate Britain's economic recovery. Moreover, it supported the British government's decision to review colonial commodity production with a view to improving the United Kingdom's balance of payments position in April 1947.[47] The Treasury did not need any persuasion. In the period before July 1947, therefore, the state of the U.K. economy, in particular, the complex preparations to meet the looming challenge of convertibility, had an important influence on the changes in imperial policy toward colonial sterling balances. Some of the conservatism in the colonial government's approach to the utilization of their sterling balances was directly associated with the fiscal initiatives worked out between the Treasury and the Colonial Office to facilitate the preservation of the stability of the pound and the correction of the British trade imbalance with the Dollar Area.

THE PATH TO CATASTROPHE

To facilitate a smooth transfer from sterling to dollars when the pound became freely convertible in July, Britain signed a series of bilateral agreements with Dollar Area countries. "Under these agreements balances accumulated before 15 July 1947 (with the exception of certain agreed releases for specific purposes) were segregated and, except by mutual consent could not have been drawn upon for any payment within or without the Sterling Area."[48] As a result of these agreements the free conversion of sterling was extended over a wide area before Britain's obligations under the Loan Agreement became effective. The impact of this policy on the drain of Britain's gold and dollar reserves is difficult to determine. Nevertheless, it is interesting to note, as Gardner does, that "in 1946 when the convertibility requirement had hardly begun to take effect, the monthly dollar drain was $75 million. In the first half of 1947, as convertibility was extended over a wider area, the monthly drain was $315 million."[49] Fforde notes further that an approaching shortage of dollars had become visible to the U.K. authorities in the autumn of 1946, when the forecasts for 1947 showed that a manageable external deficit overall was likely to be accompanied by a much less manageable deficit with the Dollar Area. He adds that other countries were also becoming very short of dollars and the provision of early postwar relief by the United States was running out. To make matters worse the election of a Republican congress in November 1946 reduced the likelihood that relief would continue and the decontrol of the U.S. economy led to a sharp increase in the price of dollar foods.[50] The growing deficit of the Sterling Area in its trade with the Dollar Area together with the drain on Britain's resources resulting from the release of sterling balances meant that the return of sterling to full international convertibility was implemented at a very inopportune time. The situation was aggravated further by a bad harvest in the autumn of 1946 and a severe winter in 1946–1947. The latter precipitated "a fuel crisis which held up production and transport and was estimated to have cost £200 million in exports."[51] In addition, "invisible earnings were disappointing, and the terms of trade turned sharply against the United Kingdom, adding £329 million to the import bill of 1947."[52] When Britain's convertibility obligations became due on 15 July 1947, its creditors had many reasons to abandon the pound. The implementation of free convertibility of sterling was tantamount to a referendum on the stability of the pound sterling as a major currency in world trade.[53] The vote of no confidence was unanimous "as almost every country with sterling hurried to convert it into dollars, with which so many more useful purchases could be made."[54]

The net drain on Britain's gold and dollar reserves increased from £226 million for the year in 1946 to £381 million between July and September 1947. Part of this dramatic increase was due to the fact that "convertibility was not being restricted to the current account."[55] It is estimated that the drain of dollars to Transferable Account countries rose from £49.3 million in the first six months of 1947 to £75.8 million in the period between 1 July and 20 August.[56] While Belgium had an agreement with Britain to limit gold and dollar transactions to £15 million annually it converted £34.4 million during the six weeks of convertibility.[57] It is evident, therefore, that "Britain's creditors passed an unfavorable judgement on Britain's economic prospects and employed every available means of exploiting their convertibility privileges before it was too late."[58] By 16 August 1947, there was only $850 million of the American loan left. To avert the collapse of the British economy, the free convertibility of the pound sterling was suspended on 20 August 1947.

HALTING THE SLIDE: AUGUST 1947–SEPTEMBER 1949

The convertibility debacle represents a milestone in imperial policy toward the colonial empire. In its aftermath, Britain decided to place greater emphasis on the use of colonial resources to promote its program for economic reconstruction. This thrust in colonial economic policy was considered at the highest level of the government. In September 1947, Foreign Secretary Ernest Bevin informed Prime Minister Clement Attlee that he had asked the secretary of state for the colonies to establish an interdepartmental committee to handle balance of payments questions. "It seems to me," he said, "that the same committee should have its terms of reference widened to take into consideration the development of the empire, as well as development at home; so as to earn by the production of raw materials a large contribution to the balance of payments."[59] Bevin added that a variety of raw materials possessed by the empire (such as coal, chrome, copper, asbestos, diamonds, lead, rubber and tin) were in short supply in the Dollar Area and suggested that the proposed committee should have been charged with establishing priorities for the development of these commodities.

The prime minister responded, "I agree entirely that we must see that any schemes for the development of the empire's resources which will earn or save dollars should be actively pursued and I will see that this point is kept in mind by the new organization."[60] Bevin also called for an intensification of efforts to develop the colonies to assist British reconstruction. He suggested as an example that the coalfields of Southern Rhodesia should be developed to sell coal to Argentina. This, he said, "would help us indirectly to get food for the UK."[61] Attlee agreed and added that this matter should be energetically pursued once the proposed committee began functioning.[62] The prime minister and the foreign secretary added another dimension to the existing concept of colonial development. The latter was now interpreted as being synonymous with the expansion of the production of dollar-earning or dollar-saving commodities produced in the colonies.

While Britain had clearly intended to develop the human and physical resource potential in the colonial empire in the early postwar period, one of the immediate objectives of the development process following the crisis of July 1947 was, undeniably, the expansion of the production of dollar-earning or dollar-saving commodities. Attlee and Bevin were not alone in their interpretation of colonial development. Their view was shared by officials from the Board of Trade and the Colonial Office. Ivor Thomas, the parliamentary under secretary of state, stated candidly:

The position of the Colonial Office in this matter is very clear. The colonies have three different but closely related functions to perform in our joint campaign to get our economy on even keel again. In the first place they must produce the things which they themselves need so as to diminish imports particularly from dollar countries; in the second place they must produce the things the UK needs to import, and is at present importing from foreign countries, and in particular dollar countries; in the third place they must produce more of the goods which can be sold for dollars.[63]

To achieve the immediate imperial objective for colonial development, an export drive committee was established in September 1947 to spearhead the government's initiative to earn dollars to assist in resolving its balance of payments deficits. The crisis of 1947 had therefore revitalized what had always been the major underlying tenet of British imperial policy, that is, that the colonies existed primarily for the benefit of the metropole. However, as was the case with the passage of the Colonial Development Act of 1929, the underdeveloped state of the colonies was advanced in conjunction with the problems affecting the British economy as justification for the mobilization of colonial resources.

The most detailed enunciation of this policy was given by Sir Stafford Cripps, the minister of economic affairs, in an address to the African Governors Conference on 12 November 1947. In his elaboration on the development of the British colonies in Africa, Cripps stated:

We have for a long time talked about the development of Africa but I do not believe that we have realized how much from the point of view of the world economy that development is absolutely vital. . . . The further development of African resources is of the same crucial importance to the rehabilitation and strengthening of Western Europe as the restoration of productive power is to the future progress and prosperity of Africa. . . . In Africa indeed is to be found a great potential for new strength and vigour in the Western European economy and the stronger that economy becomes the better of course Africa itself will fare. It is the urgency of the present situation and the need for the Sterling Group and Western Europe, both of them to maintain their independence that makes it so essential that we should increase out of all recognition the tempo of African economic development. We must be prepared to change our outlook and our habits on Colonial Development and force the pace so that within the next 2–5 years we can get a really marked increase in the production of coal, minerals, timber, raw materials of all kinds and foodstuffs and anything else that will earn or save dollars.[64]

The crisis of July 1947 forced the British government to acknowledge the inadequacies of the existing level of development in its dependent territories and provided a powerful incentive for it to accelerate the development process. It was also clear that as long as the benefits to the United Kingdom could be justified Britain was prepared to allocate the financial resources necessary for colonial development. The "dollar crisis" also silenced, at least for the time being, British government officials who felt that the thrust of imperial policy was tantamount to economic exploitation of the colonies. The consensus was that the colonial economies were appendages of the imperial economy, and their survival was inextricably linked to the recovery of the British economy. Furthermore, colonial development, especially that of the African colonies, was linked to the maintenance of economic stability in the United Kingdom. The latter was in jeopardy as long as Britain and the rest of the Sterling Area continued to require large supplies of dollar imports. Thus, the aim of imperial policy was to augment and accelerate the production of colonial primary commodities which would enable Britain either to save or to earn dollars while simultaneously restricting colonial expenditure in the Dollar Area.

Colonial expenditure on foreign trade was also dictated by the requirements of the British economy. In terms of expenditure, colonial governments were asked to provide estimates of their imports from the Western Hemisphere for 1948. "These hurriedly compiled estimates were subsequently imposed as 'ceilings' to their [dollar] expenditure on imports from the Western Hemisphere."[65] This system of 'dollar ceilings' was controlled from London by the Colonial Dollar Drain Committee, which comprised representatives from the Treasury, the Colonial Office, the Board of Trade and the Bank of England. These 'ceilings' were set as follows: Malaya $74 million, the West Indies including Bermuda $107 million, West Africa $29 million and East Africa $19 million.[66] The secretary of state for the colonies was sensitive to the unsatisfactory features of these 'ceilings.' He explained, "actually when the telegram was drafted it had not been my intention to use the estimates in such a way, but the direction which events are developing seems to have no alternative to the adoption of such measures as indicated above, very rough justice though it may entail."[67]

The convertibility crisis of July 1947 also had repercussions on the independent sterling countries which had become by this time less amenable to the dictates of imperial policy. At an emergency meeting in September 1947, these countries reviewed their export and import programs in the light of the dollar crisis. In a communiqué issued at the end of the meeting they promised to "report to their respective governments, which will be able to consider what reductions in hard currency are possible and what assistance can be given in other ways to the strengthening of the area's gold and dollar reserves."[68] Also, "the various Dominions announced their intention to live within their current dollar incomes and so avoid drawing upon their accumulated sterling balances."[69]

The drain of Britain's gold and dollar reserves between July and August 1947 raised questions about the feasibility of the nondiscrimination clause of the Loan Agreement. Although the prime minister admitted that up to 6 August 1947, the clause "had been hardly operative at all,"[70] the prevailing "dollar shortage" and Britain's adverse balance of payments deficits were sufficient to justify the elimination of this clause. Following discussions with the United States in September 1947, it was agreed finally to allow Britain to discriminate against American goods in favor of supplies from the non-Dollar Area.[71] This represented a radical check to the American attempt to secure Britain's participation in multilateral trade. This was aptly summarized by Gardner, who wrote that "the Loan Agreement designed to foster multilateralism had precisely the opposite effect. Not only did it fail to effect any permanent change in British trade or financial policy, it shook the faith of many in the desirability of multilateralism and greatly strengthened the hand of the traditional critics of the objective."[72]

The attempts to rescue the pound sterling were not limited to the measures to maximize the production of "dollar earning" or "dollar saving" commodities in the colonial empire or a reduction in dollar expenditure by independent Sterling Area countries. Nevertheless, these measures ensured that the dependent members of the Sterling Area bore the brunt of the burden in Britain's campaign to achieve a surplus in dollar transactions among Sterling Area members. If one excludes the gold sales to the United Kingdom from the rest of the gold sales from the Sterling Area, the dependent territories of the Sterling Area were the only members of the "sterling bloc" with a surplus in their transactions with the "dollar pool" in 1947. This surplus was US$40 million in 1947 and US$206 million in 1948. Britain and the independent Sterling Area had a combined deficit of US$3,331 million in 1947 and US $1,485 million in 1948.[73] In addition the proportion of Britain's merchandise dollar deficit covered by the dollar trade surplus of the dependent Sterling Area grew from 4 percent in 1946 to 23 percent in 1948.[74]

The dollar crisis enhanced further the case for increased American financial assistance to both Britain and Western Europe. By this time the postwar split between Eastern and Western Europe was confirmed "and in the emergent 'cold-war' the economic prosperity of the West suddenly acquired strategic significance for the U.S.A."[75] Before the end of the year President Truman was authorizing "interim aid" while putting before Congress a total demand of $17 billion for European recovery.[76] In April 1948 Marshall Aid was approved by the U.S. Congress, and $17 billion was channeled into the cause of European recovery. For Britain this meant that it was able to cover its dollar deficits while it pursued economic reconstruction. Together with the measures taken by the British government "Marshall Aid" enabled Britain to reduce the burden on its gold and dollar reserves.[77]

BRITAIN, AMERICA AND EUROPE: 1947–1949

The collapse of efforts to restore sterling to full convertibility in 1947 did not put an end to American pressure to dismantle the system of trade restrictions that the United Kingdom had established to defend sterling. Britain was still obliged to fulfill its commitments under the Loan Agreement of 1945. However, the crisis of July 1947 forced the Americans to ignore discriminatory practices by Britain in its transactions with the Dollar Area. For its part, Britain was steadfast in its opposition to any plan or measure that threatened to undermine its gold and dollar reserves. Within Europe itself, there was a recognition that some level of cooperation was necessary for Western Europe to recover from the devastation wrought by the war. Kaplan and Schleiminger noted that as some European statesmen struggled to overcome their economic problems, they were prepared to yield much of their newly regained sovereignty to a supranational state. They were attracted by the prospect of markets that would have been easier to penetrate than the North American market, a better division of labor and a more efficient use of resources. They also felt that the free movement of goods, money and people would have been beneficial to all the participating countries.[78] The need for a United Europe was also supported by the United States. The United States believed that European integration was a necessary part of the economic foundation that would herald a new era of lasting peace and prosperity in Western Europe. It was also seen as a crucial element in counterbalancing the threat posed by the Soviet Union to American interests in Europe, and correcting what the United States saw as a "basic" structural flaw in the Western European system, "its division into a ëmultiplicity' of economic sovereignties."[79]

To facilitate cooperation in Europe the Committee for European Economic Co-operation (C.E.E.C.) was established in July 1947. It comprised 16 European countries including Britain, France and Germany.[80] By April 1948 after protracted negotiations, the Organization for European Economic Co-operation (O.E.E.C.) was created. The accord establishing it called for the integration of Western Europe and the maximization of efforts to develop production, modernize systems and eliminate all abnormal restrictions on the exchange of goods, services and labor.[81] In 1948 and 1949 the members of the O.E.E.C. signed two Payments and Compensation Agreements in an attempt to resolve the problems created by bilateralism in commercial and financial transactions. Although these agreements made it easier for individual member countries to settle bilateral balances, they did not provide for the settlement of net balances between member countries as a whole. Further, European currencies were still nontransferable. Consequently, member countries were hardly encouraged to apply measures to liberalize trade.

The establishment of the O.E.E.C. represented an important shift toward multilateralism in trade and financial transactions in Europe.[82] Although Britain was reluctant to lead this move, as a member of the O.E.E.C. it was going to be difficult for it to ignore its commitments to the organization. However, multilateralism in trade was antithetical to the tenets that were then guiding the imperial policy in the British empire. Thus, ultimately, Britain had a choice to make regarding its future relations with Europe and its colonial empire. For the moment, at least, with the effects of the abortive attempt at convertibility in 1947 still fresh in its mind, the British government had complete faith in the viability of its colonial empire.

THE POLITICAL CHALLENGE TO IMPERIAL RULE: 1948

In the wake of the convertibility crisis of 1947, Britain found itself confronted by political developments in its colonial empire which were to have profound consequences for the future of imperial control. To Britain decolonization in its dependent territories was contingent upon their rate of social and economic progress in colonial territories. During World War II the British government was forced to introduce a number of reforms and give assurances for postwar changes in policy to appease some of its colonies. In this respect the reforms and commitments in its Southeast Asian dependencies were in stark contrast to those Britain undertook in its African and West Indian colonies. In India, the British government was desperate to coax the leaders of the Congress Party into an agreement when the Japanese were moving through Malaya and Burma. Therefore, according to Darwin it "promised unequivocally to facilitate complete Indian self-government as soon as the war ended. They thus surrendered control over the timing of constitutional change in what was certain to be an extremely turbulent postwar period."[83] In 1943 Britain promised Burma, which was under Japanese control between 1942 and 1945, "complete self-government as ёsoon as circumstances permitted."[84] In May 1943 it assured Sri Lanka (Ceylon), a strategically vital part of its defense sea communications with India, and an important source of rubber after the fall of Malaya to the Japanese, that Sri Lanka would be granted full internal self-government at the end of the war.[85]

British policy in Southeast Asia was not meant to be a precedent for colonial reform in other parts of its empire. Britain responded to the threat to imperial authority evident in the West India Riots of the late 1930s, and the heightened colonial expectations for reforms which were sparked by the war in a measured, tentative manner. In Africa and the British West Indies, Britain did not agree to self-government after the war. In 1942 Lord Cranborne, the colonial secretary, "approved the appointment of unofficial African members to the executive councils of Nigeria and the Gold Coast."[86] This meant that Africans were involved in the executive, as opposed to the legislative, process of British colonial rule for the first time.[87] There were also reforms in the British West Indies. For instance, a limited form of responsible government was introduced in Jamaica under the constitution of 1944.[88] Unofficial members were allowed a majority on the executive council in Trinidad from 1941, and universal adult suffrage was introduced in Jamaica and Trinidad in 1944. In the British West Indies and British Africa, demands for self-government were not seriously entertained.

At the end of the war the British government struggled to cope with the postwar political realities in the colonies. In this respect its handling of developments in India, Burma and Sri Lanka contrasted sharply with its approach in parts of the empire such as the Gold Coast, Nigeria, Malaya and the British West Indies. In India and Burma it was forced to accept the inevitability of independence. The nationalist momentum for Indian autonomy was enhanced by the fact that India ended the war as a creditor of Britain. In addition, "the war had brought about a sharp and involuntary acceleration in the Indianization of the army and civil service which could not easily be reversed."[89] According to Darwin when British officials were considering how to fulfill their promise of self-government to India "in a way that was compatible with Britain's own interests, they found the basic elements of India's political life had changed and that the instruments of authority upon which they had chosen to rely were cracking in their hands."[90] This apart, by 1947 Britain did not have substantial economic motives for retaining India.[91] The war had destroyed the remnants of India's value as a repository for Britain's old staple manufactures. Likewise, from the point of view of the needs of sterling, India was no longer a net contributor to the dollar pool. Britain was also reluctant to promote exports to India because it felt that Indian demand for capital goods hindered domestic reconstruction, and it was better to direct exports to areas where they could earn dollars.[92] On the other hand, while the size of the Indian sterling balances was a threat to the stability of sterling, the danger was averted because Britain and India agreed on a formula for reducing the balances. Therefore, Indian independence in August 1947 did not endanger the welfare of the British economy.

Britain resisted Burma's independence, because it believed that changes in Burma would have had adverse repercussions on its policy in Sri Lanka and Malaya. Thus, it tried in vain to coopt the Anti-Fascist People's Freedom League (AFPFL) and its leader, Aung San. Eventually, it was forced to accept the fact that events during the war had destroyed the economic and political basis for British colonial rule. Thus, it capitulated and the Burmese were granted independence under a republican constitution incompatible with their membership of the British Commonwealth.[93] In Sri Lanka the United Kingdom was able to secure its economic and strategic interests because the "friendship between the British and Sinhalese politicians comfortably survived the stresses of World War II."[94] In addition, the landowning class wanted to preserve Sri Lanka's preferential export market in Britain. The Sinhalese majority also saw cooperation with Britain as its best guarantee of security against perceived threats of Indian domination. In these circumstances, therefore, Britain was able to fulfill the promise it made on self-government in 1943 without jeopardizing its political or economic interest.

Between 1945 and 1947 the momentum for change in other parts of the British empire was not as intense as it was in India, Burma and Sri Lanka. Although there was discontent, nationalist forces were not considered a serious threat to Britain's continued presence in the colonies. Thus, it felt secure in its view of political change in the colonial empire and assumed that it could regulate the forces that determined the devolution of political power. Given the state of economic underdevelopment throughout the British empire, British officials were convinced that the dependencies were not ready for full self-government, much less independence. In British Africa, for instance, the goal was self-government, but it was not something to be hurried.[95] In general, speculation was that it would have taken a generation for the principal colonial territories to attain "or be within sight of the goal of full responsibility for local affairs [i.e., internal self-government]."[96] In the interim Britain was not prepared to grant any concessions beyond allowing unofficial membership of colonial executive councils and the creation of unofficial majorities in the legislative councils.[97]

These reforms failed to satisfy the nationalist expectations. Moreover, Britain's postwar colonial economic policy had repercussions that were antithetical to the maintenance of political stability. For most dependencies, the effects of worldwide shortages in capital and consumer goods were made worse by the constraints imposed by Britain on their trade with the Dollar Area. Reports indicate there was practically no aspect of economic activity in the colonies that was not affected by basic shortages of imported materials.[98] The economic policies pursued by Britain in its dependencies also added to the tension and discontent within them in the postwar period, and in the final analysis, assisted in precipitating the unrest that threatened colonial rule in 1948.

The most famous were the Accra riots in the Gold Coast in February 1948. The political climate in the Gold Coast was destabilized by the "worldwide inflationary pressures [that] after 1945 became more acute in the Gold Coast. High prices for cocoa meant more money in circulation at a time when few goods were available, and the resulting inflation brought severe hardships to many sections of the community."[99] In June 1948 a Chinese-led communist insurrection began in Malaya. The circumstances that led to the confrontation were exacerbated by Britain's colonial economic policies. The group leading the insurrection, the Malayan Chinese, were among the subgroups "hardest hit by postwar inflation and shortages."[100] Thus, when the Malayan Union—a partial safety valve for the discontented Chinese elements—collapsed, it simply added to the sense of frustration and deprivation already being experienced by some Chinese, driving them to join forces with the communist guerrillas.[101] The reverberations from colonial economic policy also contributed to the 1948 strikes in the sugar industry in Trinidad, Antigua and St. Kitts and made the radical Zikists in Nigeria into a potentially dangerous foe. The widespread unrest in the colonial empire in 1948 undermined the imperial assumptions about containing or regulating the forces of change, without making any significant concessions to nationalist agitators, in the early phase of the devolution of power. Thus, even though the colonies had not achieved the type of advance that the Colonial Office thought was necessary for the transfer of power to be accelerated, the threat posed to colonial control by events in some colonial territories made this qualification unnecessary. The events of 1948 therefore redefined the political context in which Britain struggled to reconstruct its postwar economy and restore sterling to full international convertibility. If properly mobilized, the nationalists in the colonies were potentially a serious threat to the future of imperial rule. Henceforth, Britain could no longer ignore or overlook the political consequences of its economic policies toward the colonial empire. To successfully ward off the nationalist challenge, Britain had to address the mounting demands for meaningful political reforms, as well as the need for development finance in the colonial empire.

THE CONVERTIBILITY CRISIS AND COLONIAL ADMINISTRATIVE REFORM: 1948–1949

The remedial measures taken to stem the drain on Britain's gold and dollar reserves led to a proliferation of committees and other bodies to superintend imperial policy.[102] In January 1948 the Central Economic Planning Staff (C.E.P.S.) was established to coordinate economic policy in the colonies. The main function of the new division was to keep in touch with major developments affecting U.K. economic policy and ensure that any colonial implications of such developments were not overlooked, either by the rest of the United Kingdom or by the Colonial Office and colonial governments.[103] The overall emphasis on colonial economic affairs was such that six of the nine specialist committees administered by the Central Economic Planning Staff were related to colonial affairs.[104] By1949 all economic departments administering the colonial empire were drawn together in an Economic Intelligence and Planning Division, accounting for one-third of the administrative establishment of the Colonial Office, which oversaw colonial economic planning.[105]

In 1948 the imperial government established also the Colonial Development Working Party (C.D.W.P.) "to review and make recommendations regarding the arrangements for determining the allocation of capital goods required for the maintenance and development of colonial resources."[106] Sydney Caine, the deputy under secretary of state, commented:

The recommendations of this Working Party may be of first importance in establishing satisfactory machinery for ensuring that colonial capital investment projects receive proper consideration and that colonial development is not impeded by failure to get its due share of capital equipment which is also urgently required for investment projects in the UK or for export to hard currency countries.[107]

The creation of the C.E.P.S. and C.D.W.P. and other bodies to oversee and organize colonial economic affairs was a manifestation of the increasing level of importance the British government attached to these matters. This was confirmed in a note on "Economic Development in the Colonies" by the secretary of state, which was submitted to the prime minister on 5 February 1948. Following discussions, government ministers decided that "they should have applied themselves more energetically to the task of economic development in Africa and the other Colonies."[108] They agreed to prepare "overall plans for co-ordinating and intensifying development planning in the Colonies and for integrating colonial plans with economic policy in the UK."[109]

There was also growing concern about the inability of existing policies and organizational structure of the Colonial Office to cope adequately with the demands made upon it by the "dollar crisis." The Select Committee on Estimates contended in April 1948 that there was nothing to suggest that there was a coherent strategy for economic planning underlying the extensive colonial development schemes which were being undertaken or contemplated under the 1945 Act.[110] Officials from the Colonial Office were also unhappy. Gorell Barnes, an assistant under secretary, claimed that despite considerable progress there was a feeling of dissatisfaction within the Colonial Office.[111] When this memorandum was discussed officials from the Colonial Office, the Treasury and the Board of Trade agreed "that there was a clear need for some improvement on the present ad hoc arrangement for relating these needs to the maintenance of existing economic activity in the colonies."[112]

Structural changes in the organization of the Colonial Office were matched by other measures and policy statements emphasizing the trend of imperial policy. One of the most significant developments was the passage of the Overseas Resources Development Bill (O.R.D.B.), which established two corporations: the Colonial Development Corporation (C.D.C.) and the Overseas Food Corporation (O.F.C.) in February 1948.[113] The main difference between the two corporations appeared to be their spheres of operation. The C.D.C. was created specifically to promote developments within the colonial empire. The O.F.C.'s area of operation was more general, and it could participate in colonial development only at the invitation of the secretary of state for the colonies.

It was argued that this bill was "as much designed for the purpose of meeting the needs of the world as it is of meeting the special needs of colonial peoples."[114] Creech Jones, the colonial secretary, claimed that it represented

a further big step forward in our conception of colonial development. The Colonial Development and Welfare Acts of 1940 and 1945 were of great importance because of the planning involved under them in respect to social and economic development. . . . We now have the opportunity of carrying economic development a stage beyond that, in so far as we are able to encourage enterprise, of both a private and public character, in order to increase the economic wealth and exploit the resources for the general development of these territories.[115]

He also made what can be considered the most crucial point underlying the formation of the C.D.C.

It is sometimes little recognized that so far, in Colonial Development only a comparatively small sum has been invested for the purposes of exploiting territorial resources. . . . Indeed, a great deal of investment was switched away from Africa and our Colonies for use in South America and the American Continent. To that extent, we have not given to the development of these territories the attention which we should have given in days gone by.[116]

The British government clearly intended to make a virtue of necessity. The colonial secretary painted a picture of methodology and altruism in Britain's approach to colonial economic development which did not exist at this time. The reality was that the rapid expansion in the dollar-earning capacity of colonial territories required by the "dollar crisis" of July 1947 could not have been accommodated by the existing imperial arrangements for colonial expenditure. There were no specific provisions for expanding the production of the major export-earning commodities in the colonies in the Colonial Development and Welfare Acts of 1940 and 1945. The "dollar crisis" of 1947 exposed Britain to the legacy of lethargy and indifference that had hitherto characterized the imperial policy toward the development of colonial resources. When the United Kingdom turned to its African colonies in its hour of need, it was clear that without a massive injection of capital help would not be forthcoming. This capital inflow was provided under the auspices of the C.D.C. and O.F.C.

At the African Conference in October 1948, the British government clearly intended to continue emphasizing one of the main themes of imperial policy, namely, the role of the empire in the reconstruction effort.

The draft brief of the speech prepared for the chancellor of the Duchy of Lancaster, Hugh Dalton, reviewed the events that preceded the crisis of 1947 and the measures taken to resolve it. It stressed that existing measures "must be maintained and, wherever possible intensified."[117] This draft also provides useful insights into the forces that shaped imperial policy at the time. In his comments on the draft, the private secretary to the chancellor of the exchequer stated that while the Treasury agreed with its general gist, it wanted to see the "dollar earnings" or "dollar savings" aspects of colonial development given greater emphasis. He also hinted that there were limits to what the United Kingdom would do to promote overseas investments in the near future.[118]

The Colonial Office was more concerned with the image being created by the focus on imperial policy than with the substance of policy itself. Mr. Poynton, an assistant under secretary of state, contended, "we must avoid at all cost giving the impression that the colonies have to be content with the residue that is left over after the UK and the needs of others have been met in full. I detect this obsolete heretical doctrine in the Chancellor's Private Secretary's letter."[119] Like Poynton, the colonial secretary and other Colonial Office officials wanted other items emphasized. These included the need to improve agricultural production, the expansion of economic activities, increased health facilities and other factors which were considered fundamental to improving the standard of living in Africa.[120] One official even suggested a redraft of the section of the text that dealt with the United Kingdom and the existing financial difficulties, to stress the mutual benefits involved in Britain's mobilization of the economic resources of the colonies. In short there was consensus between the Treasury and the Colonial Office on the substance of imperial policy. The dispute was about its presentation to the colonies.

As far as Britain was concerned, by September 1949 the policies employed to restrict colonial expenditure in the Dollar Area and increase the sale of dollar-earning products had accomplished encouraging results. Reports revealed:

Between 1946 and 1948 the colonies have enormously increased their direct dollar earnings and these were running at an annual rate of from $600 million to $800 million during the first half of 1948. At the same time, expenditure by the Colonies in the Western Hemisphere has been curtailed. It fell in spite of higher prices and the necessity to increase purchases of certain equipment for development, from $500 million in 1947 to an annual rate of $473 million in the first half of 1948.[121]

The colonies also made a substantial indirect contribution to the dollar balance of the United Kingdom. Britain's imports from the colonies increased from 5.4 percent of total imports in 1938 to 9.4 percent in the first half of 1947 and 10.2 percent during the first six months of 1948.[122] It was noted "this rise has resulted undoubtedly in a considerable saving of dollars by enabling the United Kingdom to divert purchases from the hard currency sources."[123] In the months following the suspension of convertibility Britain's economic recovery was remarkable.[124] Its exports and invisible earnings increased steadily and its current account deficit was turned into a surplus.[125] More important, the deficit on Britain's current account with the Dollar Area was reduced from £557 million in 1947 to £275 million in 1948.[126] Despite this success, however, the size of the deficit continued to threaten Britain's recovery efforts because it had to be financed out of reserves. This latter situation was analogous to the one existing in the Sterling Area, where in spite of a general reduction in "dollar imports," the deficit with the Dollar Area continued to be substantial.[127] By the second quarter of 1949, the Sterling Area's overall trade balance with the Dollar Area began to deteriorate.[128]

The short-lived recession in the United States contributed significantly to the existing state of affairs. Cairncross notes that it "had serious repercussions on imports of materials from the Sterling Area, especially rubber, wool, jute and tin, reducing both the volume and price paid for them."[129] Ultimately, this led to a dramatic increase in the adverse balance of payments of the whole Sterling Area. The overall drain on Britain's gold and dollar reserves increased from £82 million in the first quarter of 1949 to £157 million in the second.[130] The doubts cast on the stability of the pound by the failure of convertibility in 1947 returned to haunt it. "Even before the quarter was completed and the extent of the loss of reserves disclosed there were signs of distrust."[131] There was an increase not only in speculation against the pound sterling in anticipation of devaluation, but "irregular markets in pounds sterling had grown up in New York and other foreign centers beyond the jurisdiction of the British Exchange Control,"[132] and the bounds of the official exchange rate. Britain's initial reaction to this crisis was to reinforce the policies already in existence. On some occasions correspondence between officials of the Colonial Office was devoid of the concerns about colonial exploitation which characterized earlier debates on colonial economic policy between the Colonial Office and the Treasury. N. Mayle, assistant secretary at the Colonial Office, stated:

I fully appreciate the political objections to putting forward proposals, which, on the face of them, might give colour to the criticism that we are attempting to exploit the Colonial Empire to help the UK out of its dollar difficulties. But the possibility of criticism should not I suggest, deter us from putting forward proposals if we consider them to be necessary to ensure the fullest contribution from the Colonial Empire to the dollar problem. It would be possible when putting the proposals to the Colonies, to meet the criticism in advance with the obvious argument that by helping the UK the Colonies are helping themselves, since it is a case of sinking or swimming together.[133]

The secretary of state informed the colonies in July 1949, "there can now be no question of increasing colonial dollar ceilings for 1949, whether to deal with the price differential problem or for any other purpose."[134] He also called for the suspension of the issuing of licences for imports from the Dollar Area "except in cases where suspension would have dire consequences."[135] In the rest of the Sterling Area Britain obtained agreements reiterating earlier commitments. But the new restrictions could affect the adverse balances only after an interval of time, and meanwhile the loss of reserves was being aggravated by a speculative movement against sterling.[136] On 18 September 1949, the pound sterling was eventually devalued by 30.5 percent.

CONCLUSION

Between 1945 and 1949 the British government struggled resolutely to remedy the problems involved in reconstructing its war-torn economy, fulfilling its obligations to the United States, maintaining the viability of the Sterling Area, restoring the pound to full international convertibility and satisfying increasing colonial demands for political and economic reform. Its difficulties were constrained further by the dynamic nature of the domestic, colonial and international conditions in which it had to operate. Between December 1945 and July 1947, the main provisions of the Loan Agreement were increasingly violated, as Britain attempted to reconstruct its war-torn economy. As the deadline for convertibility approached, efforts to safeguard sterling intensified. In addition, colonial economic policy was gradually transformed to reflect the changing economic needs of the metropole.

The collapse of sterling convertibility in July 1947 marked a turning point in the development of economic relations between Britain and its colonial dependencies. In its aftermath the benefits accruing to Britain from colonial development were easily justified. Consequently, the process was energized, more financial resources were placed at the disposal of the colonies, colonial economies were integrated into that of the metropole and a lot of emphasis was placed on expanding the production and export of "dollar earning" and "dollar saving" commodities that were produced in the colonies.

Ironically, the transformation in economic relations between Britain and its colonies occurred simultaneously with the emergence of a major nationalist challenge to colonial rule in three of Britain's most valuable colonies at this time: the Gold Coast, Malaya and Nigeria. Given the significance of their contribution to the British economy capitulation was out of the question. Nevertheless, repression was not enough to neutralize the nationalist forces. Britain was thus compelled to make some, albeit limited, concessions. By 1949, however, the full significance of the nationalist challenge to colonial rule was yet to unfold, and consequently it was not seen as a danger to the restoration of sterling to international convertibility or to Britain's economic recovery.

In retrospect, however, there was danger in store for Britain. Although officials believed that the colonial sterling balances could endanger the United Kingdom's economic stability, between 1946 and 1949 they felt that it was better to allow the colonies to continue to accumulate sterling reserves than to permit them to spend it on development. This policy was employed no doubt because the maintenance of colonial rule was Britain's guarantee that it could contain the potential danger the balances posed for its economy. By 1949, however, the bulk of the colonial sterling reserves were held by the three colonies (the Gold Coast, Malaya and Nigeria) in the forefront of efforts to accelerate the pace of political reform in the British empire. Once the momentum for change intensified, it was only a matter of time before the economic implications of the political challenge to colonial rule were realized.

NOTES

1. G.D.H. Cole, *The Postwar Condition of Britain* (London: Routledge and Kegan Paul, 1956), pp. 99–104. See also S. Pollard, *The Development of the British Economy 1914–1967* (London: Edwin Arnold, 1969) pp. 356–357 and A. R. Conan, *The Sterling Area* (London: Macmillan, 1953), pp. 3–5.

2. P. D. Henderson, "Britain's International Trade Position," in G. D. Worswick and P. H. Ady, eds., *The British Economy 1945–50*. (Oxford: Clarendon Press, 1952), p. 66. See also C. S. Newton, "The Sterling Crisis and the British Response to the Marshall Plan, *Economic History Review*, Vol. 37, No. 3, (1984), pp. 393–394.

3. R. M. Hathaway, *Ambiguous Partnership: Britain and America 1944–1947* (New York: Columbia University Press, 1981), p. 24. See also P. Burnham, *The Political Economy of Post War Reconstruction* (London: Macmillan, 1990).

4. United Nations Department of Economic Affairs, *Economic Report: Salient Features of the World Economic Situation 1945–47*, pp. 33–34.

5. D. H. Aldcroft, *The European Economy 1914–1990* 3rd edition (London: Routledge, 1993), p.105.

6. L. S. Pressnell, *External Economic Policy since the War, Vol. 1: The Postwar Financial Settlement* (London: HMSO, 1987), appendix 25, p. 423.

7. J. Fforde, *The Bank of England and Public Policy 1941–1958* (Cambridge: Cambridge University Press, 1992), p. 141.

8. P. W. Bell, *The Sterling Area in the Post-War World: Internal Mechanism and Cohesion 1946–1952*. (Oxford: Clarendon Press , 1956), p. 53.

9. For an excellent discussion of Britain's attempt to find a negotiated solution to this problem see Fforde, *The Bank of England and Public Policy 1941–1958*, pp. 95–124. See also R. N. Gardner, *Sterling Dollar Diplomacy in Current Perspective* (New York: Columbia University Press, 1980),p. 329, and Newton "The Sterling Crisis and the British Response to the Marshall Plan," pp. 399–401. There were many examples of sterling countries striving for economic independence. India proposed as early as 1946 that the pooling system for hard currencies should be terminated. South Africa withdrew from the dollar pool in 1947 and when asked to live within its dollar income in 1948, Australia expressed its inability to do so.

10. Conan, *The Sterling Area*, p. 71. He points out also that there was a technical side to the problems of sterling countries which made it difficult for Britain to impose her will upon them. Many of these countries did not possess highly organized and efficient administrative financial systems. Thus they were unable to forecast or regulate state balance of payments in order to facilitate exchange rationing. For example, in 1947–1948, after setting a limit of US$80 million for its dollar deficit, Australia found that it amounted to US$200 million. India on the other hand, spent in one year (1948–1949) the sterling released for three years. For further details see Chapter 5 of *The Sterling Area*.

11. Gardner, *Sterling Dollar Diplomacy in Current Perspective*, p. 328.

12. E. Zupnick, *Britain's Postwar Dollar Problem* (New York: Columbia University Press, 1958), p. 129.

13. *The Sterling Area: An American Analysis*. The United States Economic Cooperation Administration Special Mission to the United Kingdom (London, 1951), p. 68. For further details on the growing dollar deficit of the Sterling Area see "Post-War Dollar Deficits in International Trade," World Economic Report 1949–50 (United Nations, 1951).

14. *N.A.I.* Savingram: C.S.G., Lagos to S.N.P., S.E.P. and S.W.P. June 30, 1945.

15. Ibid.

16. *N.A.I.* Ib. Min. Agric. 1/446/3031 Vol. 12. Savingram S/S to Governor of Nigeria, 18/9/45.

17. United Nations Food and Agriculture Organisation Commodity Series, *Fats and Oils Bulletin*, no. 13 (August 1949), pp. 44–45 and 74–75.

18. Ibid.

19. *Parliamentary Papers 1945–1946*, Vol. XX 1(Cmd. 6785). World Food Shortage, p. 3.

20. Ibid., p. 6.

21. *P.R.O.* CO 852/964/3. B. A. Keen, C. E. Rooke and I. McFadyen to the Secretary of State for the Colonies (undated).

22. Zupnick, *Britain's Postwar Dollar Problems*, p. 129.

23. The British government's emphasis at this time seems to have been influenced also by the positive signs of recovery that were evident in the British economy for much of 1946 and the early part of 1947. See A. Cairncross and B. Eichengreen, *Sterling in Decline: The Devaluations of 1931, 1949 and 1967* (Oxford: Basil Blackwell Publishing Ltd., 1983), pp. 113–115; A. Cairncross, *Years of Recovery: British Economic Policy, 1945–1951* (London: Methuen, 1985), p. 130; and K. O. Morgan, *Labour in Power 1945–1951* (Oxford: Clarendon Press, 1984), pp. 335–341.

24.   *P.R.O.* CO 852/1001/2/19907/69/47 Pt. 1. Extract from a minute by C. G. Eastwood 26/4/47. The wording of this minute was very interesting. While he was obviously concerned with Britain's balance of payments problems, Eastwood placed these needs within the overall context of the world economy. He explained, "what we want to discover is on the one hand what are the world needs and the UK needs for particular commodities likely to be for a period of years, and on the other what are the technical possibilities of growing those commodities in the Colonies."

25.   *P.R.O.* CO 852/1001/2/19907/69/47 Pt.1. Minutes of the first meeting of the CPPC 29 May 1947.

26.   Ibid.

27.   Ibid.

28.   Ibid.

29.   Ibid.

30.   *P.R.O.* CO 852/1001/2/19907/69/47. Circular Telegram S/S to all Colonies (excluding Ceylon) 26/6/47.

31.   D. J. Morgan, *The Official History of Colonial Development*, Vol. 2 (London: Macmillan Press, 1980), p. 54.

32.   Ibid., pp. 54–56.

33.   *P.R.O.* CO 537/3089. Economic Policy Committee Preparations of Papers for Circulation. Practical Achievements in the Colonies since the War. Some Practical Achievements in the Colonies since the War. 7/12/48.

34.   *Parliamentary Accounts and Papers 1946–1947*, Vol. X (Cmd. 7167). Report on the Colonial Empire 1939–1947, p. 82.

35.   Morgan, *The Official History of Colonial Development*, p. 56. See also J. H. Bowden, "Development and Control in British Colonial Policy with Special Reference to Nigeria and the Gold Coast 1935–1948" (Unpublished Ph.D. thesis, Birmingham, 1980), p. 331.

36.   Ibid., p. 54.

37.   Ibid.

38.   *P.R.O.* T 236/3351. "The Treatment of Colonial Sterling Balances," draft memorandum by O. L. Williams. This was forwarded to N. E. Young with a covering letter dated 4/5/49. The memorandum itself was undated. However, the date of the covering letter suggests that it was mostly likely written in late April or the first week of May.

39.   Morgan, *The Official History of Colonial Development*, p. 57.

40.   Ibid., p. 58.

41.   Ibid., p. 58. See also p. 122.

42.   Ibid., p. 58. See also *P.R.O.* T 236/3351. "The Treatment of Colonial Sterling Balances." Draft memorandum by O. L. Williams.

43.   Ibid., p. 58.

44.   Ibid., p. 58.

45.   *P.R.O.* T 236/3351. "The Treatment of Colonial Sterling Balances." Draft memorandum by O. L. Williams.

46.   Ibid. This point was made in O. L. Williams' first draft, but was omitted from subsequent drafts.

47.   *P.R.O.* CO 852/1001/2. Extract from a minute by E. G. Eastwood, 26/4/47.

48. *The Sterling Area: An American Analysis*, p. 98. Britain negotiated these agreements because "the quantity of British exports which would have been claimed, had all the holders been free to draw on their accounts without restraint, would have been far larger than Britain could make available out of current production," p. 180. In order to freeze or "block" balances, two accounts were set up in England for the central banks of the countries concerned. One account contained Sterling balances accumulated before the signing of the Loan Agreement, July 1946. These were frozen and could be released only by the mutual agreement of Britain and the country concerned. The other account contained the balances released by mutual agreement together with those accumulated after the signing of the agreement.

49. Gardner, *Sterling Dollar Diplomacy in Current Perspective*, p. 315. See also *P.R.O.* CO 852/1040/3. "United Kingdom Balance of Payments 1946 to 1949."

50. Fforde, *The Bank of England and Public Policy 1941–1958*, p. 141.

51. Pollard, *The Development of the British Economy 1914–1967*, p. 360.

52. Ibid.

53. Fforde claims that in February 1947 George Bolton, adviser to the Bank of England, had predicted that "the effect of convertibility will be to add substantially to the drawings on US dollar credit without giving any off-setting advantages of any kind." Thus, he proposed: a renegotiation of the Loan Agreement; full restoration of the United Kingdom's right to a transitional period under the Bretton Woods agreement; a tightening up of the Sterling Area; fresh discrimination in trade arrangements with Western Europe; and consideration of a 20 percent devaluation. Bolton added that if Washington refused to negotiate, Britain's only choice would have been to abandon the international institutions and repudiate its various obligations. See *The Bank of England and Public Policy 1941–1958*, p. 143.

54. Pollard, *The Development of the British Economy 1914–1967*, p. 360.

55. Gardner, *Sterling Dollar Diplomacy in Current Perspective*, p. 317. See also R. G. Hawtrey, *Towards the Rescue of Sterling* (London: Longmans, 1954), pp. 21–25.

56. Ibid., p. 317. These accounts facilitated the free transfer of sterling earned on current transactions, regardless of the country of residence of the account holder. See also Newton, "The Sterling Crisis and the British Response to the Marshall Plan," pp. 400–401.

57. Zupnick, *Britain's Postwar Dollar Problem*, p. 168. See also J. R. Sargent, "Britain and Europe" in G. D. Worswick and P. H. Ady, eds., *The British Economy 1945–1950* (Oxford: Clarendon Press, 1952), p. 513.

58. Gardner, *Sterling Dollar Diplomacy in Current Perspective*, p. 318. See also Hawtrey, *Towards the Rescue of Sterling*, pp. 24–25.

59. *P.R.O.* CO 537/3047/19128/71. Minute by E. Bevin to Prime Minister Attlee. 13/9/47.

60. Ibid., Prime Minister to Bevin. 16/9/47.

61. Ibid., Bevin to Prime Minister, 15 September 1947.

62. Ibid., Minute by Prime Minister to Secretary for Overseas Trade, 16 September 1947.

63. *P.R.O.* CO/537/3027/19128/71. Ivor Thomas to Stafford Cripps, 17/9/47.

64. *P.R.O.* CO 852/1000/3. Speech by the Rt. Hon. Sir Stafford Cripps K. C., Minister for Economic Affairs, to the African Governors Conference on 12 November 1947.
65. *P.R.O.* CO/852/889/19339/3/48. "Economic Planning in the Colonies," memorandum by Gorell Barnes 3/8/48.
66. *P.R.O.* CO 537/3095/19144. Secret "Dollar Drain Committee" progress report by the Treasury, 10/12/47.
67. Ibid., Outward telegram S/S to all colonies 3/12/47.
68. Gardner, *Sterling Dollar Diplomacy in Current Perspective*, p. 329.
69. Ibid., p. 330.
70. Ibid., p. 331.
71. Ibid., p. 332. Gardner argues that American concurrence on this matter was very significant, "in view of the fact that American antipathy to discrimination was originally caused by preferential practices in the Colonial Empire." This can be interpreted as an indication of the Americans' acceptance of the gravity of Britain's economic position.
72. Ibid., p. 342.
73. Zupnick, *Britain's Postwar Dollar Problem*, p. 129.
74. Ibid., p. 143.
75. Pollard, *The Development of the British Economy 1914–1967*, p. 361. See also Newton "The Sterling Crisis and the British Response to the Marshall Plan," pp. 401–407.
76. Ibid.
77. *P.R.O.* CO 852/1040/3. "United Kingdom Balance of Payments 1946–1949."
78. J. J. Kaplan and G. Schleiminger, *The European Payments Union* (Oxford: Clarendon Press, 1989), pp. 7–27. See also Vanthoor, *European Monetary Union Since 1848: A Political and Historical Analysis* (London: Edward Elgar, 1996.)
79. M. J. Hogan, *The Marshall Plan: America, Britain and the Reconstruction of Western Europe, 1947–1952.* (Cambridge: Cambridge University Press, 1989), p. 91. See also Chapter 3.
80. Hogan, *The Marshall Plan*, pp. 60–61.
81. Ibid., pp. 125–128. See also Cairncross, *Years of Recovery*.
82. Ibid., chs. 3–5.
83. J. Darwin, *Britain and Decolonisation* (London: Macmillan, 1988), p. 87.
84. Ibid., p. 98.
85. Ibid., p. 103.
86. M. Crowder, "The 1939–45 War and West Africa," in J. F. Ajayi and M. Crowder, *A History of West Africa*, Vol. II (London: Longman, 1974), p. 615.
87. Ibid.
88. M. Ayearst, *The British West Indies* (London: George Allen and Unwin, 1960), pp. 71–74.
89. Darwin, *Britain and Decolonisation*, p. 88.
90. Ibid., p. 89.
91. P. J. Cain and A. G. Hopkins, British Imperialism: Crisis and Deconstruction 1914–1990 (London: Longman, 1993), p. 96.
92. Ibid.
93. Darwin, *Britain and Decolonisation*, pp. 100–101.

94.   Ibid., p. 105.
95.   R. Hyam, "Africa and the Labour Government," *Journal of Imperial and Commonwealth History*, Vol. 16, no. 3 (May 1988), p. 153.
96.   Ibid., p. 152.
97.   See O. Aluko, "Politics of decolonization in British West Africa," in Ajayi and Crowder, *History of West Africa*, pp. 627–653.
98.   *Parliamentary Papers 1946–1947*, Vol. X (Cmd. 7167), p. 82.
99.   D. Rooney, *Sir Charles Arden-Clarke*. (London: Rex Collings, 1982), p. 84.
100.   R. F. Holland, *European Decolonization 1918–1981: An Introductory Survey*. (New York: St. Martin's Press, 1985), pp. 106–107.
101.   Ibid.
102.   A. Thurston, *Records of the Colonial Office, Dominions Office, Commonwealth Relations Office and Commonwealth Office*, Vol. 1 (London: HMSO, 1995), p. 315.
103.   Bowden, "Development and Control in British Colonial Policy, with Special Reference to Nigeria and the Gold Coast," p. 342.
104.   Ibid. These were: The Colonial Development Working Party, the Colonial Economic Development Council, the Review of Programs and of Colonial Capital Investment Requirements, the Colonial Dollar Drain Committee, Colonial Aspects of the Economic Activities of the United Nations and the Colonial Primary Products Committee.
105.   *Thurston, Records of the Colonial Office, Dominions Office, Commonwealth Relations Office and Commonwealth Office*, p. 315.
106.   *P.R.O.* CO 852/873/1/19298/63/12. S/S to the Officer Administering the Government of Nigeria. Outward telegram 24/1/48.
107.   Ibid.
108.   *P.R.O.* CO 537/3030/18706/9/92. "Economic Development in the Colonies" a Note by the Secretary of State for the Colonies. 5 Feb. 1948.
109.   Ibid.
110.   *P.R.O.* CO 852/855/4, Select Committee on Estimates, Fifth Report.
111.   *P.R.O.* CO 852/889/19339/1948, Re-organisation of Economic Planning in the Colonies, memorandum by Gorell Barnes, 3 August 1948.
112.   Ibid.
113.   *P.R.O.* CO 852/867/4/19286/7/2. "The Colonial Development and Welfare Act and the Overseas Resources Development Act" a Note by the Colonial Office. 17/4/48.
114.   *House of Commons Debate*, Vol. 446, col. 134, 20 January 1948.
115.   Ibid.
116.   Ibid.
117.   *P.R.O.* CO 852/1052/3. "The Colonial Empire and the Economic Crisis." Conference Discussion Paper A. C. (48)5, with the draft brief for Dalton's speech on 7 October, "The Economic Position of the United Kingdom in Relation to the Colonies," dated 22 September 1948.
118.   Ibid., Letter from Secretary to the Chancellor of the Exchequer to Mr. Mason. 4 Oct. (N. D. Mason was Private Secretary to the S/S.)
119.   Ibid., minute by Poynton to Watson. 6/10/48.
120.   Ibid., W. H. Watson to N. D. Mason. 6/10/48.
121.   *P.R.O.* CO 537/3089/19128/89/2/3. Economic Policy Committee.

Preparation of Papers for circulation. Practical achievements in the colonies since the war. 7/12/48.

122. Ibid.

123. Ibid.

124. *The Sterling Area: An American Analysis*, p. 69.

125. A. Feavearyear, *The Pound Sterling: A History of English Money*. (Oxford: Clarendon Press, 1963), p. 417.

126. *The Sterling Area: An American Analysis*, p. 192.

127. Ibid.

128. Conan, *The Sterling Area*, p. 104.

129. Cairncross, *Years of Recovery: British Economic Recovery 1945–51*, p. 203.

130. *P.R.O.* CO 852/1040/3. United Kingdom Balance of Payments, 1946–49.

131. Hawtrey, *Towards the Rescue of Sterling*, p. 30.

132. Ibid. See also Fforde, *The Bank of England and Public Policy 1941–1958*, pp. 219–249.

133. *P.R.O.* CO 852/1039/6/97304/68. Minute by Mayle to Eastwood.

134. Ibid. Circular telegram S/S to all Colonies. 4/7/49.

135. Ibid.

136. Hawtrey, *Towards the Rescue of Sterling*, p. 33. See also A. Cairncross and B. Eichengreen, *Sterling in Decline: The Devaluations of 1931, 1949 and 1967* (Oxford: Basil Blackwell, 1983).

Recovery and Relapse:
British Imperial Policy, 1949–1952

The devaluation of September 1949 put an end to speculation against the pound, and stimulated a general improvement in the economic conditions in Britain and the Sterling Area in the months prior to the outbreak of the Korean War.[1] Despite this, the British government was concerned that the impending cessation of Marshall Aid was going to make it difficult for the United Kingdom to endure any future drain on its gold and dollar reserves.[2] The Treasury also argued that "the existence of large accumulations of sterling balances, enhanced the dangers involved in any restoration of the free convertibility of sterling."[3] The recovery of the British economy occurred at a time when the movement for trade liberalization in Europe was gathering momentum. This was evident in the establishment of the European Payments Union (E.P.U.) in September 1950. Under the terms governing the operations of the E.P.U., member countries "entered into an agreement to authorize without delay the transfer of foreign exchange required to settle on due date all regularly authorized transactions."[4] The E.P.U. effected the settlement of all accredited trading and invisible transactions between O.E.E.C. countries and their associated monetary areas. Thus, European countries finally had an instrument that could facilitate decisive progress toward multilateralism in trade.[5] Bilateral deficits between member countries were automatically offset against credit balances with others. In addition, using quotas calculated on the basis of the total payments and receipts in respect of the visible and invisible trade of each member country and its associated monetary area, transactions were settled partly in credits and partly in gold. This arrangement was enhanced by the fact that the Union had access to capital made available by the United States to enable it to make payments in gold or dollars.[6] Thus, once they maintained their quotas E.P.U. member countries could have safeguarded their reserves of gold and convertible currency.

The creation of the E.P.U. had important consequences for imperial policy. In 1950 O.E.E.C. countries agreed to eliminate quantitative restrictions on 60 percent of their private imports from each other. This was to increase to 75 percent by 1 February 1951.[7] They also agreed that trade liberalization and nondiscrimination should occur simultaneously. In addition, all existing and future measures for liberalization were to be applied equally to imports from states belonging to the E.P.U.[8] Members of the E.P.U. that faced a serious drain on their gold and dollar reserves were exempted from its rules on trade liberalization. Although there was some flexibility to enable it to cope with serious balance of payments difficulties, the code of liberalization of the E.P.U. meant that the Americans notwithstanding, Britain was now under pressure in Europe to the eliminate the trade barriers that it had established to protect sterling. Given that the measures to safeguard sterling were an integral part of colonial economic policy, in order to fulfill its obligations to the E.P.U., Britain had to liberalize its policies with regard to colonial trade.

Expectations of early moves to liberalize British trade were dashed by the economic crisis that followed the outbreak of the Korean War in June 1950. During this conflict Britain endorsed American action to oppose North Korean aggression and increased its expenditure on defense under a three-year plan from £3,400 million in September 1950 to £4,700 million in January 1951. According to Morgan, "the entire foreign and defense policies were suddenly being recast, with grave consequences for its [Britain's] economic strategy and political future."[9] As a result of the increase in expenditure on defense "a violent and disastrous change took place during 1951 in the overseas balance of payments of the United Kingdom."[10] Thus, as Fforde aptly concludes, "instead of looking forward to steadily rising output, with external balance and without undue inflationary pressure, the electorally precarious government had now to contemplate a resumption of shortages and bottlenecks . . . and the threat of renewed external weakness."[11]

By the middle of 1951 the increase in the prices of goods and services caused by the Korean War had reached astronomical levels. As a result the sterling value of British imports of raw materials from all sources rose from £690 million in 1949 to £960 million in 1950 and £1,572 million in 1951.[12] Overall in 1951 the volume of imports was about 46 percent more than it was in 1950 and import prices had increased by 60 percent. This "massive increase in UK import prices for 1951 dislocated the British balance of payments that had been strengthened in 1950."[13] Britain's plight was accentuated by the fact that rising imports from the O.E.E.C.

together with a vast increase in Sterling Area imports from the Dollar Area resulted in a further loss of dollars.[14] As a result the United Kingdom's gold and dollar reserves moved from a surplus of US$414 million (£147 million) in the first half of 1951 to a deficit of US$1,578 million (£563 million) between July and December,[15] and overall Britain's gold and dollar reserves moved from a surplus of US$3,300 million (£1,178 million) in 1950 to a deficit of US$1,164 (£415 million) in 1951 (Table 3.1).

Table 3.1
The Drain on the United Kingdom's Gold and Dollar Reserves, 1949–1951

(US million) Deficit(-) Surplus (+)

Year	Reserves
1949	1688
1950	3300
1951 (first half)	414
July–September	–638
October	–320
November	–248
December	–372

Source: P.R.O. T236/4348. Key Statistics on Overseas Finance Mid-January 1952. H. M. Treasury copy no. 20.

The figures for the United Kingdom's trade deficit were just as alarming: "starting with the extreme severity in August, the deficit climbed to the extraordinary total of £424 million, with a total of £521 million for the year as a whole."[16] Britain's dollar balance moved from a surplus of £308 million in 1950 to a deficit of £561 million in the second quarter of 1951.[17] The stability of the British economy was threatened yet again.

This strengthened further Britain's resolve to continue relying on the resources of its colonial empire. The secretary of state pointed out in a circular dispatch to all colonial territories that "there was during the second and third quarter of 1951 a sharp deterioration in the dollar surplus earned by the Sterling Area in comparison with the two preceding quarters and this trend was expected to continue."[18] He continued, "in these circumstances I fear that there is no prospect of any substantial relaxation of control of dollar spending in the Sterling Area being possible in the near future."[19]

In October the new chancellor of the exchequer, R. A. B. Butler, told the cabinet "we are in a balance of payments crisis, worse than in 1949, and in many ways worse than in 1947. Confidence in the sterling is impaired, as witness the large discounts on the forward sterling in New York, and speculation against it is considerable, increasing the deficits and the drain on our gold and dollar reserves."[20] He claimed that the drain on the United Kingdom's gold and dollar reserves was more intense than at any other time since the war, and noted that the very serious deterioration in the United Kingdom's position, coming as it did, at the inception and not during the rearmament program, threatened the whole of the sterling position of the United Kingdom.[21]

Britain's dilemma at this time was made worse by the Iranian seizure of the Abadan oil fields and the consequent loss of a further £120 million annually in invisible earnings. In addition, toward the end of 1950, interest and the amortization on U.S. and Canadian loans costing "over £75 million annually were due and this would have seriously depleted the invisible earnings, especially since Marshall Aid had been terminated."[22] Further, the recovery of West Germany and Japan from the devastation wrought by war and the United States from the mild recession of 1949 meant that Britain was assured of intense competition in international markets from 1950 onward. As Burnham so succinctly puts it, "an exceptional conjunction of unfavorable developments in the second half of 1951 intensified the pressure on sterling."[23] Even though the situation in 1951 was not as grim as it was in 1945 or 1947, given the context within which the Tories inherited power, immediate steps had to be taken to protect sterling. At the beginning of the 1950s, therefore, there were no fundamental changes in the economic conditions in the United Kingdom that shaped colonial economic policy. Thus, the measures employed by the British government to channel colonial resources toward the defense of sterling remained the same.

THE POLITICAL AND ECONOMIC CHALLENGES IN THE COLONIES: 1949–1951

The volatility in the British economy between 1949 and 1951 coincided with a period of acceleration in the process of political reform in the British empire, especially in the principal dollar-earning colonies, the Gold Coast, Nigeria and Malaya (the colonial empire's largest dollar earner). Between 1949 and 1951 these colonies' share of the accumulated colonial sterling balance increased from 37.5 percent to 41.7 percent. During this period Nigeria was the largest holder of accumulated colonial balances with about 16.5 percent of the total balances. Next were the Gold Coast with about 12.5 percent and the Federation of Malaya with just over 10 percent.[24] Despite the significant percentage of the total colonial balances held by these colonies, their continued growth and the territories' rapid advance toward self-government, between 1949 and 1951 government officials were not concerned about the implications of these developments for the British economy.

In the period between 1949 and 1951 the colonial government in the Gold Coast came under relentless pressure, primarily from the left-leaning Convention People's Party (C.P.P.), to establish through a general election a constituent assembly that would determine full self-government for the colony.[25] The C.P.P.'s "Positive Action" (a nonviolent civil disobedience campaign of agitation, propaganda, strikes, boycotts and noncooperation) won mass support, and some demonstrations resulted in looting and rioting in many parts of the colony. In an attempt to stem the rising tide of nationalist revolt and dictate, if not derail, the campaign for self-government, the colonial government clamped down on press freedom and jailed the principal leaders of the C.P.P.[26]

In January 1951 a new constitution was introduced and in the elections that followed in February, the C.P.P. swept the polls, even though its leaders were imprisoned. Under the 1951 constitution official representation in the Legislative Council was abolished, a ministerial system was introduced, and Africans had a majority on the Executive Council that was responsible not to the governor alone, but to the Legislative Council as well. Although the C.P.P. controlled five of the eight ministerial posts, and was the governing party, it did not have full control of the colonial government. The key portfolios of defense, foreign affairs, justice and finance were the responsibility of ex-officio members appointed by the governor. To Kwame Nkrumah, the C.P.P. leader, the provisions of the 1951 constitution represented a transitional stage in the path of independence. From his anti-imperialist rhetoric it was clear that Nkrumah was not going to be satisfied with anything less than independence for the Gold Coast. In the context of the existing Cold War, this prospect was not very appealing to the British government. Nkrumah's left-wing tendencies together with his anti-imperialism aroused fears that the colony may have been vulnerable to communist penetration. The latter held all sorts of horrendous prospects for Britain because the Gold Coast was an important dollar earner and it was one of Britain's largest colonial creditors in terms of accumulated sterling balances.

The situation in Nigeria was not as volatile as that in the Gold Coast. Nevertheless, both the British government and the colonial government believed that events in the Gold Coast played an important role in the impetus for change in Nigeria. Thus, they tried to ensure that constitutional reform in Nigeria did not lag too far behind those in the Gold Coast. A new constitution was promulgated in Nigeria in January 1951. Although universal adult suffrage was not introduced, Nigerians played a greater role in the appointment of their representatives to the central legislature. In addition, the principal instrument of colonial government policy was now a council of ministers presided over by the governor. However, ministers were appointed by the governor or lieutenant governor (in the regions), subject to an affirmative vote by elected representatives in the regions concerned. Further, defense external affairs, the public service, finance and justice remained the purview of ex-officio members appointed by the governor.

In Malaya the communist war of national liberation continued unabated in 1951. At this juncture the anti-communist elements were all devoted to the defeat of the communist insurgents. Nevertheless, Malayan nationalists used the emergency to strengthen their demands for independence, "maintaining that the Communist charge that the rebels were fighting against 'imperialism' would lose its force if the government were Malayan and not British."[27] In addition, under the terms of the agreement it signed with the Malay rulers in 1948, Britain was committed to the introduction of elections for the legislatures in the federation as a first step toward the eventual granting of self-government. By 1951 the elective principle was being used to choose municipal representatives. These elections signaled the beginning of the dismantling of the system in which political activity was limited to making representations to the government or organizing public demonstration in protest over various issues.[28] Unlike the Gold Coast and Nigeria, a ministerial system in which nominated members of the Legislative Council were responsible for various departments and functions of government was introduced into Malaya in 1951. However, ultimate responsibility for colonial administration continued to rest solely with the ex-officio official members and the high commissioner, Britain's representative in the federation. They also had the power to veto decisions of the Legislative Council.

Political reform in the Gold Coast, Nigeria and Malaya established an important basis from which the nationalists could make further demands for political autonomy. Even though Britain was losing control of the pace of political transformation in the Gold Coast and struggling to hold back the winds of change, or at least moderate their intensity, in Malaya and Nigeria, it was keen to ensure that the process was not detrimental to its economic well-being. Given the instability surrounding sterling at this juncture, it was clearly not prepared to grant concessions that would have enabled Nigeria, Malaya and the Gold Coast to subvert its ability to channel their resources to assist in the defense of sterling or correcting its trade imbalance with the Dollar Area.

However, it was proving increasingly difficult to constrain the forces of change. In Nigeria, for example, unofficial members of the Legislative Council were becoming impatient with the pace of economic development. They criticized the emphasis that was being placed upon agricultural exports and called on the colonial government to begin a program of industrialization.[29] Governor Macpherson acknowledged that the growing level of discontent was "forcibly brought to my attention during my first wide tour of the country."[30] As a result in March 1949 Regional Production Development Boards were established in the three regions of Nigeria and a Colony Development Board to incorporate Lagos. These boards were funded from the proceeds of the existing marketing boards in accordance with the main crops produced in each region. A formula was devised through which 70 percent of the boards' surpluses was retained as sterling reserves, for price stabilization, 22.5 percent for regional development and 7.5 percent for research.[31]

Pressure from nationalist agitators had therefore coerced the Nigerian colonial government into modifying the British government's policy toward the use of the sterling reserves accumulated by the marketing boards.[32] Hitherto, apart from small sums allocated for research and disease control, the bulk of the marketing boards' surpluses were held in London as reserves to facilitate price stabilization in the colonies. Even though there was as yet no indication of serious concern, developments in Nigeria suggested that alterations in colonial policy toward the preservation of sterling were an inevitable consequence of the process of political reform. There were also other changes that accompanied the transfer of political control. By 1951 the colonial secretary's control was confined to broad issues of fiscal policy, measures against inflation, exchange and currency control, development finance and loan policy. Control over annual budgetary estimates rested with the Standing Finance Committee of the Legislative Council. The colonial secretary also dispensed with responsibility for writing off loans, approving expenditure from public funds and the formal approval of annual budgetary estimates. These were now handled by the Legislative Councils.[33]

By 1951 most colonies had established organizations geared to service industrial development, and several had made significant strides in this area. In Nigeria, the Federation of Malaya, Singapore, Jamaica and Trinidad, the production of electricity had increased from a combined total of 402.1 million kilowatt hours in 1947 to 1,219 million kilowatt hours in 1951.[34] In Uganda projects were underway for the manufacture of textiles, safety razors, iron and steel. In Jamaica a new cement factory was under construction and was expected to begin operations shortly. Factories producing gypsum plasters, blocks and laundry blue were also under consideration. In Trinidad legislation was passed designating new industries as "pioneer" and the government was empowered to grant them tax and duty concessions. Margarine, butter substitutes, cotton shirts, recorder machines, boxes and cartoons were also being manufactured. In the Gold Coast there were a number of industrial enterprises including three timber mills, six printing presses and two textile factories.[35]

As was the case with the political changes that were occurring in the British empire, economic diversification had important implications for imperial policy that was geared principally toward the expansion of production of dollar-earning or dollar-saving primary exports. Taken in conjunction with the movement for greater political autonomy, it was clear that the nationalist forces in the colonies were intent on reconstructing the nature of economic relations between Britain and colonial territories. In addition, in the emerging dispensation they were not prepared to continue merely as sources of the raw materials needed by British or European industries. However, the depth of the integration of the metropolitan and colonial economies, a lack of capital, dependency on British and Sterling Area markets, a shortage of skilled personnel and Britain's determination to retain control, or at the very least, influence over the process of change in colonial economies guaranteed that alterations to colonial economic relations would be very difficult.

Given the changing political and economic order in some colonial dependencies in 1951, it was not surprising that the position of the colonial secretary and the U.K. Treasury in constitutionally advanced territories was the subject of much concern within imperial and colonial circles. The colonial dilemma was epitomized in discussions that occurred in the Federation of Malaya.[36] As the federation moved toward self-government, the power of the colonial secretary or the Treasury to enforce the will of the British government was no longer thought to be vested in exercising a veto, but in the cold political facts. Simply put, the issue now was whether the Malayan Federation required assistance from Britain, which the latter had the power to withhold. If the answer to this was affirmative, it was believed that the effective power of the British government could be assumed for years to come. This did not mean that the colonial secretary or the Treasury could only hope to make an impression by threatening to withhold financial assistance. On the contrary, Britain wanted to safeguard its interest by consultation rather than a trial of strength.[37] But it was quite prepared to use economic leverage if the situation warranted it.

The changing political and economic climate in the colonial empire did not affect Britain's response to the balance of payments crisis of 1951. At the onset of the deterioration in Britain's gold and dollar reserves in July 1951 the ceiling on colonial expenditure on dollar imports was set at US$199 million, an increase of 22.6 percent over the US$154 million that was set in 1950 (Table 3.2).

Table 3.2
The Performance of the U.K. Colonies Relative to the Ceilings on Their Dollar Expenditure, 1948–1952

(US $ millions c.i.f)

	Aggregate Ceilings	Actual Expenditure
1948	348	330
1949	217	241
1950	154	120
1951	199	194
TOTAL	928	885

Source: *P.R.O.* T 236/3563. A. K. Potter minute to Sir L. Rowan 26/10/51.

The colonial secretary outlined the policy implications of Britain's difficulties for the colonies. He explained that rearmament in Western Europe was reducing the supplies of raw materials and manufactured goods available for export to the markets overseas. Furthermore, the dollar surplus of the Sterling Area had declined so sharply during the second quarter of 1951 that the possibility of a relaxation in dollar restrictions was ruled out.[38] In addition, the outlook for 1952 was for a continuance of the dollar drain on reserves and a downturn from net dollar surpluses to a substantial dollar deficit and this called for remedial action. Consequently, colonial dependencies were warned that the existing situation ruled out the substantial relaxation in dollar restrictions that was thought possible at the beginning of the year.[39]

The volume indices for colonial exports of primary products revealed a significant increase in colonial mineral exports from 114 points in 1949 to 137 points in 1951. Oilseeds, vegetable oils and whale oil exports increased from 127 in 1949 to 131 in 1950 before declining to 101 in 1951. The export of foodstuffs other than edible oils increased from 111 in 1949 to 115 in 1951 (Table 3.3).

Table 3.3
Volume Indices of Colonial Exports of Primary Products, 1936 and 1946–1953
(1948=100)

Year	Minerals	Oilseeds, Vegetable oils, and whale oil	Foodstuffs other than edible oils	Other agricultural and forestry products	Total
1936	89	118	116	64	90
1946	59	76	97	61	71
1947	81	95	95	94	91
1948	100	100	100	100	100
1949	114	127	111	109	113
1950	136	131	114	110	120
1951	137	101	115	108	117
1952	145	120	116	101	119
1953	149	129	127	104	125

Source: The Colonial Territories 1954–55 (Cmd. 9489).

While the colonial empire was forced to practice economy in its dollar expenditure, then, its exports were expanding, and more significantly, it continued to enjoy a growing surplus in its transactions with the Dollar Area. The colonial surplus increased from US$210 million in 1948 to US$410 million in 1950. For the first half of 1951 it was US$357 million and US$480 million for the year as a whole (Table 3.4). It is important to emphasize that the colonial surplus with the Dollar Area was greatest between 1950 and 1952, a time of major crisis in the U.K. economy. For the period as a whole the surplus was US$1,257 million. During the critical years 1951–1952 it was US$847 million (Table 3.5).[40]

The limitations on colonial spending were heavily criticized in some parts of the colonial empire. In Nigeria, for example, Nnamdi Azikiwe, the leader of the National Council for Nigeria and the Cameroons, a prominent nationalist party, complained that although Nigeria was a major dollar earner because of cocoa, oil palm produce and timber exports, it was unable to spend the dollars it earned. He contended, "our needs are greater than those of the British, yet all we get in return is pounds sterling and high prices on imports."[41] He accused Britain of exploitation and threatened to pull out of the commonwealth and establish a republic in Nigeria after independence.[42] Bangura claims that in the Gold Coast there was a groundswell of opposition from "nationalist quarters against the policy of import controls and dollar rationing."[43] The latter was resented because it was felt that dollar discrimination was inimical to cooperation with the United States in finance and commerce, areas thought to be vital to the colony's

Table 3.4
Colonial Transactions with the Dollar Area, 1948–1951
(Estimated Payments and Receipts)
$million

	1948			1949			1950			1951		
	1st half	2nd half	Year	1st half	2nd half	Year	1st half	2nd half	Year	1st half	2nd half	Year
Payments for Imports (f.o.b.)												
West Africa	15	10	25	15	10	25	10	10	20	11	17	28
West Indies	75	60	135	55	45	100	35	30	65	42	48	90
Far East	70	45	115	35	25	60	10	10	20	20	36	56
Other	20	20	40	20	15	35	15	10	25	14	20	34
TOTAL	180	135	315	125	95	220	70	60	130	87	121	208
Receipts from Exports												
West Africa	80	45	125	60	25	85	65	35	100	104	31	135
West Indies	25	25	50	30	30	60	25	35	60	34	28	62
Far East	145	150	295	125	95	220	115	190	305	255	143	398
Other	15	15	30	15	5	20	20	20	40	20	28	48
TOTAL	265	235	500	230	155	385	225	280	505	413	230	643
Other Transactions, net (receipts)												
All territories	10	15	25	10	20	30	20	15	35	31	14	45
SURPLUS	95	115	210	115	80	195	175	235	410	357	123	480

Source: Colonial Territories 1949–50 (Cmd. 7958); *Colonial Territories 1950–51* (Cmd. 8243);
Colonial Territories 1951–52 (Cmd. 8553); *Colonial Territories 1953–54* (Cmd. 9169),
gold sales not included.

development objectives. To resolve this problem nationalist leaders tried to persuade the colonial government to release more dollars for expenditure on colonial development, remove all import restrictions and issue more import licences.[44]

THE STERLING CRISIS AND COLONIAL STERLING BALANCES POLICY: 1950–1952

With regard to its policy for managing the colonial balances, the British government's predicament was complicated further after the outbreak of war in Korea in June 1950. The tremendous rise in world

Table 3.5
Colonial Transactions with the Dollar Area, 1951–1953[1]
Estimated Payments and Receipts

	1951			1952			1953		
	1st half	2nd half	Year	1st half	2nd half	Year	1st half	2nd half	Year
Imports (f.o.b.)									
West Africa	11	17	28	14	8	22	14	11	25
West Indies	42	48	90	50	50	101	45	48	93
Far East[2]	20	36	56	22	17	39	11	14	25
Other	14	20	34	17	11	28	14	14	28
TOTAL	87	123	208	103	87	190	84	87	171
Exports (f.o.b.)									
West Africa	104	31	135	87	45	132	76	62	138
West Indies	34	28	62	25	31	56	34	25	59
Far East[2]	255	143	398	140	118	258	101	64	165
Other	20	28	48	24	36	70	20	45	65
TOTAL	413	230	643	286	230	516	231	196	427
Other Transactions[3] net receipts	17	30	20	20	14	34	20	20	40
Current Account Surplus[3]	343	112	455	202	157	359	165	129	296
Gold sales to UK	14	11	25	8	–	8	–	–	–
TOTAL	357	123	480	210	157	367	165	129	296

Source: *Colonial Territories 1953-54* (Cmd. 9169).

[1] Including also transactions in gold.
[2] Excluding Hong Kong's transactions financed through the unofficial market.
[3] These figures differ from those on pages 24–5 and page 41 Cmd.9119. The latter includes certain items of a captial nature.

commodity prices triggered by the war, coupled with the restraints on colonial expenditure imposed by Britain, resulted in significant increases in the colonial sterling balances. They increased from £582 million in 1949 to £735 at the end of 1950. In addition, whereas in 1949 they accounted for 12.2 percent of Britain's total sterling liabilities, in 1950 they accounted for 19.6 percent. While the British government struggled to find a solution to the dilemma posed by its colonial sterling liabilities, the magnitude of the problem was escalating.

In January 1950 the colonial balances were disaggregated by the Colonial Office to enable it to better appreciate the potential for colonial development finance. Using figures at October 1949 when the balances totaled approximately £620 million, assistant under secretary of state at the Colonial Office responsible for finance H. T. Bourdillon stressed "that while the colonies as a whole are substantial holders of sterling, this amount covers the holdings of well over fifty different territories, and no single territory holds a very large balance. Consideration in the aggregate should not obscure this vital factor."[45] This was not true. By 1950, 10 colonies (about 20 percent of Britain's colonies) accounted for 81.6 percent of all the sterling balances accumulated by colonial territories. These were: the Gold Coast, the Malayan Federation, Nigeria, Hong Kong, Kenya, Uganda, Singapore, Tanganyika, Trinidad, and Malta. Moreover, three of these ten colonies—the Gold Coast, the Malayan Federation, and Nigeria—accounted for 38.5 percent of the total colonial balances.[46] Given this distribution of the colonial balances, it was clear that it was impossible for most of Britain's dependencies to maintain or increase their level of development without greater access to U.K. or foreign sources of capital.

Toward the end of 1951 the Colonial Office became worried that the British government would have found it increasingly difficult to continue to obtain support for its policy either from colonial legislatures or from colonial people in general, if more of the funds that were accumulated through past taxation were not spent on development.[47] Therefore, amid the turbulence in the British economy, the secretary of state for the colonies asked the cabinet to consider using colonial sterling balances to provide funds for development and thereby reduce the demand placed upon the London money market by the colonies.[48] As a result a working party was established to consider the colonial secretary's request.[49]

Despite this A.H. Poynton, assistant under secretary of state at the Colonial Office, was not convinced that the utilization of colonial sterling reserves for development financing would solve the problem of funding in the colonies.[50] Poynton warned that "in terms of borrowing over the next 3 or 4 years the Treasury and the Colonial Office have hitherto been thinking in terms of a gap of some £40 million (perhaps more) between the needs of the colonies and the absorptive capacity of the London market."[51] He argued, "it would, I fear, be over optimistic to suppose that the colonies will not require every penny that the London market can make available to them."[52] He concluded that "finance would remain a real problem because the costs of development plans are increasing daily."[53]

Although the Colonial Office accepted that the colonies should assist Britain in resolving its balance of payments problems, it wanted the British government to be more accommodating in its policy toward the colonies. The Colonial Office thus pressed for a clarification of Britain's position on the role of the colonies in the balance of payments crisis.[54] In October 1951 officials from the Colonial Office and the Treasury met to discuss the colonial empire's role in the economic thinking then prevailing in the United Kingdom. In the end they agreed that the government needed to decide whether or not it was going to be lenient in its treatment of the colonies before deciding on the scope of measures that it was going to employ to resolve the crisis.[55] This issue was addressed by the new colonial secretary Oliver Lyttelton, in a submission to the British cabinet on 19 November 1951.[56] The Colonial Office was opposed to the imposition of further restrictions on colonial imports to assist the Sterling Area to correct the overall deficit. While the Colonial Office did not underestimate the importance of the economic well-being of the Sterling Area to the welfare of the colonies, it argued that there was a growing feeling of discontent and dissatisfaction in the colonies, at the way in which progress was being hampered by decisions taken in the United Kingdom.[57]

The essence of colonial dissatisfaction was the belief that the current imperial policy limited the freedom of colonial people to use their monetary and financial resources for their own development. The Colonial Office therefore wanted the British government to recognize the colonies' claim to a volume of imports that permitted progress in development to continue and allowed some improvements in the standard of living even during rearmament. It warned the government that serious political consequences would follow if Britain was unable to satisfy the economic needs and aspirations of colonial peoples beyond the provisions made so far.[58] The shortage of imported goods to the colonies was a particularly vexing issue at this time. In 1951 the flow of imported goods was limited by the outbreak of war in Korea and the rearmament in Britain. Heavily demanded goods such as iron and steel, semimanufactured nonferrous metals and sulphur containing chemicals all reached the colonies in limited supplies. Britain had found it virtually impossible to maintain the export of semimanufactured steel at the 1950 level. Thus, it reintroduced controls over the use of steel and cut colonial exports below the 1950 level. It also asked colonial governments to exercise economy in their use of steel and to ensure that imports were put to their best advantage.[59] Cement, copper, copper alloy, zinc, aluminium and consumer durables such as cotton were also in short supply. Moreover, even if the goods could be acquired, restriction on transactions with the Dollar Area prevented the colonies from satisfying their demand from this source. From a colonial viewpoint, therefore, it was easy to link the shortages in the supply of colonial imports to the subordinate position of the colonies in relation to Britain.

The Treasury disagreed with the position of the Colonial Office as it was set out by the Colonial Secretary.[60] The Treasury believed that the Colonial Office was either ignoring or misjudging the implications of the balance of payments crisis for the Sterling Area in general. Thus, the Treasury opposed allowing the colonies to use the large surpluses that they enjoyed in their transactions with the Dollar Area in 1950 and 1951 to expand their dollar imports. To the Treasury, this surplus was an important element in assisting the United Kingdom to resolve the Sterling Area's deficit in its trade with the rest of the world. The latter had resulted in a loss of nearly 40 percent of Britain's gold reserves in the last six months (of 1951), and the use of £300 million credit in the E.P.U. Therefore, the Treasury wanted the colonies to keep broadly the same dollar ceilings in 1952 as obtained in 1951, and limit their imports from dollar and nonsterling sources. It concluded "their contribution will be a continued surplus with the Dollar Area and a small surplus with the whole of the nonsterling world, and a surplus with the rest of the Sterling Area."[61] The Treasury believed, therefore, that the defense of sterling and the needs of the metropole, the dominions and the independent members of the Sterling Area took precedence over those of colonial territories. The Treasury was keen to utilize the surplus in colonial transactions with the Dollar Area, because in 1950, 143 percent of Britain's merchandise dollar deficit was covered by the surplus of the dependent territories in the Sterling Area. It fell to 86 percent in 1951 (Table 3.6).

Table 3.6
Proportion of Britain's Merchandise Dollar Deficit Covered by the Dollar Trade Surplus with the Dependent Sterling Area

Year	Percentage
1935–39	27
1946	4
1947	2
1948	23
1949	14
1950	143
1951	86

Source: E. Zupnick, Britain's Postwar Dollar Problem, p. 143.

The British government was not eager to make fundamental alterations in its colonial sterling balances policy. Despite the large increases in the colonial balances in 1950 and 1951, in December 1951 the Treasury stated that the colonies were not going to be allowed to use their balances to expand their expenditure on imports because of the crisis that faced the British economy. The Treasury added that the colonies "will keep to broadly the same dollar ceilings in 1952 as in 1951, and they will take steps to limit the growth of imports from the non $ [sic] non £ [sic]

countries. Their contribution will be a continuous surplus with the dollar area, a small surplus with the whole non £ world, and a surplus with the other £ areas."[62] In 1952 the ceiling on colonial dollar expenditure was fixed at US$200 million, US$1 million more than the US$199 set in 1951. It was also agreed that the colonies could have spent a maximum of US$215 million.[63]

This was one of the most unequivocal declarations of the extent to which the state of the U.K. economy determined its policy toward the use of colonial sterling balances. It was clear that the relaxation or the abandonment of import restrictions was a prerequisite for stemming and/or reducing the growth of the colonial sterling reserves. On the other hand, once Britain's gold and dollar reserves remained threatened, the limits on colonial expenditure that helped to stimulate the growth of the colonial sterling balances were going to continue. This was done not only because Britain was unable to meet colonial demands for imported goods, but also because it enhanced the supply of dollars that the British government needed to improve its balance of payments position. The size of the colonial sterling balances was therefore, in part, a manifestation of the degree of sacrifice imposed upon the colonies by the United Kingdom to obtain urgently needed dollars and other hard currencies.

When the secretary of state for the colonies outlined the justification for the dollar ceilings to the colonies in January 1952, he echoed the Treasury's arguments for giving the needs of the United Kingdom and the Sterling Area priority over that of the colonies. Colonial governments were reminded of their obligations as members of the Sterling Area and their interest in the strength of sterling, to which their currencies and their monetary reserves were held. Most of the colonies also depended on a small range of major products liable to market fluctuations, as well as the free movement of capital between the United Kingdom and the colonies.[64] In March 1952 the colonies were asked to "reduce by the second half of 1952 their own non-sterling imports to 85 percent of the 1951 level"[65] in order to facilitate Britain's balance of payments problems.

The chances for a reversal, if not a modification, in policy were quashed when following a meeting on colonial dollar imports the Treasury and Colonial Office concluded that the existing programs for economy in colonial dollar expenditure should continue. Their decision was prompted by the fact that they thought the existing programs helped to draw the attention of the colonies to alternative sources of supply and U.K. industries to the colonial needs. They claimed also that this was particularly important at a time when every effort was being made to expand the scope and quantity of the U.K. exports in order to help relieve the Sterling Area's balance of payments difficulties.[66]

CONCLUSION

After the devaluation of sterling in 1949, Britain continued to emphasize the same policies it had employed following the convertibility crisis of 1947 to ensure that its dependencies assisted in the correction of its trade deficit, and that of the independent members of Sterling Area, with the Dollar Area. The economic recovery that followed devaluation was short-lived; by the middle of 1951 Britain found itself in the throes of another crisis, precipitated this time by the aftereffects of the Korean war of June 1950. Crisis in the United Kingdom meant that the colonial territories were not given any respite from stringent controls on expenditure, particularly with respect to the Dollar Area.

Between 1949 and 1951 the contribution of the Gold Coast, Nigeria and Malaya toward the Sterling Area's deficit with the Dollar Area was too important for nationalist forces to be trusted with full self-government. Their demands, however, could not be ignored. Next to the guerrillas whom it was fighting in Malaya, Nkrumah's C.P.P. represented the most serious threat to the continuation of British colonial rule in these three colonies. Despite the clamor for change, from the reforms introduced during this period, it was clear that Britain's central aim was to safeguard its economic interest by attempting to dictate the pace of the reforms, rather than submitting to pressure from the nationalists. However, the C.P.P.'s victory in the general elections of 1951 signaled that militant nationalists in the Gold Coast were gaining the upper hand in their struggle with Britain for self-government.

In Nigeria, on the other hand, the balance of power was also shifting toward the nationalist elements. Even though there was generally, an absence of the militancy that characterized the transition in the Gold Coast, after the Accra Riots of 1948 Britain was forced to become proactive in its policy toward the decolonization in Nigeria. Thus, to neutralize opposition to colonial rule, it had to ensure that political changes in Nigeria were in line with those taking place in the Gold Coast. In Malaya, Britain had responded positively to the nationalists who had used the opportunity provided by the emergency to press their claims for independence. Therefore, although the United Kingdom was hanging on tenaciously, there were clear signs that major political changes were under way in Britain's most valuable colonies. By 1951 the Gold Coast, Malaya and Nigeria accounted for 41.7 percent of the sterling reserves accumulated by British colonies. While government officials were slow to react, Britain was rapidly losing political control in the very colonies with sterling reserves that were a potential threat to its economic well-being.

NOTES

1.   S. Pollard, *The Development of the British Economy 1914–1967* (London: Edwin Arnold, 1962), p. 363.

2.   Ibid., p. 363. See also *P.R.O.* CO 537/6674/97207. Extract from the *Financial Times*, 1/11/50.

3.   *P.R.O.* PREM 8/1187. J. M. Flemming to Mr. Rickett. 27/3/50, "Sterling Balances," memorandum by the Chancellor of the Exchequer, (E.P.C. (50) 40).

4.   *O.E.E.C. At Work for Europe* (Paris: Chateau De La Muette, 1960), p. 41. See also A. Cairncross, *Years of Recovery: British EconomicPolicy 1945–1951* (London: Methuen, 1985), ch. 10. The E.P.U. comprised 18 Western European countries: France, Austria, Belgium, Denmark, Germany, Greece, Iceland, Ireland, Italy, Luxembourg, Netherlands, Norway, Portugal, Spain, Sweden, Switzerland, Turkey and the United Kingdom.

5.   Ibid., pp. 40–41.

6.   Ibid., pp. 42–43.

7.   Cairncross, *Years of Recovery*, p. 287.

8.   M. J. Hogan, *The Marshall Plan: America, Britain and the Reconstruction of Western Europe, 1947–1952* (Cambridge: Cambridge University Press, 1989), pp. 324–325.

9.   K. O. Morgan, *Labour in Power 1945–1951.* (Oxford: Clarendon Press, 1984), p. 424.

10.   Ibid., p. 477.

11.   J. Fforde, *The Bank of England and Public Policy 1941–1958* (Cambridge: Cambridge University Press, 1992), p. 351.

12.   R. G. Hawtrey, *Towards a Rescue of the Pound Sterling* (London: Longmans, 1959), p. 48.

13.   P. Burnham, *The Political Economy of Postwar Reconstruction* (London: Macmillan, 1990), p.171.

14.   Morgan, *Labour in Power*, p. 477.

15.   *P.R.O.* T236/4348. Key Statistics on Overseas Finance Mid January 1952. H.M. Treasury copy no. 20.

16.   Morgan, *Labour in Power*, p. 477. See also Fforde, *The Bank of England*, p. 417.

17.   Ibid.

18.   *P.R.O.* CO 537/7589/97280/65. Circular savingram. S/S to all colonies. Gold and Dollar Reserves. 25/7/51.

19.   Ibid.

20.   *P.R.O.* CAB 129/48 (31 October–29 December 1951). C. (51) 1. 31 October 1951. Cabinet. The Economic Position: Analysis and Remedies. Memorandum by the Chancellor of the Exchequer, R. A. Butler.

21.   *P.R.O.* CAB 129/48 (31 October–29 December 1951). C. (51) 1. 31 October 1951. Cabinet. The Economic Position: Analysis and Remedies. Memorandum by the Chancellor of the Exchequer, R. A Butler.

22.   Burnham, *The Political Economy of Postwar Reconstruction*, pp. 172–173.

23.   Ibid., pp.170–176.

24.   *P.R.O.* T 236/3562. Sterling Assets of the Colonial Territories 1949–1951.

25.   J. F. Ajayi and M. Crowder, *History of West Africa.* Vol. 2 (London:

Longman, 1974), pp. 627–635. See also D. Austin, *Politics in Ghana 1946–1960* (Oxford: Oxford University Press, 1964).
26.   Ibid. See also D. Rooney, *Sir Charles Arden-Clarke* (London: Rex Collings, 1982), chs. 5–6.
27.   R. S. Milne, *Government and Politics in Malaysia* (Boston: Houghton Mifflin Company, 1967), pp. 32–36. See also G. P. Means, *Malaysian Politics* (London: University of London Press, 1970).
28.   Means, *Malaysian Politics*, p. 132.
29.   A. E. Hinds, "British Imperial Policy and the Development of the Nigerian Economy, 1939–1951" (Ph.D. thesis, Dalhousie University, Halifax, Nova Scotia, Canada, 1985), p. 262.
30.   Ibid.
31.   Ibid., p. 264.
32.   Ibid., p. 263.
33.   *P.R.O.* CO 852/730/5. Circular dispatch 16/6/48. Financial devolution in Africa.
34.   *Digest of Colonial Statistics*, no. 29 (London: HMSO, 1956), Table 33.
35.   *Parliamentary Papers 1950–1951. The Colonial Territories 1950–51*, XXVI (Cmd. 8243), 1. pp. 79–80.
36.   *P.R.O.* CO 1025/125. Financial Control in Constitutionally Advanced Territories. Memorandum on Financial Procedure and Control in the Federation of Malaya. Undated.
37.   Ibid.
38.   *P.R.O.* CO 852/1139/5. Circular savingram from Secretary of State for the Colonies 31 July 1951.
39.   *P.R.O.* T 236/3563/OF 25/219/019. Draft for Treasury concurrence. Draft Circular savingram to all Colonies. This was sent by A. H. Poynton to H. Brittan on 9 October 1951. Poynton said that this was a draft of what "we should like to send on a secret and personal basis to all colonial governors."
40.   The slight differences in the figures for 1951 found in Table 2.9 and Table 2.10 are due to the fact that the data in Table 2.9 were converted from dollars into pounds.
41.   *P.R.O.* CO 537/4630/30654. Extract from the *Chicago Daily News* 26/5/49.
42.   Ibid.
43.   Y. Bangura, *Britain and Commonwealth Africa: The Politics of Economic Relations 1951–1975* (Manchester: Manchester University Press, 1983), p. 45.
44.   Ibid., p. 46.
45.   *P.R.O.* T 236/3351. H. T. Bourdillon 10/1/50.
46.   *P.R.O.* T 236/3562. Sterling assets of the Colonial Territories December 1950.
47.   A. N. Porter and A. J. Stockwell, eds., *British Imperial Policy and Decolonisation 1938–1964*, Vol. 2 (London: Macmillan, 1989), Doc. 3 "Balance of Payments of the Colonial Territories." Cabinet Memorandum by the Secretary of State for the Colonies 19 November 1951, CAB 129/48, p. 107. I have not found any evidence that suggests that there was a lot of agitation in the colonies that was specifically related to the manner in which Britain was managing colonial sterling balances. Nevertheless, Gorell Barnes noted that from his conversations with governors and other colonial officials on leave in Britain, his impression was

that there was always an underlying feeling among the public in the dollar earning territories "that they were turning in a lot of dollars to London and getting nothing in return." See *P.R.O.* CO/852/1139/5 W. L. Gorell Barnes to Martin Flett 29/11/51.

48. This is quoted from *P.R.O.* T 236/3352. "Colonial Sterling Balances," A. K. Potter to Mr. Flett, 21/3/53.

49. *P.R.O.* T 236/3351. Secret C.C (51) 9th Conclusions, Tuesday 20 November 1951.

50. *P.R.O.* T 236/3351. A. H. Poynton to A. Johnson 21/11/51.

51. Ibid.

52. Ibid.

53. Ibid.

54. *P.R.O.* T 236/3563. Minute by M. T. Flett 20 October 1951.

55. Ibid.

56. *P.R.O.* CAB 129/48. C (51) 22, 19 November 1951. Cabinet. Balance of payments of the Colonial Territories. Memorandum by the Secretary of State for the Colonies.

57. Ibid.

58. Ibid.

59. Ibid.

60. *P.R.O.* T 236/3564. Commonwealth Finance Ministers Meeting. Brief on objectives and general policy 20 December 1951.

61. *P.R.O.* T 236/3564. Commonwealth Finance Ministers Meeting. Brief on objectives and general policy 20 December 1951.

62. *P.R.O.* T 236/3564. Commonwealth Finance Ministers Meeting. Brief on objectives and general policy. Note by the Treasury, 20/12/51.

63. *P.R.O.* T 236/3355. Minute by Mr. Clowser 27/6/52.

64. *P.R.O.* T 236/3564. Outward telegram Secretary of State to all Colonies 2/1/52.

65. *P.R.O.* T 236/3355. Minute by Mr. Clowser 27/6/52.

66. *P.R.O.* CO 852/1141/8. Ms. A. M. Jenkins (Treasury) to Mr. J. G. Stott (Ministry of Supplies) 17/6/52.

4

Sterling and Colonial Resource Mobilization: The Crucial Years, 1945–1951

THE EXPANSION OF COLONIAL COMMODITY PRODUCTION, 1945–1947

During the early period of postwar economic recovery and reconstruction, bulk purchasing agreements and exchange controls were maintained as crucial features of Britain's colonial economic policy.[1] Before the convertibility crisis of July 1947, there were clear indications that economic instability in the United Kingdom was affecting colonial economic policy. In November 1945 the British government appealed to colonial governments to consider its financial position when requesting assistance in their plans for development and welfare. They were reminded that

The contribution to be made from the Imperial Exchequer is a real burden on the United Kingdom taxpayer, to be borne at a time when the resources of the United Kingdom external as well as internal, have been heavily strained . . . the financial burdens borne by the United Kingdom have been very much greater than those which have fallen on any other part of the Commonwealth. They have been greater absolutely, and they have entailed a most serious worsening of the external financial position of the United Kingdom quite unparalleled in any other part of the Commonwealth or in any Allied country.[2]

As the realities of Britain's balance of payments problems unfolded, the Colonial Office was in the vanguard of imperial attempts to determine the extent to which colonial resources could be mobilized to assist in alleviating Britain's trade imbalance. By April 1947 it had initiated plans for a review of colonial commodity production which took into account the United Kingdom's balance of payments difficulties and the world shortage in many commodities.[3] Its aim was to discover "what are the world needs and the UK needs for particular commodities likely to be over a period of years, and . . . what are the technical possibilities of growing these commodities in the colonies."[4] The deliberations within the Colonial Office were consistent with the overall shift in British imperial policy toward the acquisition of commodities produced in the colonial empire at this time. The situation was explained succinctly by Creech Jones, the colonial secretary. He stated that

at the beginning of 1947 it was abundantly clear that the world-wide economic disturbances caused by the war needed bold action . . . among the remedies a quicker tempo in colonial development was obviously called for. . . . In addition, therefore, to the development work already planned and launched it became necessary to ask what more was possible to strengthen the economies of the territories to meet their needs, and to increase the production of foodstuffs and raw materials in short supply in the world. . . . The world's needs became the colonial empire's opportunity.[5]

This trend in policy was formalized with the establishment of the Colonial Primary Products Committees (CPPC). This heralded the introduction of a more systematic approach to the investigation, identification and acquisition of primary commodities produced in the empire. The formation of the CPPC coincided with the continuing deterioration in Britain's balance of payments and was part of the government's overall strategy to facilitate economic recovery. In order to mask its primary concerns, the terms of reference of the CPPC were couched in a manner which implied that the planned expansion in commodity production for export in the colonial empire was a joint initiative between Britain and its dependent territories. The inaugural meeting of the CPPC was concerned mainly with reviewing products that were established colonial exports and making plans for exploring new sources of raw materials. By June 1947 members of the CPPC agreed on a list of commodities and the order of priority in which they were to be discussed. They were placed in four categories. Top priority was given to animal products (such as meat, dairy products and poultry), grains (such as rice, maize and millet), oilseeds (both edible and inedible), timber, fertilizers and fibers. Next in the order were fruits, fruit juices and tanning materials. They were followed by bagasse, dried fruits and starches. The lowest in the order of priority were hides and skins, beverages (such as cocoa, tea and coffee), spices, sugar, molasses, insecticides, gum and resins.

The list of priorities compiled by the CPPC was to a large extent a reflection of the international state of commodity production at this time. By 1947 world agricultural production was still recovering from the devastation wrought by war. Recovery was exacerbated by poor weather conditions. Preliminary estimates of crop production in the Northern Hemisphere in 1947 forecasted "a gloomy picture of the world's food production until the harvest of 1948."[6] Agricultural production in Europe was particularly hard-hit by adverse weather conditions. An unusually severe winter had damaged or destroyed millions of hectares of fall seeded crops, and an extremely dry summer cut yields of all important crops. The resultant reduction in food supplies also had a serious effect on livestock products.[7] The crops most seriously affected were potatoes and grains such as wheat, barley, rye, oats and maize (Table 4.1).

Table 4.1
Annual Production of Selected Grain Crops in Europe: Prewar Average, 1946 and 1947
(millions of metric tons)

	Prewar average 1934–38	1946	1947
Wheat	42.3	32.9	25.8
Rye	19.1	11.2	10.5
Barley	14.4	11.7	11.7
Oats	22.9	17.8	16.9
Maize	7.3	7.9	15.3
Potatoes	134.2	100.3	98.0

Source: *Economic Report. Salient Features of the World Economic Situation, 1945–1947*, p. 193 (New York: United Nations Department of Economic Affairs, 1948). Figures for the USSR and Albania are not included because of inadequate information.

Projections showed also that for many countries in Western Europe, total feed supplies in 1946/47 were about 85 percent of their prewar average relative to the number of animals, and concentrated food supplies were only about 65 percent as large. The net result of this was expected to be shortages in the supply of meat. In fact in the period 1934–1938 Europe, excluding the Union of Soviet Socialist Republics (USSR), was responsible for 43.7 percent or 12,245 metric tons of world meat production. This had fallen to 27 percent or 7,553 thousand metric tons in 1947. The world production of fibers was also below prewar levels. By 1947 10,550 million metric tons of fiber were produced as opposed to 12,655 metric tons, on average, between 1934 and 1938. In the case of cotton, a major British import, in 1946 world production was less than 75 percent of the average for 1934–1938.[8] Major shortfalls were also predicted for the world supply of oils and fats.[9]

The situation in the United States was markedly different from that in Europe. The index of farm production revealed that the production of all major food crops and food livestock was well above prewar levels (Table 4.2).

Table 4.2
Index of the Volume of Farm Production in the United States, 1944–1947
(1935–39 = 100)

Year	Total farm production	All crops	Food crops	Food livestock
1944	136	128	129	141
1945	133	122	129	141
1946	136	135	144	138
1947a	136	136	148	138

Source: *Economic Report: The Salient Features of the World Economic Situation 1945–1947* (New York: United Nations Department of Economic Affairs, January 1948), p. 33.
a. Preliminary.

In 1946 and 1947 food crop production was more than 40 points above the prewar average and livestock production was 38 points in excess of the prewar average. In the case of wheat, production had increased from 741 million bushels in 1939 to 1,407 in 1947. Meat production in the United States increased from an average of 7,783 thousand metric tons between 1934 and 1938 to 11,300 metric tons in 1947. The production of oats had increased from 958 million bushels in 1939 to 1,232 bushels in 1947.[10] The United States was also one of the principal producers of cotton and other fibers traded on the world market at the end of World War II. Unlike Europe, therefore, between 1945 and 1947 the United States was a major source of supply for many of the commodities that were traded internationally. The problem was that U.S. supplies had to be paid for in dollars, a transaction that seriously aggravated the United Kingdom's balance of payments position. Thus, the intention of the CPPC was to identify alternative sources of supply within Britain's colonial dependencies.

COLONIAL EXPORTS AND BRITAIN'S BALANCE OF PAYMENTS, 1947–1949

Despite the emphasis on the duality of metropolitan and colonial needs contained in the terms of reference of the CPPC, it was clear that colonial needs were tangential in the mobilization of colonial resources through the CPPC This was evident when the issue of producing dollar-earning commodities in the colonies was addressed in a memorandum to the British cabinet in August 1947. According to this memorandum, Britain's trade imbalance with the United States was directly responsible for the initiatives sanctioned by the British government with respect to the expansion of export production from the colonies.[11] The government's aim was to try to "re-establish, and indeed improve upon, the pre war position in which exports of primary produce from the colonies to America were among our principal earners of dollars."[12] Similar concerns were manifested in the first report of the CPPC in January 1948. The increase in colonial export production was not regarded "merely as a measure to meet the immediate dollar emergency but as a long-term contribution to the stability of the Sterling Area and to European reconstruction plans."[13] According to the CPPC, the colonial contribution was central to Britain's efforts to develop alternative sources to supplies from the Dollar Area. The CPPC explained that "it will remain necessary to develop supplies outside of the Western Hemisphere and reduce Europe's dependence upon foodstuffs and raw materials from that area [the dollar], if the pattern of world trade is to be restored to equilibrium and Europe is to recover the ability to meet its dollar needs from current earnings."[14]

The importance which was attached to the mobilization of colonial resources after July 1947 was evident in the agencies that made submissions to the CPPC The CPPC reviewed memoranda and suggestions for the development and mobilization of colonial commodities from the Board of Trade, the Ministry of Food, the Foreign Office and the Colonial Office and the Empire Cotton Growers Association. The common link among these submissions was the emphasis on the need to reduce Britain's dependence on commodities supplied by the Dollar Area. One of the main concerns of the Board of Trade was the need to increase colonial cotton production.[15] As a result of the return of labor lost to munitions during the war, the raw cotton consumed by the textile industry was expected to increase from 320,000 tons to 400,000 tons per year. The satisfaction of the increased demand was a major problem because in 1945–1946 about 51 percent of the cotton imported into the United Kingdom came from U.S. and Brazilian sources and was paid for in dollars. On the other hand, 67 percent of the cotton consumed in the United Kingdom was the American type with a staple length ranging from ⅛th of an inch to 1⅛th inches. This was the principal type of cotton produced in the colonial empire. However, with the exception of India (8 percent), the major cotton-producing areas in the British empire, East and West Africa, supplied only 4 percent of the cotton demanded in the United Kingdom in the period 1945–1946 (Table 4.3).[16]

Table 4.3
The Main Sources of Britain's Cotton Imports, 1935–1950
(Metric tons)

Country	1935–1939 Average Imports	%	1945–1946 Average Imports	%	1946–1947 Average Imports	%	1947–1948 Average Imports	%	1948–1949 Average Imports	%	1949–1950 Average Imports	%
USA	257	40	102	30	81	22	84	21	116	26	208	42
Brazil	48	7	56	17	67	19	81	20	94	21	40	8
India & Pakistan	93	15	26	8	33	9	40	10	31	7	36	7
Br. East Africa	8	1	9	3	12	3	13	3	14	3	15	3
Br. West Africa	5	1	2	1	4	1	6	1	8	2	8	2
Belgian Congo	–	–	18	5	19	5	14	3	17	4	15	3
USSR	27	4	11	3	17	5	14	3	7	2	4	1
TOTAL AMERICAN TYPE	438	68	224	67	233	64	252	61	287	65	326	66
Egypt	132	21	65	19	73	20	95	23	90	20	114	23
Sudan	30	5	35	10	39	11	46	11	44	10	30	6
Peru	40	6	13	4	18	5	19	5	16	4	18	4
Br. West Indies			1		1		1		1		1	
Br. East Africa *	**	**	**	**	**	**	**	**	3	1	5	1
TOTAL EGYPTIAN TYPE	202	32	114	33	131	36	161	39	154	35	168	34
GRAND TOTAL	640	100	338	100	364	100	413	100	441	100	494	100

* Figures for British East Africa from 1948/49 distinguish between BP 52, which is an Egyptian-type cotton, and the other Ugandan-type cottons, which are American types.

** Included in British East African type.

Source: P.R.O. CO 852/965/3. Cabinet Imports Diversion Committee Working Group on Cotton. Notes on statistics provided by the Board of Trade.

The Board of Trade thus felt that Britain's efforts to reduce its dependence on cotton imports from the United States and Brazil should focus on expanding cotton exports from East and West Africa. Nigerian cotton was said to be the ideal substitute for the medium staple consumed in the United Kingdom. The Board of Trade therefore contended:

It is unnecessary to measure the theoretical ceilings of Lancashire's demand for Nigerian cotton as no expansion scheme which would reach it is likely to be undertaken. Subject, therefore, to the quality being maintained and the price being competitive there should not be any risks in the foreseeable future of Nigeria without a ready market for the expanded production she may achieve.[17]

There were also other savings which could have stemmed from expanding cotton production for export from Nigeria. Whereas in 1947 the f.o.b. price of American cotton was 20d per pound and Brazilian cotton was 18d per pound, Nigeria's was only 11d per pound.[18]

The Ministry of Food was also worried about the purchase of wheat from the Dollar Area. In 1946–1947 the United Kingdom obtained most of its wheat from the United States and Argentina, both of which were hard currency areas. The ministry felt that this situation was undesirable and it called for a greater effort to ensure that a larger proportion of Britain's wheat supplies was obtained from commonwealth sources.[19] The Colonial Office, on the other hand, took a general interest in the expansion of commodity production throughout the colonial empire and stressed the importance of remedying the food situation in Britain and the need to conserve dollar imports. The Foreign Office focused on the raw materials that were in short supply in the United States and called for a revision of the priority grading for nonmineral.[20] It divided the raw materials that were needed in the United States into three categories: minerals (such as tin, copper, nickel, lead, bauxite, and industrial diamonds), vegetable products (such as rubber, coffee, sugar, oils and fats, rice and cordage-fibers) and animal products (such as silk, wool, furs, hides and skins). American dependence on the importation of these materials had increased greatly since 1940, and this trend was expected to continue. During the war the United States had consumed over 5 million tons of domestically produced ore, and by the end of the war its reserves of mercury and platinum were virtually exhausted. It was also heavily dependent on foreign sources for nickel, chromite, tin, long fiber asbestos, industrial diamonds and quartz crystals.

The Foreign Office contended that while the U.S. demand for sugar, vegetable oils and fats, sisal coffee and industrial diamonds could be satisfied from sources within the U.S. sphere of influence such as the Philippines and parts of Central and South America, colonial produce competed successfully with goods produced in these regions.[21] The United States was also deficient in minerals in which the British colonies were richly endowed, particularly tin (Malaya and Nigeria), copper (Northern Rhodesia), bauxite (British Guiana), asbestos and chrome (Southern Rhodesia), manganese (Gold Coast), industrial diamonds (Gold Coast, Sierra Leone and Southwest Africa) and graphite (Ceylon). While many of these minerals could also have been found in the self-governing dominions, India and Burma, the Foreign Office wanted emphasis to be placed on the development of minerals found in the colonial empire.[22]

The submission of the Foreign Office led to the establishment of the CPPC Minerals and Metals Panel which was also chaired by Eastwood, chairman of the committee for agricultural products. He explained that when the CPPC was established, initially it was decided "to concentrate on agricultural commodities and leave metals alone for the time being."[23] He added, "we are now convinced that, particularly from the point of view of dollars, an early review of the colonies metals and minerals is essential."[24] At the first meeting of the CPPC Minerals and Metals Panel, Eastwood reiterated the importance of Britain's balance of payments difficulties to the formation of the minerals and metals panel. He stated that the panel "would examine the production in the colonies of the metals and minerals known to be available in the colonies with particular reference to those which we are likely to earn dollars directly by export to the USA or to save dollars by substituting in the United Kingdom those at present procured in dollar areas."[25] By August 1947 therefore the British government had created mechanisms to ensure that all colonial products that could either earn or save the dollars required to assist in resolving Britain's balance of payments problems were identified so that steps could have been initiated to expand production.

At the end of 1947 the CPPC had examined commodities produced in the colonies under five headings: animal products, food grains, industrial fibers, citrus, juices and fertilizers.[26] Although it recommended that the Colonial Office should send a mission to investigate diseases, storage and marketing in African territories where pastoralism was important, the committee did not think that there was much potential for increasing beef or poultry production in the colonial empire. On the other hand, it felt that rice production should be encouraged to the maximum extent possible. It noted that even though it may have been difficult to generate a surplus for export, increased production in the colonies would have reduced dependence on imports and would have saved dollars. Cotton was identified as the most important of the industrial fibers. The CPPC thus suggested that the production of cotton of a staple length of between $^{15}/_{16}$th of an inch and $^{11}/_{16}$th inches should have been expanded as rapidly as possible. While the findings of the CPPC were a major source of information on the potential for expansion in selected agricultural commodities produced in the British colonial empire, its recommendations did not have much of an impact. In most cases by the time they were published the expansion of production in the commodities identified was already being actively encouraged. Moreover, the committee did not make recommendations for oilseeds because attempts to expand production were too well known.

The CPPC Minerals and Metals Panel was less active than its counterpart which investigated agricultural commodities, and by November 1947 it had faded as an effective body.[27] Committee members complained about their frustration "in getting things moving when we have a demand and a workable deposit."[28] One of the principal obstacles to mining was the British government's policy of recognizing the rights of local people to maximum benefits from the exploitation of their resources. This policy discouraged speculators at a time when colonial people were unable to undertake these ventures on their own. The Minerals and Metals Panel also felt marginalized because it did not have any input into the decisions regarding the exploitation of the major dollar-earning or dollar-saving minerals. This was determined at the highest levels of the British government. In addition, the development of the resources which it identified suffered because of the shortages of plant and equipment. Consequently, one official lamented that although increased mineral production was important "there is perhaps not the same urgency about it . . . as there is for increased food supplies in this country."[29]

The British government's attempt to expand production for export of selected commodities from the colonial territories was not limited to the identification of products for expansion. The commodities identified formed the basis of projections on the extent to which colonial production could be expanded to assist Britain in resolving its trade balance. The principal items for which the British government felt increased production was necessary were: oilseeds, especially groundnuts, oil palm produce and copra, sugar, bananas, cocoa, rice, cotton, hard fibers, rubber, hardwoods, tin and copper.[30] With the exception of groundnuts, sugar, rice and cotton, an expansion in the export of the main agricultural products of the colonial empire could not be achieved by increased cultivation in the short run. Oil palm and cocoa trees took four to five years to mature, coconuts six to ten years, hard fibers three to four years and rubber five years. In the case of these crops the best that the British government could hope for was an increase in output by improving the methods through which existing crops were produced, processed and transported to the point of export (Table 4.4).

Table 4.4
The Period of Growth of the Main Colonial Exports

Crop	Period of Growth Before Bearing
Oilseeds	
Groundnuts	Annual crop
Palm Products	4–5 years (10 years for full bearing)
Coconut Products	6–10 years
Sugar	18 months°
Bananas	Annual crop*
Cocoa	4–5 years
Rice	Annual crop
Cotton	Annual crop
Hard Fibers	3–4 years
Rubber	5 years

° Any number from one to six ratoon crops may be taken up, according to local circumstances, but the average appears to be about three, giving a life cycle of four years.

* Propagated by suckers.

Source: P.R.O. CO 852/1001/2. Colonial Production Forecast. Tables 4.1 to 4.9 were also taken from the same source.

The imperial authorities expected a greater increase in the export of crops that were planted and harvested annually than they did for crops that took a couple of years to mature before they could be harvested.

In July 1948 colonial production was forecasted to easily satisfy the Sterling Area's demand for cocoa, hard fibers, rubber and tin; and between 70 and 90 percent of its requirements for oilseeds, bananas, and copper between 1950 and 1953. Export production in the colonial empire was therefore essential to the well-being of the Sterling Area in general, and Britain in particular (Table 4.5).

The indices showing export trends (by volume) for selected colonial commodities 1936=100 revealed that oilseed exports were expected to increase 293 points by 1950–1953, substantial increase when compared with the 112 points in 1946 (Table 4.5). The centerpiece of the government's projections was the East Africa groundnut scheme which was expected to boost the output of East and Central Africa from 12,000 tons in 1946 to 460,000 tons in 1953. Overall groundnut exports were expected to grow from 329,000 tons in 1946 to 870,000 tons in 1953 (Table 4.6).

Table 4.5
The Index of Colonial Production Trends for Selected Exports, 1946–1953
(1936=100)

	Foodstuffs			
	1 1936	2 1946	3* 1950/53	4 Col. 3 as a % of probable Sterling Area needs in 1950/53
Oilseeds	100	112	293	93 (in terms of oil)
Groundnuts	100	112	100	
Palm Oil	100	77	130	
Palm Kernels	100	75	130	
Copra and Coconut Oil	100	41	84	
Sugar	100	90	140	48
Bananas	100	29	81	75
Cocoa	100	77	72	182
Rice (production)	100	95	140	**
	Raw Materials			
Cotton	100	62	111	15–20
Hard Fibers	100	110	121	175 (approx.)
Hides and Skins	100	77	102	Below 1
Rubber (production)	100	109	206	286
Timber (hardwoods)	100	112***	155	Not estimated
Tin (production)	100	47	133#	220 (1950)
Copper (production)	100	129	227	78

*   Unless otherwise stated the figures in the columns under the heading 1950/53 represent the maximum figures to be reached in these years.
**   Negligible quantities available for export.
*** 1947 figures
\#   1950 figures

Table 4.6
The Colonial Groundnut Export Forecast, 1946–1952/53

	Exports ('000 of tons decorticated)		
	1936	1946	Estimated 1950/53
Nigeria	218	288	350
Gold Coast	–	–	10
Gambia	50	29	50
East and Central Africa	27	12	460x
TOTAL	295	329	870

x = 1953 figure

Together with the export of copra, coconut oil, palm oil and palm kernels, groundnuts from the colonial dependencies were expected to satisfy about 93 percent of the Sterling Area needs by 1953 (Tables 4.7 and 4.8).

Table 4.7
The Colonial Coconut Production Forecast, 1946–1950/53
(Copra and Coconut Oil in Terms of Copra)

	Exports ('000 of tons)		
	1936	1946	Estimated 1950/53
Malaya	150	53	150x
North Borneo	8	2	10
East Africa(including Zanzibar)	21	10	15z
West Africa (mainly Gold Coast)	2	2	2
Mauritius	1		
Seychelles	5	6	6
B.W. Indies and America	6		
Western Pacific	86	41	50
TOTAL	**279**	**114**	**233**

°   1947 figure. 1946 statistics incomplete

x   1953 figure

z   ¾ of this production may be consumed in East African Colonies

Table 4.8
The Colonial Production Forecast for Oil Palm Produce, 1946–1950/53

	Exports ('000 of tons)		
	1936	1946	Estimated 1950/53
	(A) Kernels		
Nigeria	386	308	380
Sierra Leone	85	49	90
Gold Coast	11	6	10
TOTAL	**482**	**363**	**480**
	(B) Oil		
Nigeria	163	112	200
Malaya	29	35+	50
TOTAL	**192**	**147**	**250**

+ = 1947

Sugar exports were projected to reach 140 points in 1950/53, compared with 1946 when they were 10 points below the figure for 1936. This meant an increase from 881,000 tons in 1946 to 1,380,000 tons in 1950/53 (Table 4.9).

Table 4.9
The Colonial Sugar Production Forecast, 1946–1950/53

	Exports ('000 of tons)		
	1936	1946	Estimated 1950/53
East Africa	19	10	20
Mauritius	274	230	400
Fiji	141	106	160
British Guiana	176	148	
Barbados	98	96	
Jamaica	78	148	800
Leewards	46	53	
Windwards	8	3	
Trinidad	143	87	
TOTAL	983	881	1,380

The largest increase was anticipated from the British West Indies: 800,000 tons by 1950/53, 265,000 tons more than the 535,000 tons produced in 1946. As an incentive to increase production the Ministry of Food promised a guaranteed market for colonial sugar producers between 1948 and 1950, and was considering extending it when the guarantee expired. To achieve the projected output for sugar exports the government intended to improve plant equipment and machinery at sugar factories. In 1953 colonial sugar exports were expected to supply 48 percent of the Sterling Area's demand (Table 4.9).

Cotton exports were forecasted to increase from 119 million pounds in 1946 to 213 million pounds in 1950/53 (Table 4.10). The largest increase was expected from production in Uganda. This was forecasted to move from 88 million tons in 1946 to 130 million tons in 1950/53. It was hoped that this would meet 15–20 percent of the Sterling Area's needs (Table 4.10). Vast increases were also expected in rubber production, especially in Malaya. About 88.4 percent of the projected increase in colonial rubber production was expected to come from Malaya (Table 4.11).

Table 4.10
The Colonial Cotton Production Forecast, 1946–1950/53

	Exports ('000 of tons)		
	1936	1946	Estimated 1950/53
Uganda	129	88	130
Tanganyika	25	9	
Kenya	6	1	40
Nyasaland	5	4	
Nigeria	25	15	40
West Indies	2	2	3
TOTAL	192	119	213

Table 4.11
The Colonial Rubber Production Forecast, 1946–1950/53

	Exports ('000 of tons)		
	1936	1946	Estimated 1950/53
Malaya	364	404	720
North Borneo	8	5	25
Sarawak+	21	9	55
Brunei	1	1	2
Nigeria+	2	11	12
TOTAL	396	430	814

+ Figures are exports not production

° Small quantities of rubber are produced in a number of Colonies other than these shown above, but the figures are not significant.

Tin production was expected to increase by 56,900 tons between 1947 and 1950, from 36,100 tons to 93,000 tons. Malaya was also expected to supply the bulk of the increase in the output of tin that was forecasted (Table 4.12).

Table 4.12
The Colonial Tin Production Forecast, 1946–1950

| | Production ('000 of tons of tin contained in ore) | | | | |
| | 1936 | 1946 | Estimated | | |
			1948	1949	1950
Malaya	67	27	45	57.5	84
Nigeria	10	9.1	8	8	9
TOTAL	77	36.1	53	65.5	93

Cocoa was the only major dollar-earning export for which production was expected to decrease. It was expected to decline from 306,000 tons in 1945–1946 to 285,000 tons in 1950/53. This forecast was based on assumptions about the effect of diseases such as swollen shoot on production in the Gold Coast, the empire's leading cocoa exporter (Table 4.13).

Table 4.13
The Colonial Cocoa Production Forecast, 1946–1950/53

| | Exports ('000 of tons) | | |
	1936	1946	Estimated 1950/53
Gold Coast	290	204	175
Nigeria	92	94	100
Trinidad	12	4	5
Grenada	4	4	5
TOTAL	398	306	285

While a lot of emphasis was placed on increased efficiency in the production of primary exports to assist in redressing Britain's trade imbalance with the Dollar Area, there were obvious limits to the viability of this strategy. In the short run the expansion of production for export was impossible for most of the commodities exported from Britain's colonial dependencies. Moreover, for the commodities where expansion was possible, it was dependent on a number of variables, some of which were beyond the control of the British government. Thus, Britain could not rely solely upon increased efficiency in production to achieve its objectives.

One of the organizations that was key to the success of the expansion of the production of dollar-earning or dollar-saving commodities was the Colonial Development Corporation. The formation of the CPPC and C.D.C. aroused the interest of the press both in Britain and in the colonies. Among the many commentaries, two opposing opinions captured the ensuing debate over the motives underlying the mobilization of colonial resources. The *Daily Telegraph*, a conservative newspaper published in Britain, reported:

Out of Britain's need is arising the structure of an economic partnership with people of Africa rich with possibilities for the future of the whole world. . . . It has become necessary to apply principles of the old nineteenth century expansionism to new fields and in a new manner. The problem is to raise the standard of living of the world's backward peoples in such a way that they can absorb and benefit from the vast industrial production that is seeking markets.[31]

The article contended further that the shortages of primary products and foodstuffs in Britain were making a revolution in agricultural production in Nigeria possible. It claimed that once the revolution was under way and the vicious circle of peasant poverty was broken "new forms of enterprise would be drawn by the centripetal action of a rising spiral of living standards."[32] It concluded "nothing could be more abhorrent than a suggestion that these schemes are merely exploitation to solve our own immediate difficulties. Yet there may be unfriendly minds who will conceive such charges."[33] Given the vast sums at the disposal of these corporations and the circumstances in which the Overseas Resources Development Bill was passed, the underlying motive for the bill was challenged. In Nigeria an editorial in the *West African Pilot*, a newspaper owned by Nnandi Azikiwe, strongly condemned both the O.F.C. and the C.D.C. It contended that

Colonialism is aimed at developing the resources to expand the production of foodstuffs and raw materials which Britain needs badly to carry out her socialism at home. . . . It is irrefutable that some crumbs do fall in our empty mouths while British housewives enjoy their promised much bigger margarine and fat ration next year. We may concede also that our economic affiliation with Britain is in some respects beneficial to us, but we maintain . . . our economic development, if it is really ours, cannot be carried out to our best interest without our consultation and participation . . . our country has enough mineral and vegetable resources which we can use as collaterals in raising a billion pounds from abroad and from home to finance these projects.[34]

The *West African Pilot* also published a series of articles condemning the thrust of the British government's policy. One observed, "every month that passes brings along one long-term proposal or another, each in reality directed toward relieving the mother country, though ostensibly meant for the welfare of colonial peoples."[35] It added that while the ventures contained employment opportunities "these were merely incidental in comparison with the main purpose of feeding British industries."[36] The editorial felt that Britain should be assisted, but wanted aid to be given "with a definite understanding that our people are not sacrificed to the avidity of capitalist Europe which is only now roasting in its own fire."[37] It contended "the deeper the octopus sinks its tentacles into the economic fabric of Nigeria, the more difficult the task becomes of cutting off those tentacles."[38] These sentiments were echoed by the *Ashanti Pioneer*, a newspaper published in the Gold Coast. It commented:

Lest she might be identified with exploiting the Colonies Britain, as is her wont, judiciously looks at the brighter side of things. She sees through the gloom the unparalleled and unprecedented opportunity to develop the Colonies economically. . . . We in the Gold Coast proudly welcome this singular opportunity of being able materially to help Britain, the brave, courageous and adventurous crusader, in this her supreme hour of need. All we demand is a clear straight forward statement of the tremendous issues involved. What use is "diplomacy" in this purely economic affair?[39]

From the outset the British government was concerned about the type of reception that would have been given to the C.D.C. Foreign Secretary Ernest Bevin stressed that the government should ensure that its colonial development plans could not in any way be represented as springing solely from Britain's own selfish interest.[40] Presentations were thus to be devoid of any possible suggestion of the exploitation of colonial populations. Moreover, to neutralize criticism all schemes undertaken by the C.D.C. were to emphasize raising the standard of living of colonial peoples in addition to obtaining the foodstuffs and raw material needed by Britain. Bevin's advice was included in the Colonial Office's offensive against allegations that the formation of the C.D.C. was associated solely with the need to resolve ongoing problems in the British economy. The Colonial Office claimed that it was evident for some time that the finance available to colonial governments under the Colonial Development and Welfare Act and from other sources was only sufficient to establish and develop basic economic services. Furthermore, the organs of government were not well fitted to undertake economic projects of a commercial character. Consequently, it was decided to establish the Colonial Development Corporation to remedy these anomalies.[41]

This explanation gives the impression of a degree of altruism that was clearly absent in the formulation of this policy. The fact is the C.D.C. was established because the level of expansion in colonial exports required to assist in alleviating Britain's balance of payments difficulties could not be met out of existing financial provisions for colonial development. Also, in the role it established for the colonies, Britain intended to develop projects that were geared specifically to earning or saving dollars. The needs of the British economy provided the motive, and the developmental needs of the colonies were used as the justification for the policy. The Colonial Office was simply trying to make a virtue out of necessity. Despite numerous declarations of its intentions to consult colonial peoples and promote development through Ten-Year Development Plans, it was clear that, in the short term at least, colonial development under the Labour government was synonymous with the expansion of export production in commodities which it felt could make a significant contribution to redressing Britain's trade imbalance. As the Colonial Development Working Party put it, "the colonies in their own interest as much as in the interest of the United Kingdom, should aim to make the maximum contribution that their resources permit to the early attainment of a balance in the external payments of the Sterling Area."[42]

The British government's policy with respect to the use of colonial resources was also stoutly defended by the chancellor of the exchequer, Hugh Dalton. In his address to the African Governors conference in October 1948, Dalton claimed:

in our consideration of the economic position of the United Kingdom it was explained how vital to our recovery and to the stability of the whole of the Sterling Area it is that we should develop during the next few years new sources of supply of our essential raw materials and foodstuffs in areas outside the Dollar Area. This means that the new resources which are being made available for colonial development should, wherever possible, be devoted to the production of such commodities, and in order to ensure that the potentialities of the various territories are carefully considered in relation to the needs of the Sterling Area as a whole the Colonial Primary Products Committee has been established.[43]

Dalton dismissed the substance of allegations of colonial exploitation that were being leveled against British policy on the grounds that they were "based on the assumption that the production in the colonies of foodstuffs and raw materials for sale to overseas countries is in itself undesirable and that it would be preferable for the minerals to remain untouched in the ground or for the bush to remain uncleared and infested with tsetse [flies]."[44] A lot of emphasis was placed on the benefits accruing to the colonies from developing their resources to assist Britain in resolving its trade imbalance. However, the chancellor chose to ignore the fact that whenever there was a clash between metropolitan and colonial needs, the latter were always subordinated to the former. Moreover, the colonies were shouldering an unfair amount of the responsibility for defending the pound sterling and achieving a surplus in the Sterling Area's balance of trade with the Dollar Area. As the chancellor of the exchequer himself so aptly put it, the "considered view of the United Kingdom Government is that the development of the economic resources of the colonies . . . is one of the most important means by which, in the long term, it may be possible to bring the balance of payments of the Sterling Area as a whole, once more into equilibrium."[45]

The British government stressed that its policies were mutually beneficial to Britain and colonial peoples alike. Colonial commentators were nevertheless understandably suspicious. To begin with, in the short run the trend of the existing policy was toward a greater integration of colonial economies into the British economy[46] and these commentators were convinced that without political control they had no means of ensuring that their interest in any economic venture would have been protected. They were aware also that their own development plans were being stymied by continued shortages of capital and consumer goods and very little was being done actively to encourage the development of the local industries in the colonies that had flourished during the war.

The concerns of colonial commentators were also shared by government officials. Gorell Barnes, assistant under secretary in the Economic Department of the Colonial Office, believed that the most important thing, from an imperial point of view, was to maintain a balance between political and economic considerations, the viability of the colonial contribution to the United Kingdom and the direct interest of colonial peoples, production for export and production for the improvement of nutritional standards in the colonies. He warned that it was dangerous to place "exclusive emphasis on the first of each of these pairs."[47] The colonies had managed to increase their net dollar earnings both by increasing their production of goods for export to the Dollar Area and by restricting the import of nonessential goods from it. Gorell Barnes thus contended "the colonies cannot continue to contribute to European viability on such a substantial scale, both as dollar savers and as earners, unless the United Kingdom and other countries outside the Dollar Area pay for colonial exports both to the non-dollar and the Dollar Area by exporting to them adequate supplies of consumer and other goods of the type they require."[48] From Gorell Barnes' memorandum it was also clear that the list of commodities prioritized by the CPPC was no longer guiding the imperial effort to maximize commodity production for export from the colonial empire. Instead, the commodities that were identified by the Economic Intelligence Department of the Foreign Office as being in short supply in the United States were targeted for expansion.

These included oilseeds, especially groundnuts, sugar, rice, cocoa, cotton, rubber, cobalt, tin, bauxite and copper.[49] These commodities were all dollar earners or dollar savers and a programme was produced setting out the annual production targets that were expected for each of these commodities by 1952/53.

The expansion of export production in the colonial empire led to higher incomes for primary producers and increased demands for capital and consumer goods in the colonial territories. This added to Britain's difficulties because the growth in colonial demand for capital and consumer goods could have been satisfied, for the most part, only by increased imports, either from the United States and other hard currency sources or from the United Kingdom. The former meant a loss of scarce currency. The latter could have been achieved only at the expense of exports to other areas, particularly hard currency destinations, or the already inadequate levels of investment and consumption in United Kingdom.[50] Colonies were warned, therefore, that regardless of the effort made by the United Kingdom to remedy the shortages in the supply of capital and consumer goods, in the immediate future, supplies were not likely to be sufficient to support all the projects for colonial development even though they appeared desirable. Similarly, it was not going to be possible to enable increased incomes to be fully reflected in a correspondingly increased standard of living.[51] Thus, despite their increased earnings the colonies were called upon to control imports, especially of consumer goods that had to be paid for in hard currencies, and to implement measures to economize in the use of capital goods and scarce materials such as iron and steel.

The achievement of the imperial policy in the colonies since the war was assessed in a paper submitted to the Cabinet Economic Policy Committee by Creech Jones, the colonial secretary, in December 1948.[52] The paper concentrated on the contribution of the colonies to the export drive and the establishment of a sound balance of payments for the U.K./Colonies.[53] It was revealed that the drive to expand colonial exports over the period 1946–1947 was very successful. Exports of most commodities had increased over the 1946 figure. In addition, "between 1946–48 the colonies have enormously increased their dollar earnings and these were running at an annual rate of from US$600 to US$700 during the first half of 1948."[54] At the same time colonial expenditure in the Western Hemisphere fell from US$500 million in 1947 to an annualized rate of US$473 million in the first half of 1948. This decline occurred despite the fact that the price of their imports had increased and the colonies had to increase their purchases of certain equipment for development. Creech Jones stated, "this fall shows the first result of the imposition, in the autumn of 1947, of a system of dollar ceilings, the full effects of which (because of the time lag in working off existing licences) should begin to show in the second half of 1948."[55]

The colonies also made a substantial indirect contribution to the dollar balance of the U.K./Colonies group. Colonial imports from U.K. sources rose from 5.4 percent in 1938 to 9.4 percent in the first half of 1947 and 10.2 percent in the first half of 1948. This increase led to "a considerable saving of dollars by enabling the United Kingdom to divert purchases from hard currency sources."[56] Colonial products such as tin, rubber, sisal, cocoa and oilseeds also figured prominently in the successful negotiation of bilateral trade agreements with European countries for increased supplies of foodstuffs for the U.K.[57] By employing a twin strategy of limiting colonial imports from the Dollar Area and expanding colonial exports to that area, the British government had succeeded in directing colonial resources toward resolving its trade imbalance with the Dollar Area. By the end of 1948, therefore, dollar-earning and dollar-saving commodities were the primary focus of imperial attempts to expand resource production in the colonies to meet Britain's balance of payments needs.

In 1949 the British government continued to focus on projects to promote the production of dollar-saving commodities in the colonies.[58] The latter was also the subject of talks between U.S. and U.K. officials in Washington in September 1949. The British government reiterated its contention that the economies of the colonies were based on the production of primary commodities that were complementary to those of the United Kingdom and Western Europe. Increases in the production of colonial primary products that provided an alternative to supplies from the Dollar Area were welcomed because such increases would have assisted in correcting the trade imbalance between Western Europe and the Dollar Area. Colonial production was seen as assisting the trade balance with the Dollar Area in one of three ways: by reducing the need for colonies themselves to import from the Dollar Area, particularly in the case of foodstuffs for internal consumption as these accounted for a large proportion (about 40 percent) of colonial dollar expenditure; by earning dollars through direct sales to America and other dollar account countries; or by saving dollars through providing an alternative source of supply to the Dollar Area for the rest of the world. It was extremely difficult to place any one commodity precisely within only one of these three categories, because the United Kingdom often had a choice between the use of increased colonial dollar production to earn or save dollars. Cocoa, for example, was said to be primarily valuable as a dollar earner, while sugar and cotton were primarily thought to be valuable as dollar savers.

The strategy to expand commodity production for export from the colonies involved much more than merely attempting to improve the production of the individual commodities themselves. Since the bulk of agricultural activities in the colonial empire was done by peasants, the British government decided to devote a lot of its effort to increase the production of dollar-saving commodities to improving peasant production. This was not done through a series of special projects, but through general programs which fell within the purview of the agricultural departments in the colonies. These included schemes to enable the peasants to acquire tools and other capital equipment and marketing arrangements designed to provide incentives to peasants.[59] This apart the government developed colonial infrastructure to facilitate projects that contributed either directly or indirectly toward earning or saving dollars. These included: The East African Railways and Harbour Development, which was designed to expand transport facilities to enable a greater outflow of oilseeds, minerals and other exports and a speedier inflow of heavy imports; general road construction in the Gold Coast, to enable increased outflow of exports; and the groundnut scheme in Tanganyika, East Africa, which opened up tsetse- and bush-covered areas to the large-scale production of groundnuts. By 1949, therefore, the British government was involved in a comprehensive initiative that encompassed projects and schemes geared toward alleviating its trade problems with the Dollar Area. Driven by the conviction that colonial resources were vital to its strategy for economic recovery, Britain was determined to ensure that these resources were tapped to the fullest extent possible.

STERLING AND THE MARKETING OF COLONIAL PRODUCE: 1946–1951

The expansion of commodity production for export from the colonial empire also led imperial government officials to reexamine the mechanisms for marketing colonial produce. By 1951 bulk purchase arrangements for rubber, sisal, tin and tea were abolished. They were retained, however, for important colonial products such as oilseeds and vegetable oils, sugar, cotton, coffee, bananas and copper.[60] This meant that the Ministry of Food, the Board of Trade, the Ministry of Supply and the Colonial Office continued to play a significant role in the purchase of colonial produce. As a result of the gradual removal of national and international controls over commerce at the end of World War II, especially the price ceilings in the United States, by 1946 "something approaching an international market for many colonial exports began to be re-established."[61] Thus, the wartime method of determining prices for colonial plantation and mining exports on the basis of cost of production became unattractive. Equally, the arbitrary method of fixing prices for peasant produce employed during the war also became untenable. As far as the British colonies were concerned the buying prices of all major colonial agricultural products and some of nonagricultural products were below, and in some instances substantially below, existing international prices. This apart, in the postwar era Britain was under pressure from foreign buyers and colonial producers to abandon the policy under which it reserved, in whole or in part, colonial export surpluses.

These developments occurred at a very awkward time for Britain, where one of the principal postwar concerns was the trade imbalance with the United States and dollar countries. In these circumstances it was important for the British government to regulate the price it paid to colonial producers, to ensure that its balance of payments position was not jeopardized. As Creech Jones so aptly put it, "to this country in its present difficulties, any reduction of price and the consequent reduction in pressure on the balance of payments and in the burden of internal price controls must be welcome."[62] Nevertheless, he recognized that, being underdeveloped and for the most part desperately poor, the colonies were dependent for the future on a rise in income and the beginnings of an accumulation of capital; therefore they welcomed higher prices. A conflict of interest was thus inescapable.[63] Creech Jones felt that the issue of producer prices affected the United Kingdom in two ways. First, if "higher prices for colonial products are made immediately available for expenditure by the producer, the inflationary potential in the colonies is increased and the strain on the UK exporting power intensified." The second "is that the higher the prices fixed for certain colonial products, the greater will be the amount of dollars earned by the sale of those products to hard currency countries."[64] Like other aspects of colonial policy, then, the marketing of colonial produce was also influenced by developments in the wider metropolitan economy. Moreover, given the gravity of the problems in the postwar British economy and the importance of price as one of the incentives to increase colonial export production, the government was faced with a conundrum.

Throughout most of 1947 officials from the Colonial Office criticized the British government's policy for fixing the prices paid to colonial producers. The Board of Trade and the Ministry of Food were singled out for making first claims on colonial exports at prices considerably below world market prices "through the use of the colonial export licensing system and other government sanctions."[65] Before the sterling crisis of July 1947, the Colonial Office was under pressure from the Treasury and the Ministry of Food to conclude a long-term contract aimed at securing U.K. requirements of West African cocoa during periods of shortage, at an advantageous price when compared with free-market values. Eugene

Melville, assistant under secretary at the Colonial Office, believed that there would be prima facie evidence of exploitation if Britain subscribed to any marketing arrangement which, all things considered, did not constitute a good business deal for the colonial producers concerned.[66] Therefore Melville called on the Colonial Office to dissociate itself from any arguments advanced by the Treasury and the Ministry of Food "which savour in any way of exploiting the special position of the UK to the disadvantage of the colonies."[67]

Gerard Clauson, assistant under secretary at the Colonial Office, was not in favor of fixing the export prices of colonial produce to world market prices, because for most commodities this was tantamount to American market prices. The problem was that prices on the American market were very unstable. Clauson argued that Britain should continue to control the marketing of colonial produce "and interpose a shock-absorber between the world price and the local price."[68] He called for the establishment of a marketing arrangement either akin to the one governing the marketing of cocoa, or government purchase and resale or a sales body representing the industry as a whole. This body would have fixed the price paid to local producers below the world market price and would use the difference to establish a fund to protect local producers from fluctuations in the world price for their produce. He concluded, "we should not be too good-natured to the purchasing departments of His Majesty's Government. Even if the present world prices are much cost of production in the colonies . . . we should still charge the full market price and bank the proceeds against a rainy day later."[69] Clauson clearly envisaged the creation of marketing boards along the lines of those which eventually became a feature of the arrangements for marketing colonial produce in the postwar era. Yet, as far as pricing policy was concerned he was sympathetic to the Treasury. He stated, "I do not underestimate the difficulty which we should have in doing this where world prices are so high as to bring the Treasury in to support the purchasing departments on the grounds of balance of payments considerations."[70] As far as Clauson was concerned, therefore, ultimately the need to safeguard Britain's trade balance should have taken precedence over the needs of the colonial producers in the determination of the pricing policy for colonial exports in any new marketing arrangement.

To the colonial secretary existing pricing arrangements were a legacy of the war, and "now their only justification is the financial advantage of the United Kingdom."[71] While he accepted that it was important to keep Britain's overseas payments to a minimum, he did not believe "that this justifies action which is contrary to the policy of opposition to colonial exploitation for which the Labour Party has always stood."[72] He added, "we should not, by means of colonial export licensing and other controls, force sales to this country at less than fair market price. I recognize the danger that the acceptance of these rules may adversely affect the United Kingdom's balance of payments, but consider that the danger can best be met by broader arrangements for dealing with the disposal of colonial sterling balances."[73] Creech Jones called for the establishment of a territorial marketing board operating a price stabilization fund, to give producers in a particular area an effective cushion against price fluctuations while permitting their products to be sold freely and without discrimination on a world market at varying prices from day to day. He also recommended the payment of the full market value of their products to colonial producers; the determination of market value by free negotiations between buyers and sellers, with the British government scrupulously eschewing the exercise of pressure or the use of constitutional pressure to impose a settlement in its own interest as a consumer of colonial products; and, finally, making colonial products available to all potential buyers on the basis either of freely negotiated contracts or of an internationally agreed allocation scheme. The submission of these recommendations to cabinet was eventually deferred because Creech Jones thought that it was better to await an improvement in the general atmosphere for its discussion. To him, "in view of the development of the economic situation [in the early months of 1947] it was inopportune to raise these general issues."[74]

By May 1947 it was reported that there was a slight change in the attitude of the Treasury toward the marketing of colonial produce. According to Melville, "in so far as the Treasury were behind the buying ministries in enforcing a policy of low prices for colonial products, there has been a slight softening of heart on one issue in particular which this problem raises namely, the colonies' dollar enforcing capacity."[75] The Treasury suggested "drawing a line between colonial commodities of which we are, as an empire, net exporters and those of which we are as an empire net importers."[76] Net exports were to be traded at the highest market price possible.[77] For the net imports the Treasury plan involved a "low price policy even if this meant colonies having to accept less than what might be argued to be a fair market price."[78] As the sterling crisis of July 1947 approached, therefore, the Treasury modified its position relative to the marketing of colonial produce to ensure that the United Kingdom benefited to the maximum from the prices offered for colonial exports. Thus in the case of cocoa, a net export, prices were high for both the Ministry of Food and foreign buyers. On the other hand, in the case of oilseeds (a net import), exports from West Africa were purchased at prices far below world market prices. The pattern for cocoa and oilseeds was roughly the same throughout the whole field of government-traded exports.

Because of the stance taken by the Treasury, the Ministry of Food was "unrepentantly opposed" to the Colonial Office's claim that colonial producers should have been offered the full market price for their crops, even though it had reluctantly accepted the principle of a stabilization fund.[79] The Ministry of Food, the Ministry of Supply and the Board of Trade also insisted on having a specified part of colonial production reserved for the United Kingdom by export licensing or other means. The convertibility crisis of 1947 therefore played a crucial role in shaping the principles that governed imperial policy toward the marketing of colonial produce. Commodities in which the colonial empire was a net exporter were to be traded at the highest market price possible to facilitate the maximum acquisition of hard currency. Those for which the empire was a net importer were to be traded at below world market, to ensure savings in hard currency.

In September 1947 cocoa marketing boards were established in Nigeria and the Gold Coast. In Nigeria the Cocoa Marketing Board comprised six members (three official and three nominated), who were appointed by the governor. In the Gold Coast up to 1951 the board comprised twelve members, six Africans and six Europeans. Four of the Europeans were official members.[80] The establishment of these boards did not lead to any fundamental changes in the existing arrangements governing the bulk purchases or producer prices. In addition, like their predecessor the West African Cocoa Control Board, they continued to purchase the cocoa crop from producers at prices that were below world market prices. The establishment of the marketing boards did not prevent the British government from trying to justify its policy on bulk purchasing. In September 1948 bulk purchase in the form of negotiated long-term agreements was officially proclaimed as a method for furthering colonial development by giving colonial producers the assurance of a market for their goods for some years to come. According to Leubuscher this made wartime changes in the organization and direction of their trade more or less permanent.[81]

By 1949 further changes were made in the arrangements for the marketing of colonial produce with the establishment of the Oil Palm Produce and Groundnut Marketing Board in Nigeria, the Gambia Oilseeds Marketing Board, the Sierra Leone Produce Marketing Board and the Gold Coast Produce Marketing Board. The influence of factors in the wider metropolitan economy on the operations of the marketing boards is borne out in the evidence presented by Leubuscher.[82] In the case of cocoa she noted that between 1947 and 1950, when private importation was restored, balance of payments considerations were a determining factor in both the buying and selling of cocoa. The Ministry of Food's selling price for cocoa increased from £119 in March 1947 to £225 10s in

December 1947 and was £208 6s 8d when private purchases were restored in November 1950. Also "outside the bulk purchase by the Ministry of Food, the prices at which the marketing boards sold cocoa, especially in 1949 and 1950, differed considerably according to whether the buyer was domiciled in a hard or a soft currency area."[83]

In the case of oilseeds between 1947 and 1951 the Ministry of Food paid considerably higher prices to India for groundnuts and the Belgian Congo for palm oil than it paid to producers in the colonial empire. In 1948, for example, it purchased Nigerian palm oil at £70 per ton while it paid £122 15s 7d per ton for palm oil from the Belgian Congo. In 1951 it paid £110 per ton for the highest grade of Nigerian palm oil and £171 8s 10d per ton for the equivalent from the Belgian Congo. In 1947 the Ministry of Food's purchase price for Nigerian groundnuts was £28 8s per ton while that for Indian groundnuts was £58 14d 10s per ton. In 1951 when the price paid for a ton of Nigerian groundnuts had increased to £70, that for Indian groundnuts was £99 13s 3d.[84] This apart in the case of Nigeria's oil palm produce, benniseed and groundnuts, the Ministry of Food secured contracts for the entire exportable surplus that was produced. Moreover, the fact that it offered Nigerian producers an assured market for the entire available surplus of palm oil produce was regarded by the Ministry as entitling it to pay prices below the open market value.

The purpose and policies of marketing boards have provoked much controversy. In their analysis of the genesis and functions of marketing boards, scholars such as Bauer and Helleiner contend "the policies of the marketing boards cannot be explained satisfactorily in terms of the argument usually advanced, which are more nearly in the nature of retrospective rationalization of the policies rather than any effective supporting arguments."[85] Bauer asserts also that many of the arguments advanced to explain the policies of marketing boards "are contrary to the aims of statutory marketing as laid down in the Cocoa White Papers, nor were most of them advanced at the time when the policies were adopted."[86] He adamantly rejects suggestions that the marketing board policies may have been linked to the need to reduce demand on the Sterling Area and Britain's foreign exchange reserves. He claims that "while these policies were no doubt welcome to the British authorities by reducing claims on the British economy, there is much evidence to suggest that the British authorities were prepared to make additional resources available to West Africa, and that accordingly the restriction of incomes was not required by a shortage of imports."[87] He concludes, "the widespread belief that the British authorities have influenced the marketing boards or their price policies is unfounded."[88] Helleiner argues along similar lines. He claims that "the accumulation of huge trading surpluses in the first few years of the marketing boards' operation was, in large part, accidental and that they were, with the possible exception of those earned from trading in cotton, not primarily originally intended to be used for purposes other than stabilisation."[89]

These arguments contain many weaknesses. To begin with, they leave the distinct, though erroneous, impression that the aims of statutory marketing outlined in the Cocoa White Papers are the only criteria with which one can and should evaluate the function of marketing boards in colonial economies. However, it is clear that although the Cocoa Marketing Board outlined in the White Papers served as a prototype for the marketing boards established at this time, colonial governments extended their functions into areas not originally envisaged. In April 1946, the governor of Nigeria in a dispatch to the Secretary of State sought approval "for a policy involving a considerable increase in the export price of oilseeds and cocoa, whilst reserving the power to establish development funds or price stabilisation funds . . . as a safeguard against inflation or disruption of the internal economic balance."[90] The use of marketing boards to regulate local economies was also cited by the Select Committee on Estimates. In its comments on the pricing policy for oilseeds it reported: "in order, however, to lessen the danger of inflation arising from the shortage of consumer goods the full market price was not paid to the producers, with the result that, in spite of the higher prices, there was still considerable dissatisfaction."[91] In his speech to the Nigerian Legislative Council in August 1948, Governor Macpherson noted with respect to cocoa prices:

it [the Cocoa Marketing Board, C.M.B.] has had to take into account the fact that the high prices will accentuate the existing inflationary tendency, although it is hoped that this tendency will be countered to some extent by a better supply of consumer goods, the stubborn fact remains that in times of short supply increased prices by themselves do not bring corresponding benefits.[92]

In the case of Nigeria, therefore, available evidence does not support Bauer or Helleiner's assertions on the function of marketing boards. It is clear that in addition to stabilizing producer prices the colonial government saw marketing boards as mechanisms for regulating consumer demand within the colonial economy. This added function transcended the purpose of the boards originally outlined in the "White Paper on Cocoa."

Bauer's claims that the British authorities were prepared to make additional resources available to West Africa are totally unfounded. The evidence of Britain's inability to satisfy colonial demands on its resources adequately is overwhelming. In the case of Nigeria the period 1946–1948 was characterized by particularly chronic deficiencies in the supply of capital and consumer goods. These shortages can be traced to two main factors, both related to the state of the imperial economy: a rapid expansion in domestic demand in the metropole and the limits imposed on colonial imports from the Dollar Area, the principal alternative source of capital and consumer goods. The impact of imperial economic problems on the Nigerian economy was a concrete manifestation of the extent to which the colonial economy was incorporated into that of the metropole. Consequently, the Nigerian colonial government's use of marketing boards to regulate colonial demand and control domestic inflation must be seen as an important part of the collective imperial and colonial government initiative designed to restore equilibrium to the imperial economy.

Moreover, when one considers the vigor with which the Colonial Office pursued the development of colonial resources to assist in reducing Britain's trade deficit and the ceilings that were imposed on colonial imports from the Dollar Area, it seems highly unlikely that the marketing boards would not have been utilized to regulate the burden of colonial demands on the pound sterling. These boards were among the principal levers controlling the colonial economies. Bauer himself noted:

quantitative information alone does not convey adequately the significance of these organisations. Their decisions in fixing the prices paid to producers are a major factor in determining the levels of incomes, the standard of living and the ability of people to save. . . . By prescribing producer prices they exercise a potent influence on the production of different crops.[93]

In view of the marketing boards' ability to manage colonial economies and the compelling need for such control in the metropole, especially after the convertibility crisis of July 1947, the Nigerian government's use of the boards to regulate consumer demand was clearly influenced by imperial considerations. It seems futile—as Bauer suggests—to search for official documentary evidence to substantiate allegations that the marketing boards were influenced by official pressure designed to minimize claims on Sterling Area resources and foreign exchange reserves. In Nigeria the colonial government clearly endorsed pricing policies for the marketing boards that were influenced by metropolitan considerations. Even Bauer admits that "these policies were no doubt welcomed by the British authorities."[94] Moreover, in these circumstances there was no reason for the imperial government to coerce the marketing boards, because the Nigerian colonial government policies were consistent with the requirements of the imperial economy. Here again Bauer agrees. He wrote, "quite possibly pressure in this direction would not have been necessary (even if thought desirable), since the policies of the marketing boards would have forestalled the need for it."[95]

In the postwar period, therefore, the pricing policies of the marketing boards must be analyzed within the overall context of imperial and colonial policies geared toward both the stabilization of producer and consumer prices and the regulation of demands made on the Sterling Area's resources and foreign exchange reserves. The pricing policies of the marketing boards in Nigeria clearly reflect the colonial government's perception of its function in contributing to the restoration of the British economy. A substantial portion of producer income was withheld by these boards during the period 1947–1951. The breakdown was as follows: 39.2 percent for cocoa, 49.5 percent for groundnuts, 32.5 percent for palm oil, 33.6 percent for palm kernels, and 47.5 percent for cotton. Whether such large withdrawals were justified will always be debated. Nevertheless, this policy clearly facilitated a substantial reduction in Nigeria's demands on scarce imperial resources.

In addition, although the sums accumulated were eventually repaid, the investment of marketing board surpluses in British securities enhanced imperial attempts to stabilize the pound sterling, at a time when independent members of the Sterling Area were increasing their demand on sterling resources and foreign exchange reserves. By 1951, Nigeria's marketing boards had invested a combined total of £61,539,614 in British securities. These investments exceeded the total sum of £55 million allocated for expenditure under the Nigeria Ten-Year Development Plan. It is evident, therefore, that the colony made a significant contribution to the restoration of the imperial economy at a time when it was most needed.

STERLING AND COLONIAL RESOURCE MANAGEMENT, 1947–1949

The importance of colonial resources to Britain's strategy for economic recovery prompted a review of the machinery for colonial economic planning as well as an intensification of British endeavors to develop colonial resources. In September 1947, the Colonial Economic Development Council was reconstructed to enable it to bring all aspects of colonial development into focus.[96] At the end of the year Sydney Caine, the deputy under-secretary of state, submitted a detailed proposal for strengthening the Economic Division of the Colonial Office. This was motivated principally by the fact that the existing organizational structure could not cope with the increasing pressure for rapid economic development in the colonies.[97] Caine recommended the reorganization of the Economic Division and the creation of an Economic Intelligence and Planning Department to coordinate colonial economic problems. These proposals formed the basis for subsequent changes.

Following discussions, British government ministers agreed in January 1948 that the government should have applied itself more energetically to the economic development of Africa and other colonies; they also called for the preparation of overall plans for coordinating and intensifying development planning in the colonies and for integrating these plans with the economic policy of the United Kingdom. Finally, the ministers recommended the strengthening of the machinery at the Colonial Office to carry out the plans outlined. Later in an update on the progress of arrangements dealing with economic planning in the colonies, Prime Minister Attlee was informed that the Economic Department of the Colonial Office was being reorganized into three main structures: Communications, Commercial Relations and Supplies headed by Sir Gerard Clauson; Production, Marketing and Economic Development (including liaisons with new corporations) under C. G. Eastwood; and Finance, Intelligence, Planning and Research headed by Gorell Barnes. The Intelligence and Planning section of the Economic Division was the new feature of the reorganization of the Colonial Office. This section was to be the center of economic planning and would liaise with all advisory committees. The overall head of the Economic Department was Sydney Caine. The colonial secretary also recognized that several special appointments were needed to ensure that close links were maintained between the Colonial Office and the agencies that had to carry out the executive operations. These appointments were a means of centralizing information on the general development programs and ensuring that information and guidance could flow from the center.[98]

The Colonial Economic Development Council was remodeled to include more senior officials from the Colonial Office, and it was placed more directly under the control of the parliamentary under secretary of state.[99] As an acknowledgment of the need to regulate the allocation of capital goods to the colonial empire, the Colonial Development Working Party was established under Sir Edwin Plowden. The importance of the colonial contribution to the British economy was also evident in the appointment of a minister of state and the creation of an Economic Intelligence and Planning Department in the Foreign Office. By the end of January 1948, therefore, the reverberations of the "dollar crisis" were such that they engineered major structural changes in the Colonial Office. As a result the Economic Division of the Colonial Office accounted for one-third of the total staff complement at the Colonial Office. The Colonial Office was also represented on a number of important planning and interdepartmental committees established by the imperial government.[100]

The crisis of 1947 also forced the Colonial Office to review its policy on colonial economic planning. Despite considerable progress, by August

1948 there was a general feeling of dissatisfaction at the Colonial Office. This stemmed from a number of issues such as: the fact that over most of the colonial field it was still not possible to relate goals very closely to resources; exceptions notwithstanding, many officials in the U.K. Departments had no interest in the colonies and felt that they had no responsibility for the effect of their decisions on the colonies;[101] London and the colonies were too remote from each other; and finally, there was still insufficient coordination of the various sectors of the economy. In its report of November 1948 the Select Committee on Estimates criticized the absence of a coherent strategy for colonial economic planning guiding the operations of the Colonial Office.[102] It contended that while the needs of the United Kingdom were integrated with those of the colonies, the requirements for colonial development were not being adequately addressed.

Gorell Barnes felt that many of these defects could have been ignored if the nature of the economic relations between Britain and its colonies had not changed between 1947 and 1948. He was particularly concerned about the problems caused by the shortages of capital goods and services. Thus, despite the dearth of statistical data in the colonies he proposed that colonial governments should prepare surveys; "the only absolutely essential point is that a survey should contain two important programmes; a programme for certain capital goods requirements for various periods up to five years ahead, and an annual programme for consumer needs."[103] These surveys were to be approved by a Colonial Economic Policy Committee. Once they were approved, the supply departments concerned were to be instructed to provide the required goods. As an alternative, Gorell Barnes suggested that quantities of capital and consumer goods should be allocated to, in a bloc, the individual colonies and then suballocated to the colonies by the Colonial Office.[104]

These proposals were considered in a meeting between the Colonial Office, the Treasury and the Board of Trade. It was agreed "that there was a clear need for some improvement on the existing ad hoc arrangements for meeting the needs of the colonies and for relating those needs to the maintenance of existing economic activity in the colonies and planned development schemes."[105] However, considering the shortage of available personnel, Gorell Barnes' proposed surveys were rejected as too ambitious to be practical. Instead the Treasury and the Board of Trade supported a modified version of his scheme, beginning with the establishment of formal import programs for each colonial territory.[106] By 1949, therefore, indications were that the British government was finally going to implement measures to remedy the shortages in supplies to the colonies.

Although political and administrative considerations ruled out direct British government involvement in the colonial economic planning process, it had clearly failed to formulate a program to satisfy colonial requirements of capital and consumer goods in the early postwar years. The Colonial Office explained:

It is, of course, true that it was not at once realized in 1945 that acute shortages of materials and manpower would continue so long after the end of the war. At that time it was assumed that Colonies would be able to implement their plans to the extent that their financial resources and assistance from the United Kingdom would permit; finance had been the main limiting factor in the period between the wars. It is easy to be wise after the event, and this miscalculation was made in other fields as well as that of colonial development.[107]

While in retrospect it is indeed incredible, the fact was that in the immediate postwar era colonial economic planning was formulated on the assumption that adequate supplies of essential materials would be available for colonial development. Thus, it took almost two years for action to be taken with respect to critical shortages in the supply of capital and consumer goods in the colonies.

The Colonial Office responded to the criticism leveled against its administration of colonial development and welfare schemes in a dispatch to colonial territories in November 1948.[108] This represented an attempt to improve the system of planning in the colonies, with a view to ensuring greater efficiency both in the utilization of resources in short supply and in the designing of schemes for colonial development. These objectives were commendable; however, they addressed only the colonial aspect of the problem. Given that the colonies were competing with domestic demands for capital and consumer goods, a program that made special provision for colonial needs was indispensable to the improvement of the situation in the colonial empire.

CONCLUSION

Between 1946 and the first quarter of 1947 the mobilization of colonial resources was not emphasized as a significant aspect of Britain's strategy to facilitate postwar economic recovery. However, as the problems with sterling convertibility manifested themselves, the British government was convinced that the development of commodity production in the colonies and the maximization of colonial exports would make a vital contribution to the correction of its own trade imbalance, and that of the general Sterling Area, with the Dollar Area. Its conviction was reinforced by the rapid drain on its gold and dollar reserves which resulted from the failure of convertibility in July 1947. Consequently, it devised an elaborate program to systematically identify and expand the export production of the commodities that were either dollar earners or alternatives to supplies that were obtained from hard currency sources. This program provided the foundation of the strategies it employed in the aftermath of the crises that followed the devaluation of sterling in 1949 and the outbreak of the Korean War in June 1950.

When the government's strategy was conceived the Colonial Office was not equipped to handle the job that was required. Thus, the effort to mobilize colonial resources triggered a major administrative reorganization in the Economic Division of the Colonial Office. While the British government was satisfied with its achievements by 1951, the colonies were forced to bear a disproportionate degree of the burden involved in defending sterling. The United Kingdom's contention that the mobilization process was mutually beneficial was intended to justify the obvious benefits that accrued to it, rather than to explain the sacrifice that was forced upon the colonies. Between 1947 and 1951 the effort and resources allocated by the British government to the expansion of colonial commodity production for export were easily justified by the dollars that were earned or saved through this process. Throughout the crises that characterized this period colonial needs were never given priority over those of the United Kingdom. If, as Britain argued, this was necessary because its own recovery was a precondition for colonial economic development, the real test of its enthusiasm for colonial dependencies was going to be its approach to colonial development when the colonial contribution to the stability of its balance of payments was no longer important.

NOTES

1. *P.R.O.* CO 852/650/14. "British Colonial Exports 1939–1945" by F. V. Meyer. This document gives a detailed account of the measures taken to mobilize colonial exports during the war. See also C. Leubuscher, *Bulk Buying from the Colonies* (Oxford: Oxford University Press, 1956) and P. T. Bauer, *West African Trade* (London: Routledge, 1969).

2. *Parliamentary Papers 1945–1996*, XIX (Cmd. 6713). Colonial Development and Welfare, dispatch dated 12 November 1945.

3. *P.R.O.* CO 852/1001/2. Extract from Minute by C. C. Eastwood 26/4/47. In May 1947 Caine pointed out that the Colonial Office officials had been considering the possibilities of increasing colonial commodity among themselves and sometimes in association with other departments for a few months prior to the review endorsed by Eastwood. See *P.R.O.* CO 852/1001/2. Caine to Rowe-Dutton 1/5/47.

4. Ibid.

5. The Colonial Empire 1947–48 (Cmd. 7433), p. 1.

6. *Economic Report 1945–1947* (New York: United Nations Department of Economic Affairs, January 1948), p. 191.

7. Ibid., p. 192.

8. *P.R.O.* CO 852/1000/2. Raw Cotton. Memorandum by the Board of Trade 30/6/47.

9. Ibid., pp. 193–194.

10. *United Nations World Economic Report*, pp. 3–26.

11. R. Hyam, ed., *The Labour Government and the End of Empire 1945–1951* (London: Institute of Commonwealth Studies, 1992), pp. 50–52. *P.R.O.* CAB 129/20, CP (47). "Production of Dollar-Earning Colonial Commodities." Cabinet memorandum by Mr. Thomas on balance of payments situation.

12. Ibid.

13. *P.R.O.* CO 852/1001/1. Colonial Primary Products Committee Interim Report, 15 January 1948.

14. Ibid., p. 5.

15. *P.R.O.* CO 852/1000/2. Raw Cotton. Memorandum by the Board of Trade 30/6/47.

16. Ibid.

17. Ibid.

18. Ibid., Raw Cotton. Memorandum by the Board of Trade 30/6/47.

19. *P.R.O.* CO 852/1000/2. Maize and Millet. Ministry of Food Views on future prospects. 19/7/47.

20. *P.R.O.* CO 852/937/3. Colonial Primary Products Committee. Raw materials of which the USA is short. W. F. Dawson. Secretary. 26 August 1947. This was the cover note to a note by the Economic Intelligence Department of the Foreign Office dated 16 July 1947.

21. Ibid.

22. Ibid.

23. *P.R.O.* CO 852/937/3. C. G. Eastwood to W. G. Ferguson 25/8/47.

24. Ibid.

25. Ibid., CPPC Minerals and Metals Panel. Minutes of the first meeting held at the C. O. Dover House, 29/8/47.

26. *P.R.O.* CO 852/1001/1. CPPC Interim Report 15/1/48. The following information is taken from the report.

27. *P.R.O.* CO 852/937/3. Willis to Morris 27/11/47.

28. Ibid.

29. Ibid., Minute by W. A. Morris to M. A. Willis 26/11/47.

30. *P.R.O.* CO 852/1001/2. Colonial Production Forecast. Revised version. The Colonial Office 15/7/48. The analysis that follows in Tables 4.1 to 4.9 is based on the figures provided in this document.

31. *P.R.O.* CO 852/1000/2. Excerpt from the *Daily Telegraph* quoted in *East Africa and Rhodesia*, 19/6/47.

32. Ibid.

33. Ibid.

34. *West African Pilot* 8 November 1947.

35. Ibid., 6 June 1947.

36. Ibid.

37. Ibid.

38.   Ibid.
39.   *P.R.O.* CO 852/1000/2. Extract from West African Press Survey no. 42. 12/6/47.
40.   Hyam, *The Labour Government. P.R.O.* FO 800/444. Definition of functions of Colonial Development Corporation and Overseas Food Corporation. Minute by Mr. Bevin to Mr. Attlee (PM/47/139), Doc. 84, pp. 52–53.
41.   *P.R.O.* CO 852/867/4/72. "The Colonial Development and Welfare Act and the Overseas Resources Development Act." A note by the Colonial Office, 17 April 1948.
42.   Ibid.
43.   *P.R.O.* CO 537/1052/3. A.G.C. "The Economic Position of the UK in Relation to its Colonies," address by Mr. Dalton to the conference 7/10/48.
44.   Ibid.
45.   Ibid.
46.   The secretary of state said, "the need to integrate the economy of the United Kingdom closely with that of Europe and, in turn, to integrate the economies of the Colonies more closely with the economy of the United Kingdom, should give the colonies opportunities which they might not otherwise have, to raise the standard of living and develop social welfare." See D. J. Morgan, *The Official History of Colonial Development* Vol. 2 (London: Macmillan, 1980) p. 67.
47.   Hyam, *The Labour Government.* T 236/694. "Colonial development": CO memorandum for the Treasury on the four-year program. Annex: indices of export targets 19 August 1948, p. 86.
48.   Ibid., p. 87.
49.   Ibid., p. 99.
50.   Ibid.
51.   Ibid.
52.   Hyam, *The Labour Government,* CAB 134/219, EPC(48)112. Practical Achievements in the Colonies since the War: Memorandum for Cabinet Economic Policy Committee by Mr. Creech Jones. 7 December 1948, pp. 111–115.
53.   *P.R.O.* CO 537/3089. Some Practical achievements in the Colonies since the war. 7/12/48.
54.   Ibid.
55.   Ibid.
56.   Ibid.
57.   Ibid.
58.   *P.R.O.* CO 537/5185. Secret W. D. (49)34. Washington Discussions—Head 3 (A)(1). Projects planned or underway in the Colonies to promote the production of dollar-saving commodities. Undated. This document was most likely written sometime in August or September 1949.
59.   Ibid.
60.   Leubuscher, *Bulk Buying from the Colonies,* p. 8.
61.   Ibid.
62.   Hyam, *The Labour Government P.R.O.* CO 852/989/3, "Prices of Colonial Export Products." Draft cabinet memorandum by Mr. Creech Jones. Annex: CO note on price fixing, pp. 34–42.
63.   Ibid.
64.   Ibid.

65. Ibid. "Marketing of colonial produce." Minute by E. Melville 14/1/47.
66. Ibid.
67. Ibid.
68. Ibid. Minute by G.L.M.C. 16/1/47.
69. Ibid.
70. Ibid.
71. Ibid."Prices of colonial export products." Draft cabinet memorandum by Mr. Creech Jones. Annex: CO note on price fixing.
72. Ibid.
73. Ibid.
74. Ibid.
75. Ibid. Minute by E. M. 15/5/47, pp. 31–32.
76. Ibid.
77. Ibid.
78. Ibid.
79. Ibid.
80. Bauer, *West African Trade*, ch. 21.
81. Leubuscher, *Bulk Buying from the Colonies*, p. 9. See also note no. 1.
82. Ibid., p. 11.
83. Ibid., p. 24.
84. Ibid., p. 160.
85. Bauer, *West African Trade*, p. 340. See also G. K. Helleiner, *Peasant Agriculture, Government and Economic Growth in Nigeria* (Illinois: Richard D. Irwin, Inc.), 1966.
86. Ibid.
87. Ibid., p. 342.
88. Ibid.
89. Helleiner, *Peasant Agriculture*, p. 159.
90. Saving no. 752 Governor of Nigeria to the Secretary of State. 10/4/46. This is quoted in the Keen Mission Report. See *P.R.O.* CO 852/964.
91. *P.R.O.* CO 852/855/4. Select Committee on Estimates Fifth Report.
92. *P.R.O.* CO 583/290/30572/40. Speech by His Excellency the Governor, Sir John Macpherson, to the Legislative Council, 17/8/48.
93. Bauer, *West African Trade*, p. 263.
94. Ibid., p. 342
95. Ibid.
96. Reconstruction was necessary also "when owing to retirements and resignations it [the C.E.D.C.] ceased to exist in its original form." For details on the operations of the C.E.D.C., see Morgan, *The Official History of Colonial Development*, pp. 63–79.
97. Bowden, "Development and Control in British Colonial Policy, with special reference to Nigeria and the Gold Coast 1935–1948," p. 341.
98. Hyam, *The Labour Government*, pp. 58–59. Prem 8/733 "Economic Development in the Colonies." Note by Mr. Creech Jones for Mr. Attlee 5/2/64.
99. *P.R.O.* CO 852/889/19339/1948. Re-organisation of Economic Planning in the Colonies. Economic Planning in the Colonies memorandum by Gorell Barnes. 3/8.48.
100. Ibid.

101.   Ibid.
102.   *P.R.O.* CO 852/8554. Departmental reply to the Fifth Report (1947–1948) from the Select Committee on Estimates. Memorandum by the Colonial Office 11 November 1948.
103.   Ibid.
104.   Ibid.
105.   *P.R.O.* CO 852/889/19339/1948. Minutes of a meeting held at the Colonial Office to discuss Gorell-Barnes' memorandum. 4/8/48. See also CO 852/889/19339, Economic Planning in the Colonies. Note of a meeting held in Sir Edward Bridges room on Friday, 13 August 1948, at 3 P.M.
106.   Ibid.
107.   Ibid.
108.   *P.R.O.* CO 852/863/2/19275/95. Circular dispatch, Lord Listowel, Minister of State for Colonial Affairs (for S/S) to the O.A.G.'s Administration of Colonial Development and Welfare Schemes. 15/11/48.

5

Britain's Postwar Crises and Colonial Development Finance, 1945–1951

STERLING AND COLONIAL DEVELOPMENT EXPENDITURE, 1945–1951

The British government's approach to colonial development finance in the postwar era was in some ways the most critical aspect of its colonial economic policy. When the plan for colonial development and welfare was announced in the British Parliament in February 1940, it was not justified on the grounds that the financial assistance provided for colonial development would be beneficial to the United Kingdom. There was also no mention of the fact that the plan was motivated in part, by the British government's alarm over the colonial unrest in the late 1930s and the need to ensure colonial support for Britain during World War II. Lord Lloyd, the colonial secretary, noted instead that most of the colonies "are wholly, or almost wholly dependent on the more limited resources derived from agriculture. . . . However able their government, however efficient their economic administration, many colonies cannot finance out of their own resources the research and survey work, the schemes of major capital enterprise, and the administrative or technical staffs which are necessary for their full vigorous development."[1] The colonial secretary focused on the core of the problem for the British government relative to colonial development. The majority of the British colonies lacked the financial resources necessary for their development and they looked to Britain for support. Colonial development was also justified on the grounds that it was pivotal to the sociopolitical advance of Britain's colonial dependencies. According to Lord Lloyd it was "the primary direction upon which advance in other directions is largely consequential. It is by their economic development that colonies will be in a position to devote their resources, to the maximum extent possible to the provision of those government and other services which the interest of the people demand."[2] The provisions for colonial development and welfare were therefore a British government initiative to create the socioeconomic foundation that it believed was necessary for the eventual transfer of political power to colonial peoples.

When Colonel Stanley, the colonial secretary, approached the chancellor of the exchequer for an increase in the financial allocation for colonial development and welfare in 1944, the provision of colonial development finance was linked to Britain's postwar financial problems for the first time.[3] Colonel Stanley pointed out "it is quite certain that within a few years after the end of hostilities, the sums required are likely to substantially exceed the £5 million per annum at present provided for."[4] Thus, he proposed that the annual limit provided for under the Act of 1940 be increased to £10 million and £1 million, respectively. In addition, he wanted the British government to commit itself to increasing the annual limit on development expenditure by stages over the next ten years. Colonel Stanley recommended that the new Colonial Development and Welfare Act "should provide for a maximum [expenditure] of £10,000,000 per annum for the first three years, i.e. up to 1948/49, a maximum of £15,000,000 for the next four years, i.e. up to 1952/53, and a maximum of £20,000,000 for the last two years, i.e. up to 1955/56."[5] He argued that the merit of his proposal was that it avoided a large increase in "the burden on the Exchequer in the early postwar years when our budgetary difficulties are likely to be greatest."[6]

In his endeavor to justify the financial increases he sought, the colonial secretary invoked the ideas that guided the Colonial Development Act of 1929. Thus, the benefits that were likely to accrue to the United Kingdom from the additional funds provided for colonial development were presented as a quid pro quo for colonial assistance in resolving Britain's sterling problems which should not be overlooked. Colonel Stanley contended that an increase in the allocation for colonial development finance "will result in a real increase in colonial production, which would strengthen our general financial position either by offering increased supplies of goods for which we shall not need to provide non-sterling currency, or by increasing our sales to foreign countries and particularly the hard currency countries."[7] While Colonel Stanley did not underestimate the magnitude and continuity of the pressure which the development needs of British colonial territories placed on the United Kingdom's financial resources, he believed that financial provision for colonial development was an inescapable part of Britain's obligations as colonial overlord. Colonel Stanley concluded, "if we are unable or unwilling to do so, are we justified in retaining, or shall we be able to retain a colonial empire?"[8] As far as the colonial secretary was concerned, therefore, the retention of Britain's colonial empire was in the final analysis inextricably linked to financial support that the British government was prepared to give to colonial territories.

The Treasury did not believe that the United Kingdom benefited from the sums it invested in colonial development. The chancellor of the exchequer claimed that "our assistance to the colonies is an external and not an internal payment and none of the compensatory benefits to which the increased expenditure gives rise would accrue to us. Thus, any increase in assistance under the Colonial Development and Welfare Act, is likely to be an addition to the adverse balance of payments which we have got to correct."[9] The Treasury was also reluctant to commit itself to future increases in development finance along the lines of those proposed by the colonial secretary. The chancellor contended that "our problem of overseas payments is likely to be one of increasing difficulties and that it would be unwise to undertake a commitment involving an increasing scale of assistance."[10] Thus, while colonial development was central to the British government's plans for social and political advance in colonial territories, for the Treasury, the availability of funds for colonial development ultimately depended on Britain's balance of position. Thus, if the difficulties forecasted for the U.K. economy in the postwar era in 1944 materialized, and the Treasury's stance was inflexible, then it was going to be very difficult for the colonies to obtain adequate finance from the British government for development and welfare. Toward the onset of the postwar era, therefore, the financial allocations for colonial development and welfare became linked to Britain's sterling policy. In addition, there was debate within the British government over the degree of financial support necessary to realize the primary objective of colonial economic policy and the financial support that Britain could afford given the constraints facing the British economy.

The Treasury and the Colonial Office were not alone in their concerns about potential problems to Britain, which were likely from fufilling its obligations on colonial development finance in the postwar era. The prime minister's personal secretary told a meeting of the Colonial Economic Advisory Committee in December 1944 that "the more generous sums that were contemplated by the government under the new Act would add up to an extremely small sum of money—a large sum for the tax-payers to contribute, but a very small fund out of which to stimulate and finance the economic development of 60 million people."[11] To the secretary it was difficult to envisage what practical policy could be pursued in view of the immensity of the problem and the scale of expenditure which was required. Although the members of the

Colonial Economic Advisory Committee were not as pessimistic as Durbin, they agreed that the sums provided for colonial development and welfare were inadequate. In spite of its incapacity to satisfy colonial demands for financial assistance, the British government made it clear that it was not going to "approach any foreign countries or any international investment fund which may be established, specifically for loans for colonial development."[12]

By 1945, therefore, it was acknowledged within British government circles that existing financial allocations for colonial development were inadequate. Also, it was clear that because of the magnitude of the expenditure anticipated and the reservations about the prospects for the U.K. economy, it was going to be very difficult for Britain to cope with future colonial demands for financial assistance. In fact, after the passage of the Colonial Development and Welfare Act of 1945, the colonies "were warned not to think of the British Exchequer as a "fairy godmother," and that although the £120 million pledged under the Colonial Development and Welfare Act was safe, it would be misleading to hold out hopes for any increased generosity from H.M.G."[13]

Colonial development finance posed an unprecedented challenge for the British government in the postwar era. The disruptions caused by World War II were a setback to the progress of development and welfare schemes. Thus, at the end of the war, poverty, squalor, disease, malnutrition and illiteracy were still widespread in the British empire.[14] Attempts to remedy these and other social and economic problems were encumbered by the difficulties involved in restoring sterling to international convertibility and the problems that confronted the United Kingdom in the early years of the transition from war to peace. The proportion of colonial expenditure represented by development and welfare grants during the war and early postwar years is difficult to estimate. However, from the ten-year development plans submitted by 1949, it is clear that dependencies such as Gambia (65.7 percent), Sierra Leone (55.2 percent), Seychelles (76.9 percent) and St. Helena (100 percent) depended more on the United Kingdom for development and welfare funding than most other colonial territories. Uganda (18 percent) and Northern Rhodesia (16 percent) were the least dependent. Overall most colonies looked to Britain for between 22 percent and 40 percent of their development finance (Table 5.1). When placed alongside its own needs this was indeed a serious strain on the United Kingdom's resources. Moreover, because of the colonies' reliance on Britain, obstacles to accessing and spending development and welfare funds were certain to have adverse effects on the progress of development and welfare projects in most colonial territories.

Table 5.1
Ten-Year Colonial Development Plans (1949)

Colony	Total plan £000	CDW £000	%	Loan £000	%	Local sources £000	%	Communications %	Economic (%)	Social (%)	Admin. & Misc. (%)
Gambia	1980	1300	65.7	250	12.6	430	21.7	4.7	14.0	80.6	0.7
Nigeria	55000	23000	41.8	16000	29.1	16000	29.1	23.7	12.4	57.3	6.6
Sierra Leone	5256	2900	55.2	1400	26.6	956	18.2	22.0	17.0	53.9	7.1
Kenya	22000	5100	23.2	7000	31.8	9900	45.0	12.0	48.0	29.3	10.7
Tanganyika	18005	7150	39.7	6879	38.2	3976	22.1	38.6	12.5	39.7	9.2
Uganda	13863	2500	18.0	2000	14.4	9363	67.5	11.7	18.0	41.9	29.4
Zanzibar	1436	750	52.2	250	17.4	436	30.4	1.6	10.1	87.3	1.0
Aden	2503	800	32.0	660	26.4	1043	41.7	20.4	28.6	44.3	6.7
N. Rhodesia	17000	2728	16.0	9000	52.9	5272	31.0	17.6	17.6	36.4	28.4
Nyasaland	8258	2303	27.9	2500	30.3	3455	41.8	20.9	18.6	45.6	14.9
Mauritius	7698	1786	23.2	3750	48.7	2162	28.1	4.3	25.3	69.1	1.3
Seychelles	325	250	76.9	–	–	75	23.1	8.7	20.2	68.8	2.3
St. Helena	200	200	100.0	–	–	–	–	4.7	40.0	54.2	1.1
Cyprus	6350	1750	27.6	3000	47.2	1600	25.2	8.3	40.1	45.5	6.1
Barbados	3411	800	23.5	1000	29.3	1611	47.2	3.5	24.0	63.2	9.3
Br. Guiana	6646	2500	37.6	2757	41.5	1389	20.9	26.5	45.7	15.0	12.8
Jamaica	23030	6350	27.6	5282	22.9	11398	49.5	8.8	29.6	56.6	5.0
Grenada	1732	382	22.1	500	28.9	850	49.1	15.0	33.2	42.7	9.1
St. Vincent	1106	346	31.3	.35.9	32.5	401	36.3	23.4	31.3	37.5	7.8
N. Borneo	3653	1150	31.5	1300	35.6	1203	32.9	28.9	10.7	21.5	38.9
TOTAL	199454	64045	32.1	63887	32.0	71520	35.9	18.96	22.5	47.1	11.5

Source: Parliamentary Papers 1948–1949. XIII (Cmd. 7715) 641. Progress report on the Colonial Territories 1948–1949, pp. 129–31.

The novel feature of colonial development financing in the postwar era was that development expenditure, whether from colonial development and welfare grants, colonial governments surplus revenues or loans raised by colonial governments, was to be put within the context of ten-year economic and social development plans drawn up by each colony and approved by the Colonial Office.[15] Of the £120 million allocated for colonial development and welfare, £35 million was retained by the Colonial Office to fund research and centrally administered schemes and to provide for contingencies. The remaining £85 million was divided among the colonies in accordance with size and population, known and potential economic resources, the existing state of development and development schemes under consideration or known to exist. By 1949 ten-year development plans were approved for 20 colonies. Total expenditure was £199,454,000. The significance of the United Kingdom's contribution was evident in the fact that 32 percent of this sum was expected to come from colonial development and welfare grants, 32 percent from loans to the colonies, and the remainder from local colonial resources.[16]

The allocation of expenditure for colonial development and welfare was also very interesting: 18.9 percent of total expenditure was for communications, 22.5 percent for economic development, 47.1 percent social, and 11.5 percent administrative and miscellaneous. The overwhelming emphasis of colonial development in the early postwar period therefore was on the provision of social amenities and services. (Table 5.1). While it was obviously necessary to improve the social infrastructure in the colonies, as a form of investment this did not produce quick returns. Thus, in the short term, at least, the majority of colonies were going to require further assistance for projects geared specifically toward economic development.

Between 1946 and 1948 the rate of expenditure on colonial development and welfare projects was seriously inhibited by Britain's economic problems. After the convertibility crisis of 1947 the Colonial Office was reluctant to approve development projects unless it was satisfied that the colonies had made every effort to make the maximum use of local resources.[17] The progress of colonial development schemes was also constrained by the continuation of wartime restrictions on the purchase of material from the Dollar Area in the postwar period. This served to intensify the postwar shortages in the supply of capital goods required for development projects in the colonies. In the case of iron, for example, the Colonial Development Working Party reported that between 1936 and 1938 iron and steel consumption in the colonies was in the order of 350,000 to 450,000 tons per annum. However, in 1947 the export of finished steel from the United Kingdom to the colonies was running at 180,000 tons per annum. It noted that "little more than one-third of the firm requirements for colonial public works are being met."[18]

Gorell Barnes, the director of the Finance, Intelligence, Planning and Research section of the Economic Department at the Colonial Office, was particularly critical of colonial development policy. He claimed that "in Whitehall not nearly enough attention is paid to the economic balance of the individual colonies and to the effect on that balance of decisions taken in London."[19] He explained that many of the defects in colonial economic policy would not have mattered too much, were it not for the change in colonial/metropolitan relations which occurred after the convertibility crisis of 1947.[20] He called on the government to approach colonial economic planning scientifically. A similar view emerged from a meeting between officials from the Treasury and the Colonial Office in August 1948. It was recognized that "colonial requirements tended to suffer, in the Whitehall allocating machinery, when they came up against either the UK requirements or requirements of foreign and dominion countries. . . . A new spirit and a better recognition of colonial needs seemed to be wanted."[21] There was also consensus "on a clear need for some improvements in the ad hoc arrangements for meeting the needs of the colonies and for relating those needs to the maintenance of existing economic activity in the colonies."[22] The failure of the U.K. government to make provisions for colonial needs resulted in the continuous underspending of the funds approved for development and welfare schemes. Of the £7,729,000 approved only 45.8 percent, or £3,547,000 was spent in 1946–1947, 38.2 percent, or £5,340,000, of the £13,967,000 in 1947–1948 and 52.4 percent, or £6,445,000, of the £12,280,000 approved in 1948–1949.[23] The first three years of the Colonial Development and Welfare Act of 1945 were the ones in which the rate of expenditure was the slowest. These were also years of great economic difficulty for Britain.

The slow rate of expenditure of funds approved for colonial development and welfare schemes worried the Colonial Office. In February 1947, the colonial secretary was advised against establishing an enquiry into the matter because everyone knew "what the colonies would tell us if we asked them for the reasons for the delay."[24] In November 1948 T. Lloyd, deputy under-secretary at the Colonial Office, noted, "we are thus in a paradoxical situation of needing more money on an ever increasing scale, while we are unable to spend the money already available."[25] The Colonial Office was particularly keen to solve this problem because it did not want to approach the Treasury for more money while existing allocations were largely unspent. Even though the restrictions imposed on colonial expenditure in the Dollar Area and Britain's inability to meet colonial demand for capital goods and services were central to the shortages experienced in the colonies, the British government looked to the colonies for solutions. In the Colonial Office it was proposed, for example, that funds already earmarked for colonial development and welfare projects should be redirected "by warning colonial governments, that unless the rate of absorption of their allocations increased within a given period, a part of these allocations would be withdrawn and placed in reserves."[26] Eventually, this was rejected because of adverse political reaction that was expected from its introduction. In addition, although the funds approved were not being spent rapidly, they were committed to projects that would have been seriously affected by fundamental alterations in expenditure.[27] Between 1946 and 1948 therefore, the British government was unable to solve the problems that seriously slowed the rate of expenditure on colonial development. Moreover, as the delays persisted it was becoming increasingly difficult for the colonies to make the kind of economic progress that was deemed necessary for their political progress.

The situation with respect to the shortage of colonial supplies of capital goods and services improved dramatically after 1948 because of the recovery of industrial production in Germany and other parts of Western Europe. However, the introduction of the rearmament program following the outbreak of the Korean War in June 1950 "led to a check in the flow of capital goods and steel from the U.K., thus the pace of development slowed accordingly."[28] The difficulties relative to the rate of expenditure of the funds set aside for development and welfare projects in 1945 helped to mask the fact that funding for development finance was inadequate. According to the Colonial Office "previous forecast for colonial development and welfare expenditure were falsified by factors which could have been hardly foreseen and which were largely outside the control of colonial governments."[29] In reality more funds were required in the colonies for new development projects, "some of it of considerable immediate importance to the whole Sterling Area."[30]

The need for capital inflows into the colonies was such that in 1949 the colonial secretary requested that the chancellor of the exchequer increase the funds allocated for research from £1 million to £2.5 million, and the annual limit for spending under the Colonial Development and Welfare Act from £17.5 million to £20 million. This approach was made at an awkward time for the British government. Following the devaluation of sterling in September 1949, it announced a £140 million package of cuts to the capital expenditure of the fuel and power industries, the expanding education program, new housing, food subsidies, school meals, transportation for pupils and the large field of miscellaneous investments.[31] A one-shilling charge was also introduced for National Health Service prescriptions. In the colonies heads of departments were asked to economize on expenditure in order to facilitate a 5 percent cut in the operating costs of the Colonial Office.[32] Overall, the British government expected to save about £100 million during financial year 1950–1951. Given the state of the British economy, therefore, and the thrust of Britain's economic policy, the parsimony toward the financial needs of the colonies seemed set to continue.

It is difficult in the context of colonial needs to understand what was expected from the modest sum requested by the colonial secretary. However, coming as it did, at a time of severe austerity in the United Kingdom, the increase seemed to be more an indication of what Creech Jones believed that Britain could afford rather than what was needed in the colonies. In the end because of the small size of the increase requested it was difficult for the chancellor to refuse. Thus, the ceiling on annual expenditure was raised from £17.5 million to £20 million and research from £1 million to £2.5 million for the period April 1951 to April 1956, an overall increase of just £20 million.[33] According to the colonial secretary the British government "appreciated that this represented only a small portion of the financial assistance which the colonial governments would need in order to implement their more important projects of development."[34]

At the beginning of the 1950s, therefore, the colonies were still being underfunded. Britain clearly felt that it was doing the best it could in the circumstances. However, in reality the gap between the United Kingdom's capacity to simultaneously satisfy its own financial needs as well as those of its dependencies was widening. The contradiction between its policy toward colonial development and its declared objective to assist the colonies in establishing the economic foundations necessary for the achievement of self-government and eventually independence was also growing. As Britain vacillated over the question of colonial development finance, the process of political reform was gaining momentum throughout most of its dependencies. Thus, the economic preconditions which it set for decolonization were gradually becoming irrelevant.

DEVELOPMENT FINANCE AND THE COLONIAL DEVELOPMENT CORPORATION, 1947–1951

Prior to the balance of payments crisis in 1947, the funding of colonial development projects was not emphasized as a mechanism that could assist Britain in resolving its problems. After the convertibility debacle the Colonial Development Corporation (C.D.C.) was established as an instrument for developing Britain's colonial dependencies.[35] The C.D.C. was empowered to raise a maximum of £110 million to finance projects for the development of colonial resources.[36] It was supposed to operate as a commercial enterprise "expected to pay its way and not as a grant providing body."[37] Lord Trefgarne, the chairman of the C.D.C., explained "there will be no profits in the sense that the corporation has any shareholders to pay dividends to, but profits in the sense of avoidance of loss . . . money earned would be ploughed back into colonial development in order to strengthen and spread its [the C.D.C.'s] activities."[38]

The deterioration of the British economy was an important factor in the imperial government's decision to establish the C.D.C. Norman Brooke, secretary to the Labour cabinet, explained the dilemma thus:

At recent meetings there has been general support for the view that the development of Africa's economic resources should be pushed forward rapidly in order to support the political and economic position of the United Kingdom . . . [This policy] could, I suppose, be said to fall within the ordinary definition of "Imperialism." And at the level of a political broadcast might be represented as a policy of exploiting native people in order to support the standards of living of workers in this country. This policy is doubtless inevitable—there are compelling reasons for it, both economic and international for adopting it. But if it is disclosed uncautiously [sic] or incidentally, without proper justification and explanation, may it not be something of a shock to Government supporters and indeed to enlightened public opinion generally? . . . It can of course, be argued that the more rapid development of Africa's resources will bring social and economic advantages to the native peoples in addition to buttressing the political and economic influence of the United Kingdom.[39]

The funds available to the C.D.C. were a public acknowledgment by the U.K. government of the inadequacy of the financial provisions it had made for the development of its colonial territories. It also exemplified the shift in Britain's policy toward colonial development which was most noticeable after the abortive attempt at convertibility in July 1947. While the British government was reluctant to increase the level of funding allocated for colonial development and welfare, it was quite prepared to make a major capital injection to facilitate the development of colonial resources because the benefits to the U.K. economy seemed attractive. It was clear that Britain wanted to encourage investments in schemes to facilitate the earning of the dollars required for the defense of sterling and its own economic recovery. In light of this it was not surprising, as Cowen points out, that "the Treasury insisted on divisibility between a British need for colonial production and a colonial need for welfare. The C.D.C. would fulfill the British need, the Colonial Development and Welfare funds would meet the colonial welfare requirements."[40]

The Colonial Office rejected this distinction, arguing once more that the metropolitan and colonial needs were mutual. The conflict prompted some colonial administrators to question whether or not colonial development and welfare funds would be used in the future to finance schemes of a commercial nature which could be undertaken by the C.D.C. The Chief Adviser on Development and Welfare in the West Indies clearly opposed the Treasury's position. He contended that its criteria "would place key projects for the development of colonial territories in the hands of an agency motivated by profits and not committed to their general welfare."[41] Moreover, it meant that colonies that offered the best opportunities for development would attract the bulk of the C.D.C.'s investment capital.

The Colonial Office's opposition to the Treasury's perception of the C.D.C.'s function represented a change from its former position. In the discussions that preceded the passage of the O.R.D.B., both parties agreed to make a joint statement during the debate on the bill "that recourse will not be had to the Colonial Development and Welfare Vote for funds for projects of a character which make them appropriate for financing by either corporation."[42] This was communicated to the colonies in a dispatch on 17 December 1947.[43] However, the ministers responsible for the colonies were unwilling to announce it during the debate because they believed that it would have been unwise for the Colonial Office to commit itself to a position of providing an alternative source of funds for projects rejected by the C.D.C.[44] By so doing they would have given the C.D.C. the power to determine what projects should be assisted from U.K. government funds.[45] This complete transfer of power was not the original intention of the British government.[46]

The volatile nature of colonial politics made it difficult for the C.D.C. to carry out the mandate of the British government. In West Africa, for example, this factor played an important role in determining the nature of relations between the Colonial Office and the C.D.C. Major schemes posed a very difficult problem. In the Gold Coast and Nigeria "there was intense suspicion about anything regarded as a form of exploitation of foreign capital."[47] Political elements did not always draw a clear distinction between a state-sponsored enterprise ploughing back profits into the territories and a purely private enterprise. This predilection together with the political situation made the C.D.C. very reluctant to invest in West Africa. It was extremely important, therefore, to dispel these doubts because "unless they [the Colonial Office] could have applied all the resources at their disposal there would have been a very big gap in the policy of developing the economic resources of the colonial empire in full."[48] This in turn would have added to the difficulty which Britain was experiencing maintaining a balance between the pace of economic development and political development. Thus, Sydney Caine contended, "I can think of nothing more important to West Africa or indeed Africa as a whole, than devising proper machinery to enable the Corporation to operate in Africa."[49]

The C.D.C. undertook a wide range of activities. By 31 December, 1948, it had considered fifty-seven projects (Table 5.2).[50]

Table 5.2
Projects Undertaken by the C.D.C. by 31 December 1948

Agriculture	11
Animal Projects	8
Forestry	3
Engineering	4
Factories	21
Financial	1
Fisheries	2
Minerals	7
Total	57

Source: *Parliamentary Papers 1948–1949*. XIII (188), 471. C.D.C. Annual Report and Statement of Accounts for year ending 31 December 1948.

Nine of the fifty-seven projects that were examined were undertaken. They were: gold mining and the development of the timber industry in British Guiana; the reorganization of the salt industry in the Turks and Caicos Islands; the rebuilding of Castries;[51] the large-scale production of tung oil[52] in Nyasaland; and the production of manila hemp in North Borneo. The capital sanctioned for these undertakings was £3,034,000, excluding the cost of rebuilding Castries.

By 31 December 1949, the corporation was committed to twenty-eight undertakings at an approved cost of £14,187,000 (Table 5.3).[53] The form of the C.D.C.'s involvement in these undertakings was very diverse: it was the sole investor and director in fourteen projects; a joint partner, but majority shareholder in seven; it had a minority in three projects; it issued debenture loans to three commercial companies; and it acted as managing agent for a colonial government in the other project.[54] By the end of 1951 the C.D.C. was committed to fifty-three projects at a cost of £35,729,294 (Table 5.4).[55] Between 1949 and 1951 the financial commitments of the C.D.C. had increased by about 250 percent.

The largest agricultural projects undertaken were rice farming in Gambia (£1,115,000) and the Vipija tung estates in Nyasaland (£1,200,000). Other agricultural projects included: the cultivation of bananas (£432,000) and the development of stock farms in British Honduras; the rehabilitation of the Kulai Oil Palm Estate in Malaya (£229,000); the development of the Kasungu tobacco estates in Nyasaland

(£173,000); and the Niger Agricultural Project near Mokwa in Northern Nigeria (£250,000). It was the sole investor in at least thirty-two of these ventures.

Table 5.3
The Financial Commitments of the C.D.C. for the Period Ending
31 December 1949

Division	Number Undertakings	Capital £	Approved % of Total
Agriculture	10	3,820,500	27
Animal Products	2	1,052,000	8
Engineering	1	–	–
Factories	4	1,605,000	11
Finance	2	4,125,000	29
Fisheries	4	771,500	6
Forestry	4	2,613,000	18
Minerals	1	200,000	1
TOTAL	28	14,187,000	100

Source: *Parliamentary Papers 1950*. VII (105), 171. C.D.C. Annual Report and Statement of Accounts for the year ending 31 December 1949.

Table 5.4
The Financial Commitments of the C.D.C. for the Period Ending
31 December 1951

	Number of Projects	Capital £	Sanctioned %
Agriculture	16	9,628,350	27
Animal Production	3	2,716,000	7.6
Factories	6	4,412,000	12.4
Fisheries	4	978,000	2.7
Forestry	4	3,934,361	11.0
Hotels	2	210,000	.6
Minerals	5	3,171,000	8.9
Works	3	233,000	.6
Others	8	8,715,283	24.4
Services	2	1,730,000	4.8
TOTAL	53	35,729,294	100.0

Source: *Parliamentary Papers 1952–1953*. VIII (158), 31. C.D.C. Annual Report and Statement of Accounts for the year ending 31 December 1952.

The projects undertaken by the C.D.C. during this period originated in a variety of ways. The majority was sponsored by colonial governments, often in consultation with the chairman and other members of the board of the C.D.C. Some were submitted by commercial concerns and others were initiated by the C.D.C. itself.[56] The criteria for the C.D.C.'s acceptance of a project varied. The C.D.C. claimed that the technical and commercial viability together with the benefits to the colony were paramount. Subject to the fulfillment of these conditions, one report stated, "the Corporation has naturally aimed at selecting the projects which show promise of either earning or saving dollars, in the interests of the territory itself and the Sterling Area as a whole."[57]

Of the twenty-eight projects undertaken by 1949 only eight were expected to earn or save dollars. Thus, although Britain's balance of payments problem was the driving force behind the creation of the C.D.C., its operations were not guided solely by balance of payments considerations. It provided loans to the Central Electricity Board in Nigeria to finance the improvement of land for industrial, business and residential purposes. It participated also with the governments of Trinidad and Northern Rhodesia in the construction of cement factories and with the Jamaican government in the establishment of a cannery and citrus processing plant.[58] Between 1949 and 1951 the C.D.C. lost a total of £1,146,624 on the projects it undertook.[59] Its biggest failure in a project came in the Gambian Eggs Project which was implemented in 1948.[60] This project envisaged producing 20 million eggs and 1 million pounds of dressed poultry for the British market. It was part of an attempt by the C.D.C. to reduce Britain's expenditure on poultry and poultry feed from the Dollar Area.[61] No research or pilot surveys were conducted and the project was executed despite the Treasury's skepticism and opposition from the Ministries of Food and Agriculture. In 1951 the project was ignominiously abandoned after the failure of the poultry feed crop and the destruction of a substantial part of the original poultry stock by fowl typhoid in 1949. An estimated £800,000 was lost on this project alone.

The operating losses incurred by the C.D.C., particularly the failure of the Gambia Eggs Project, prompted demands from the lord president of the council, Herbert Morrison, and the chancellor of the exchequer, Hugh Gaitskell, "that closer scrutiny be applied to the C.D.C. proposals when proposals were put forward for capital sanction."[62] They were supported by both the colonial secretary, James Griffith, and the new chairman of the C.D.C., Lord Reith. This marked the abrogation of the existing agreement which guaranteed limited ministerial intervention. There was also one other major change in the operating policy of the C.D.C. In its annual report for 1951 the C.D.C. acknowledged "that too much was attempted by way of direct executive management."[63] It decided that its new policy would be "to look for experienced private enterprise to share in investment and management."[64]

The financial setbacks suffered by the C.D.C. during the period 1948–1951 do not reduce the importance of its contribution to colonial development finance over this period. Although some of its projects were geared toward resolving Britain's deficit problems, in general the financial assistance provided by the C.D.C. proved a useful supplement to the expenditure allocated under the Colonial Development and Welfare Act. Apart from its contributions both directly and indirectly to the development of economic infrastructure in colonial territories, the C.D.C. supported the establishment of industries and other commercial ventures that promised long-term benefits for the colonies concerned. On the other hand, the funding required for the C.D.C. projects demonstrated in unequivocal terms the influence exerted by Britain's economic problems on colonial economic policy. It was also a manifestation of the importance Britain had attached to developing colonial resources to assist with its economic recovery. Finally, by 1951 it was clear to Britain that colonial development whether for its own benefit or that of the colonies was a very costly exercise.

FOREIGN CAPITAL AND COLONIAL DEVELOPMENT FINANCE: THE DEBATE, 1947–1950

Britain's postwar economic problems also influenced its policy toward foreign investment in its colonial dependencies. In the quest for sources to finance colonial development the British government gave serious consideration to foreign capital, especially American capital. In 1947 it was reported that American investors were excited about the prospect of investing in Africa. However, the problem for Britain was to find a means of making U.S. capital available on terms that were satisfactory, both to itself and to American investors.[65] The British government was wary of U.S. investors, because it feared that American control would inevitably accompany the provision of U.S. financial support. The Colonial Office felt that "any American finance should take the form of a contribution to general schemes such as possibly our own Colonial Development Corporation."[66] This was opposed by the Treasury, which believed that "it was not very attractive to have such American outposts working inside our colonial development schemes."[67] Sydney Caine, assistant under secretary at the Colonial Office, also preferred assistance in the form of a loan from the International Bank for Reconstruction and Development (I.B.R.D.). He argued that this would make resources available for development in areas such as technical expertise, equipment and material which were currently available only through an exchange of dollars.[68] Caine assumed that loans from the I.B.R.D. would be provided without conditions, at rates that were comparable with those in London. However, this was not the case. The I.B.R.D.'s rate of interest on loans was 4.25 percent per annum compared with 3 percent for loans raised on the London market[69] the I.B.R.D. was not well adapted to dealing with small projects. Furthermore, the bank (I.B.R.D.) insisted on putting in observers to watch how its money was being spent.[70]

In response to allegations that it was moving in a vicious circle on the question of foreign investment in colonial territories, the Colonial Office issued a memorandum on "American Private Investment in the Colonies" in January 1948.[71] It pointed out that "H.M.G., and through them colonial governments are under special obligations as regards access of foreign powers to colonial raw materials which make it politically difficult to put any special obstacles in the way of American investment in the development and production of such raw materials."[72] The Colonial Office reiterated that from a purely British point of view there were strong objections to allowing foreign investments in colonial undertakings "because in particular cases there may be greater danger of political control moving in the same direction."[73] Nevertheless it concluded "subject always to special political considerations in the individual cases, we should not as a matter of general policy pose obstacles to the investment of American capital in new productive undertakings in the Colonies."[74]

In a subsequent submission to the C.D.W.P. on "Investment of Foreign Capital in the Colonies,"[75] the Colonial Office argued that there were two very strong reasons for seeking to encourage the investment of foreign capital in the colonies. First, it would assist in alleviating the severe shortage of skilled manpower and capital and consumer goods; and second, it would reduce the burden borne by Britain for financing colonial development ventures.[76] As a general principle the Colonial Office supported private American investment in the colonial empire as long as it was on terms that made the future payment of interest and the return of capital in dollars contingent upon the success of the undertakings. However, it was not as receptive to investment by the government of the United States or institutions closely associated with it. It felt that this would lead to a high degree of interference from the American administration.[77] This was also true of its attitude toward the International Bank for Reconstruction and Development (I.B.R.D.).

Despite the reservations about foreign investments in the colonial empire, it is clear that colonial development finance was proving burdensome to the British government. In an attempt to address the problem, the British government sent Gorell Barnes to Washington in March 1948 for exploratory and informal discussions with officials of the

I.B.R.D. He was commissioned—provided the talks were reasonably satisfactory—"to endeavour to persuade the Bank to earmark from funds available to it, an amount to be agreed tentatively between $100 million and $200 million for the financing of colonial development projects to be agreed to in the next few months."[78] The Colonial Office felt at this stage "only confusion would result if other colonial governments were consulted about the possibility of their borrowing from the Bank."[79] Nevertheless, it devised a list of projects that could be financed by the I.B.R.D. These included: the extension of the Apapa Wharf in Nigeria, to cope with the anticipated increase in traffic likely to arise with an increase in Nigerian exports, and the proposed groundnut project in Damaturu in Northern Nigeria.[80]

Gorell Barnes reported that the attitude of the Loans Department of the I.B.R.D. was very encouraging. It was very impressed with the way in which Britain was handling colonial development. Although Gorell Barnes believed that the policy would be relaxed eventually, he noted that "it is still Bank policy to make loans in dollars only, to finance dollar expenditure."[81] Despite the generally favorable report, the Colonial Office was still reluctant to urge colonial governments to borrow from the I.B.R.D. Apart from the drawbacks inherent in the bank's policy on nondollar expenditure, the Colonial Office was unsure of the I.B.R.D.'s ability to guarantee colonial governments that borrowing from the bank would remedy the existing position vis-à-vis the supply of capital goods. Rather than abandon the idea of borrowing from the I.B.R.D., the Colonial Office suggested that the substance of the Gorell Barnes Report should be circulated to colonial governments for consideration.[82] Gorell Barnes' consultations with the I.B.R.D. confirm further the severity of the financial crunch facing the British government with regard to funding colonial development at this time. Yet, colonial governments were not encouraged to access funds from the I.B.R.D., because the supply of capital goods from Britain to the colonies was still a problem and the British government believed that the conditions attached to I.B.R.D. loans were inimical to its policies to protect sterling.

In its review of colonial development, the report of Colonial Development Working Party (C.D.W.P.) criticized the budgetary allocations for colonial development as an imposition on the United Kingdom's resources which would otherwise be available for domestic investment. While investment in colonial development was seen as justifiable in the long run, the C.D.W.P. noted, "unfortunately the United Kingdom is in a poor position to take this long view, without sacrificing further, its own standards of consumption or restraining the rate of investment at home."[83] Foreign investment, especially from the United States was seen as one of the principal means through which Britain could achieve economic stability without potentially lowering its standard of living. Foreign investment was also believed to be beneficial and important to the colonies themselves, because many of them were too poor to provide their own capital resources on a scale large enough to satisfy demand. Thus, the C.D.W.P. argued, "without foreign aid in finance and equipment some colonial developments [projects], which are economically desirable may have to be deferred indefinitely."[84] The C.D.W.P. believed that a major object of economic policy should have been "to encourage dollar finance for colonial projects, which promised a net return directly or indirectly (in hard currencies earned or saved) sufficient to cover the interest and amortisation charges."[85] It called on the British government to make a public declaration in support of foreign capital. Despite extensive discussions, therefore, by the middle months of 1949 Britain was still undecided about whether or not it was to encourage foreign investment, in particular, investment from the United States into the colonies.

The devaluation of sterling in September 1949 together with increasing colonial demands for development funds led the British government to revisit its policy on foreign investment in the colonial empire. By May 1950 the colonial secretary was anxious to see more overseas investment in the colonies to assist in their development and to strengthen the economy of the Sterling Area. In acknowledging the strain borne by the United Kingdom he noted "much new investment will continue to come from the United Kingdom and other sterling countries but with the present heavy burden on the Sterling Area's resources we must look increasingly for help from outside sources of capital."[86] This meant encouraging a bigger flow of private foreign capital into enterprises which brought economic benefits to colonial territories and also, as far as possible, assist the balance of payments of the Sterling Area. The colonial secretary admitted that there would have been cases of conflict between the immediate economic gain for the colonies and the balance of payments requirements of the United Kingdom. However, he contended that in the long run British and colonial objectives were one, or the same.[87]

The colonies were assured that the declared policy of the British government was "to remove exchange control barriers as rapidly as the balance of payments situation permits and to administer these controls, while they last, in such a way so as to impose the least impediment to desirable types of overseas investments."[88] Britain's economic concerns were central to its attitude toward foreign investment in the colonies. This was manifested in the principles that determined the acceptability of these investments. The colonial secretary stated that "where there is to be no net loss of foreign exchange by a new investment project, there is no exchange control objection. Where an exchange loss is likely, there must be careful weighing up of this against any immediate economic gain before a decision reflecting the common interest of the Sterling Area, can be taken."[89] He added, "of all the foreign currencies the dollar is, of course, the most important."[90]

From statements and declarations by the British government, it was very clear that its increasing inability to fund colonial development was forcing it to consider the feasibility of encouraging foreigners to invest in its colonial dependencies. However, it continued to attach important conditions to the acceptance of foreign investments. The underlying factor governing imperial policy on foreign investments was clearly and concisely stated in the British Parliament on 28 June 1950. The government noted that while American investment was welcomed, "we have to bear in mind that such investment normally carries with it a dollar liability for remittance of dividends or profits and an ultimate liability for repatriation of capital."[91] It was stressed that so long "as the dollar problem is with us our policy must be selective and we must satisfy ourselves that any given project will either give a net earning or saving of dollars, or will be of such substantial economic benefit to the colonial territory to justify any possible loss of dollars involved."[92] The U.K. government noted this aspect of policy because from 1 January 1950 any capital profits arising out of approved investments could have been repatriated. Consequently, the onus was on colonial territories to be selective in approving proposals for investments from the United States, because it could have involved a loss of dollars. Apart from this condition, American investors were subject to some of the same restrictions on other investors regarding the location of local industry, the purchase of land, the imposition of machinery which cost dollars and the employment of expatriate staff.[93]

CONCLUSION

Between 1946 and 1951 there were three critical issues facing the British government in relation to colonial development finance. First, the majority of the colonies lacked the resources necessary for their development and were relying on the United Kingdom to meet their needs. In many cases the socioeconomic position of colonial peoples had worsened because the war had inhibited the progress of the development and welfare schemes. Second, Britain lacked the capacity to fund colonial development. Moreover, because of its balance of payments problems and reservations about interference in its affairs it was reluctant to seek assistance from foreign sources, particularly the United States, the pressure on its resources increased. Third, because of the crises created by the abortive attempt at sterling convertibility in July 1947, the devaluation of sterling in September 1949, and finally the reverberations of the Korean War of June 1950, the focus of colonial development shifted from the needs of colonies to the benefits of colonial expenditure to the United Kingdom. Moreover, it was clear from the allocations made to the C.D.C. that Britain was willing to make more funds available for the development of colonial resources, if the expenditure could be justified by the returns.

At the end of World War II colonial development was still projected as the centerpiece of Britain's colonial policy. In its conception of colonial reform the British government had expected to transfer political power to its dependencies after the economic foundation necessary for self-government and independence was established. Between 1945 and 1951 the underlying philosophy governing colonial development was that colonial needs were subordinate to those of the United Kingdom. In the case of the capital goods and services required for development projects colonial problems were particularly grave during the period 1946–1948. The postwar shortages experienced by the colonies in acquiring capital goods and services were made worse by the enhancement of the restrictions on colonial trade with the Dollar Area, after the aborted attempt to restore sterling to international convertibility. Together with the United Kingdom's inability to satisfy colonial demand for goods and services, this led to a serious reduction in the rate of expenditure of the funds allocated for development and welfare projects, and an intensification of the effects of the shortages of the capital goods and services in the colonies. Thus, by 1951 the demands for political reform had outstripped the levels of economic development that Britain envisaged were necessary before major concessions could be made. As the central plank of its colonial policy collapsed Britain was forced to change its entire outlook toward its colonies.

By 1951 there were already a number of important developments that impacted on the United Kingdom's future relations with the colonies. To begin with, incessant economic instability and the internal adjustments necessary in the metropolitan economy were making it increasingly difficult to justify financial support for colonial development. In addition, while the difficulties with its balance of payments in the postwar period seriously inhibited Britain's capacity to fund colonial development, the demands for finance in the colonies were projected to increase. Finally, in spite of the expenditure on development most colonial territories continued to rely heavily on resources from the United Kingdom. The Treasury complained repeatedly about the strain this imposed upon its resources. However, as long as colonial development was seen as a burden to the United Kingdom, rather than part of its responsibility as a colonial power, ultimately the British government would have had to address the questions raised by the colonial secretary, Colonel Stanley, in 1944. If Britain was unwilling or unable to underwrite the cost of colonial development, was its status as a colonial power justified? And more important, would it be able to retain its colonial empire?

NOTES

1. *Parliamentary Papers 1939–40*, Vol. X (Cmd. 6175). Statement of Policy on Colonial Development and Welfare. Secretary of State to Parliament, February 1940.

2. Ibid.

3. Doc. no. 27. Colonial Development and Welfare. Secretary of State to Chancellor of the Exchequer 21 September 1944. CO 852/588/1. A. N. Porter and A. J. Stockwell, eds., *British Imperial Policy and Decolonisation*, Vol. 1, 1938–1951 (London: Macmillan, 1989), pp. 202–205.

4. Ibid.

5. Ibid.

6. Ibid.

7. Ibid.

8. Ibid., Document 29. Colonial Development and Welfare: Cabinet Memorandum by the Secretary of State, 15 November 1944. CO 852/588/11, pp. 208–211.

9. Ibid., Document 28. Colonial Development and Welfare: The chancellor of the Exchequer to the Secretary of State for the Colonies, 25 October 1944. CO 852/588/11, pp. 206–207.

10. Ibid.

11. Ibid., Document 31. Colonial Development: Extract from the Minutes of a Meeting of the Colonial Economic Advisory Committee, 19 December 1944. CO 852/588/2, pp. 215–224.

12. Ibid., Document 30. Colonial Development: Colonial Economic Advisory Committee Questionnaire with Colonial Office Response, n.d. (Autumn) 1944, CO 852/588/2.

13. M. Havinden and D. Meredith, *Colonialism and Development: Britain and Its Tropical Dependencies 1850–1960* (London: Routledge, 1993), p. 227.

14. For details see *Parliamentary Papers 1948–1949*. XIII. (Cmd. 7715), 641. Progress report on the Colonial Territories, 1948–1949.

15. Havinden and Meredith, *Colonialism and Development*, pp. 252–266.

16. Ibid., p. 254.

17. P.R.O. CO 852/863. Circular Dispatch, Listowel (for S/S) to O.A.G. 15/11/48

18. P.R.O. CO 852/868. Colonial Development Working Party Draft Interim Report. 10/4/48.

19. P.R.O. CO 852/889. Economic Planning in the colonies. Memorandum by Mr. Gorell Barnes 3/8/48.

20. Ibid.

21. Ibid., Economic Planning in the Colonies. Note of a meeting held in Sir Edward Bridges room on Friday, 13 August 1948, at 3:00 P.M.
22. Ibid.
23. E. R. Wicker, "Colonial Development and Welfare, 1929/1957: The Evolution of a Policy," *Social and Economic Studies*, Vol. 7, 1958, p. 176.
24. *P.R.O.* CO 852/863/2. Minute by G. Creasy to the S/S 20/2/47.
25. Ibid., T. Lloyd's memorandum on policy to be pursued in spending of colonial development and welfare monies, 10/11/48.
26. *P.R.O.* CO 852/863/2. Dispatch H. T. Bourdillon to D. B. Pitbaldo, 19/1/49.
27. Ibid., Minute by A. B. Cohen 19/10/48.
28. *P.R.O.* T 220/291. Colonial Development and Welfare Committee, 1951–1954.
29. Ibid., Review of colonial development and welfare expenditure. Colonial Office 1952.
30. *P.R.O.* T 220/290. Draft memorandum for submission by the S/S to the Economic Policy Committee, undated.
31. J.C.R. Dow, *The Management of the British Economy 1945–1960* (Cambridge: Cambridge University Press, 1970), pp. 45–46.
32. *P.R.O.* T 220/394. A. H. Clough to Mr. Mackay and Mr. Beighton 21/11/49.
33. *P.R.O.* CO 852/1355. Draft of the Secretary of State's Annual statement to Parliament, 1950–51.
34. Ibid.
35. M. Cowen, "Early Years of the Colonial Development Corporation: British State Enterprise Overseas during Late Colonialism," paper presented at the Institute of Commonwealth Studies, Postgraduate Seminar, London, 20 October 1983. See also W. Rendell, *History of the Commonwealth Development Corporation* (London: Heinemann, 1976); C. W. Dumpleton, *Colonial Development Corporation* (Fabian Series 186), (London: Fabian Colonial Bureau, 1957); E. R. Wicker, "The Colonial Development Corporation (1948–1954)", *Review of Economic Studies*, Vol. 23, no. 3, 1955/6, pp. 213–228.
36. *P.R.O.* CO 852/867/4/19286/7/2. "The Colonial Development and Welfare Act and the Overseas Resources Development Act." A Note by the Colonial Office. 17/4/48.
37. *P.R.O.* CO 537/3034/18706/9/106/48. The African Conference of 1948. Draft Minutes of the 8th Session.
38. Ibid.
39. Norman Brooke (Secretary to Cabinet) to Attlee, 14 January 1948. *P.R.O.* PREM 8/923, quoted in Cowen, "Early Years of the Colonial Development Corporation," p. 4.
40. Cowen "Early Years of the Colonial Development Corporation," p. 4.
41. *P.R.O.* CO 537/3031/18706/9/95. Development and Welfare in the West Indies. Hammond to Seel. 10/2/48. The concerns of the colonial administrators in the West Indies would have been shared most likely by their counterpart in other British dependencies.
42. Ibid., Serperl to Newton. 26/3/48.
43. Ibid., this dispatch was quoted by Hammond in his letter to Seel, Seel footnoted (86).

44.   *P.R.O.* CO 537/3031/18706/9/95. Eastwood to D. B. Pitblado. 19/4/48.
45.   Ibid.
46.   Ibid.
47.   *P.R.O.* CO 537/3031/18706/9/95. Minute by Cohen to Caine. 17/6/48.
48.   Ibid.
49.   Ibid.
50.   *Colonial Development Corporation Report and Accounts,* 1948, p. 11.
51.   Castries, the capital of St. Lucia, was destroyed by fire in June 1948. Public funds of £700,000 were made available to the government of St. Lucia to facilitate the rebuilding of the town. Since this task was beyond the technical capabilities of the colonial government, thus, the C.D.C. was invited to act as managing agents for the project.
52.   Tung oil was a chemical ingredient used in the paint industry, a substitute for linseed oil. The main source of the world's supply of tung oil was China. In the post-war period, however, China was unable to satisfy the existing world demand. To meet its own requirements, Britain turned to Nyasaland where tung oil was already being produced for export.
53.   *Parliamentary Papers 1950.* VII (105), 171. C.D.C. Annual Report and Statement of Accounts for the year ending 31 December 1949.
54.   Ibid.
55.   *Parliamentary Papers 1952–1953.* VIII (158), 31. C.D.C. Annual Report and Statement of Accounts for the year ending 31 December 1952.
56.   For details on the operations of the C.D.C. see E. R. Wicker, "The Colonial Development Corporation (1948–1954)," *Review of Economic Studies,* Vol. 23/24, 1955; and D. J. Morgan, *The Official History of Colonial Development,* Vol. 2, pp. 320–373.
57.   Colonial Development Corporation Report and Accounts, 1949.
58.   Colonial Development Corporation Report and Accounts, 1950.
59.   Colonial Development Corporation Report and Accounts 1949–1951.
60.   *Report on the Gambia Egg Scheme,* May 1952 (Cmd. 8560).
61.   Cowen, "Early Years of the Colonial Development Corporation," p. 4.
62.   Ibid., p. 5.
63.   Colonial Development Corporation Report and Accounts, 1951, p. 5.
64.   Ibid.
65.   *P.R.O.* CO 852/877/1. Extracted from note of a conversation between Mr. Rob, private secretary to minister of state, Foreign Office and Mr. Allen Dulles. 1/11/47.
66.   Ibid., S. Caine to R. M. Makins, 18/8/47.
67.   Ibid., Rowe-Dutton to S. Caine, 18/9/47.
68.   Ibid., Financial Participation of the IBRD in Colonial Development. Memorandum by S. Caine, undated.
69.   Ibid., Rowe-Dutton to S. Caine 18/9/47.
70.   Ibid.
71.   Ibid., European Economic Co-operation London Committee: American Private Investment in the Colonies. Memorandum by the Colonial Office.
72.   Ibid.
73.   Ibid.
74.   Ibid.

75. Ibid., Confidential. C.D.W.P. Investment of Foreign Capital in the Colonies. Memorandum by the Colonial Office. In its original version this memorandum represented a joint statement by the Treasury and the Colonial Office.

76. Ibid.

77. *P.R.O.* CO 852/877/1/19298/63/66. Alec Grant to S. Caine. 1/3/48 There was also a general feeling that the Americans "were inclined to leave a good deal of risk in local or British hands borrowing from banks, or on fixed interest for a large proportion of the capital, while retaining control in such a way that they have equity holdings or rights which would bring them the really large profits if the undertakings were a success."

78. Ibid., Confidential C.D.W.P. (48) no. 21. Proposals to borrow from the I.R.D.B. Memorandum by the Colonial Office. 9/3/48.

79. Ibid.

80. Ibid.

81. *P.R.O.* CO 852/877/1/19298/63/66. Secret telegram. Gorell Barnes from Washington to S. Caine at the Foreign Office. 22/3/48.

82. Ibid.

83. Ibid.

84. Ibid.

85. Ibid.

86. *P.R.O.* CO 852/1419. Circular savingram 776/53 from S/S 15/8/53. The colonial secretary quoted from circular a savingram sent by his predecessor on 19 May 1950.

87. Ibid.

88. Ibid.

89. Ibid.

90. Ibid.

91. *P.R.O.* CO 852/1419. Minute by K. G. Aston 30/11/53.

92. Ibid.

93. Ibid.

6

Sterling Convertibility and Colonial Reform, 1952–1958

Between 1952 and 1958 Britain's attempt to achieve economic stability and restore the pound to full international convertibility occurred in the context of an accelerating drive toward independence in the Gold Coast, Nigeria and Malaya. These were still the leading dollar earners and, by far, the holders of the largest portion of accumulated colonial sterling balances. In 1952 the United Malayan National Organization (UMNO) and the Malayan Chinese Association (MCA) alliance won a resounding victory over the opposition Independent Malayan Party (I.M.P.) in the municipal elections. Of the thirty-seven municipal council seats in the six cities of the federation, the Alliance won twenty-six and "although the elections during 1952 had been fought over a comparatively few and insignificant seats on municipal councils, they greatly influenced political activity both in the state and federal governments."[1]

The alliance formed a national organization in 1953 which was in the forefront of Malayan demands for full self-government. By 1953 both the UMNO/MCA Alliance and other political organizations in Malaya initiated plans for the achievement of independence in Malaya, and Tunku Abdul Rahman, the alliance leader, pressed the colonial government to make plans for federal elections. Independence was an issue that provoked deep divisions among the political parties in Malaya, and by the end of 1953 there were about four separate initiatives underway at the national level making plans for Malayan independence. In February 1954, the UMNO/MCA Alliance demanded the introduction of universal adult suffrage for all adults who were citizens, subjects of rulers, British subjects or born in Malaya and who lived there for five years; a three-fifths elected majority in the Legislative Council; a two-thirds elected Executive Council chosen solely from members of the Legislative Council; and federal elections no later than the end of 1954.[2] The UMNO/MCA Alliance claimed support from 90 percent of the potential electorate and was uncompromising in its demands. By the end of 1954 the Malayan national election campaign was on in earnest. The alliance promised the electorate self-government in two years and independence within four years, that is, by 1958. It proposed an amnesty to all the guerrillas who surrendered. For the people of the federation who were tired of the war, this proposal proved very popular. The alliance also called on voters to elect all fifty-two of its candidates "as a means of assuring the independence of Malaya."[3] In July 1955, the Alliance won fifty-one of the fifty-two seats it contested and polled over 81 percent of the total electorate, or four times the vote polled by all opposition candidates. Following its victory the alliance gave top priority to the achievement of independence. It was a demand the British government found impossible to ignore.

Between 1952 and 1954 there were further significant moves on the path of political independence in the Gold Coast. In an address to Legislative Assembly soon after the elections of 1951, Nkrumah stated his commitment to "full self-government now." He also made his intentions clear to the colonial secretary, Lyttleton, when he visited the Gold Coast in June 1952. He pressed for the abolition of the exclusion of ex-officio members from the cabinet and an end to British control over the external trade of the Gold Coast.[4] As he put it, "we would have to be responsible for our own direct representation in the foreign countries with which we trade and be in a position to protect our trade with foreign countries from discriminatory practices."[5] In July 1953, Nkrumah moved the now famous "Motion of Destiny" for independence in the Gold Coast and it was unanimously supported. The motion also called for direct elections for all members of the legislative assembly, and for members of the cabinet to be directly responsible to the assembly. In the elections that followed in June 1954, the C.P.P. was again victorious. A significant consequence of this victory in terms of imperial policy was the fact that the finance portfolio was now the responsibility of an elected representative for the first time. In addition, to facilitate control over fiscal and monetary policy Nkrumah pledged to establish a central bank in the Gold Coast. From then on it was simply a matter of when, rather than if, the Gold Coast was going to attain independence.

In Nigeria the regionally based parties were split over the independence issue. The main party in western Nigeria, the Action Group and the National Council of Nigeria and the Cameroon (NCNC), the main party in the eastern region, both called for full independence and moved a motion to this effect in the House of Representatives in

1953. However, the Northern People's Congress (N.P.C.), the dominant party in the northern region, the largest region, preferred self-government. In order to resolve this issue and diffuse the suspicion that had emerged over it, a constitutional conference was convened in 1953 and a new constitution promulgated in 1954. However, three ex-officio members still remained on the Central Executive Council. Nigerian ministers were given responsibility for individual government departments, but there was no provision for the post of federal prime minister. In 1954 the timing of Nigerian independence was the only major issue relative to decolonization in the territory about which there was doubt and debate.[6] Unlike the situation in Ghana, in Nigeria Britain was not under pressure, because the dominant N.P.C. was suspicious of the leading parties in eastern and western Nigeria. On the other hand, the British government indicated it would be prepared to consider a date for the country's independence once northern leaders showed their readiness for full self-government.[7] The constitutional advances in Ghana, Malaya and Nigeria made it impossible for Britain to ignore similar demands elsewhere in its empire. As Porter and Stockwell so succinctly put it, "concessions in one colony set precedents both there and elsewhere for supplementary political demands which from the mid-1950s hastened the pace and altered the manner of the transfer of power."[8]

By 1954, therefore, the process of political transformation in the British empire had reached a stage where the orthodoxy that economic development should precede political change was no longer relevant. According to the Committee on Commonwealth Membership constitutional development was so advanced that the "process cannot now be halted or reversed, and it is only to a limited extent that its pace can be controlled by the United Kingdom government."[9] It warned that "any attempt to retard by artificial delays the progress of colonial peoples toward independence would produce disastrous results."[10] Therefore, it recommended that constitutional change in the colonial empire should be allowed to take its natural course. The British government was therefore resigned to the fact that there was very little it could do to prevent the attainment of independence not only in the Gold Coast, Malaya and Nigeria, but throughout the empire. Consequently, it was forced to consider the dangers, if any, which colonial independence posed to the stability of the U.K. economy, particularly its plans to return sterling to full international convertibility, and the measures that were going to be required to safeguard its sterling policy.

COLONIAL INDEPENDENCE AND COLONIAL STERLING BALANCES POLICY, 1952–1956

As political transformation in the Gold Coast, Malaya and Nigeria intensified, British government officials and government agencies grew increasingly apprehensive about the likely effects of this process on the British economy, and also its implications for Britain's role in post-colonial states. This was particularly evident with respect to the colonial sterling balances. In March 1953 the governor of the Bank of England, C. F. Cobbold, compared the composition of the colonial sterling balances at the end of September 1948 with that at the end of December 1952 (Table 6.1).[11] He warned Sir Edward Bridges, the permanent secretary to the Treasury, that colonial sterling assets had doubled since 1948 "and there is a potential danger in this accumulation."[12]

Table 6.1
Colonial Sterling Balances, 1948–1952

	30 September 1948 £ million	31 December 1952 £ million
Currency funds	203	363
Government and other officially held funds		
Disposable	60	245
Non-disposable	137	230
West Africa Marketing Boards	–	101
Commercial Banks	179	262
TOTAL	579	1,201

Source: P.R.O. T 236/3352. Memorandum on the sterling balances of the British colonies.

Cobbold's alarm over the composition of the sterling balances in 1952 are best understood when one looks at the figures in the Memorandum on the Sterling Assets of the British Colonies which was published in May 1953. They revealed that the general reserves of the colonial governments, that is, assets of the governments that were available to the governments but not required for immediate needs or tied up in funds established for special purposes, increased from £59 million in 1949 to £207 million in 1952; development funds, that is, money set aside specifically to meet the cost of development, increased from £6 million to £26 million; and West Africa Marketing Boards and Uganda price assistance funds increased from £55 million to £145 million in the same period. In 1949, 17.9 percent of the total colonial sterling balances were available to

Table 6.2
Sterling Assets of All Colonies, 1949–1952: Distribution by Classes of Funds

As at 31st Dec.	Government Funds (a)								Currency Board Holdings & Currency Funds with the Crown Agents for the Colonies	West African Marketing Boards, Uganda Price Assistance Funds, etc. (c)	Funds with United Kingdom Banks, etc.	TOTAL
	General Reserve (including Current Balances) (b)	Develop- ment	Renewal	Sinking	Pension and Provident	Savings Bank	Local Govern- ment	Misc.				
1949	59	6	17	27	7	59	3	38	236	55	163	670
1950	107	8	17	26	6	60	3	38	282	86	219	852
1951	151	22	19	32	7	69	3	58	337	137	255	1090
1952	207	26	22	38	13	75	5	57	363	145	271	1222

Source: P.R.O. T 236/3352. Memorandum on the Sterling Balances of the British Colonies

(a) Including funds of other public bodies with the Crown Agents, apart from Uganda Price Assistance Funds.

(b) General funds with the Crown Agents as shown in Cmd. 8856 comprises "General Reserve (including Current Balances)" and "Development" funds, plus small amounts included under other "Government Funds" headings.

(c) Only sterling securities in the case of the West African Marketing Boards.

colonial governments at short notice. By 1952 that had increased to 30.9 percent (Table 6.2).

The governor's main worry was the increase in the funds comprising the colonial balances that were classified as freely disposable. These had increased from 10.3 percent (£60 million) of the total balances in September 1948 to at least 28.8 percent (£346) million of the balances in 1952. In addition, at the end of 1953 six territories accounted for 63.4 percent of the total colonial sterling balances: the Gold Coast £142.5 million; Nigeria £200.6 million; Kenya £91.2 million; Uganda £74.6 million; and the Federation of Malaya £132.1 million and Singapore £104.9 million.[13] The Bank of England feared that if these sterling balances were spent quickly, they could be a source of pressure on sterling internationally, and a source of difficulty if large realizations of securities were involved.[14] Hitherto, Britain had effective political control in the colonies and was therefore in a position to restrain colonial spending. The governor felt that the ongoing process of political reform heralded danger for the United Kingdom because "some of the more important colonies, at least, are moving toward independence, when restraint in spending may be less easy to obtain in time of need."[15] Thus, he questioned the wisdom of the imperial government's policy of simultaneously allowing the colonies to accumulate sterling balances and obtain loans on the London market.[16] The Bank of England believed that the potential threat to Britain's balance of payments position caused by the accumulated sterling balances could be contained if the colonies met more of their financial needs from their own resources. The Bank of England was in effect calling on the British to change its policy toward the management of colonial balances in order to deal with the possible consequences of colonial independence. It feared that once the colonies gained independence, a rapid liquidation of their sterling assets could jeopardize the international stability of the pound, and no doubt Britain's plans to restore it to full convertibility.

The Bank of England's call for a change in government policy echoed the general concern within government circles about the growing size of the colonial sterling balances in 1953. Sir T. L. Rowan, Treasury Second Secretary, argued that it was difficult to defend a policy under which three things happened simultaneously, "the colonial sterling balances grow, we make grants under the Colonial Development and Welfare Act, and some colonies come to borrow on the London market. This cannot be a sensible policy and may inflict strains on us when we may least want them."[17] Others questioned whether or not Britain was exploiting the colonies by forcing them to make loans to the British Government.[18] The supporters of the government's policy argued that the growth in the colonial balances was due not so much to austerity as to the inability of the colonial economies to absorb more than a limited number of imports coupled with the continuing high prices for their imports.[19]

As a result of the disquiet over policy the Treasury suggested that a working party should be established to examine the colonial sterling balances in detail. This suggestion was welcomed by the Colonial Office, and this working party was established on 22 May 1953. It consisted of officials from the Colonial Office, the Treasury, the Bank of England and the Crown Agents. According to its terms of reference it was to review the existing sterling balances of the colonies and probable future accruals, examine the possibility of the colonies making greater use of their surpluses, look at the policy of the backing for colonial currencies and finally review the investment policy of the Crown Agents.[20] In the meantime the Colonial Office decided to begin work on the publication of a memorandum which was aimed at exonerating the U.K. government from the charges that it was exploiting the colonies.

The Working Party reported in September 1953. It noted that the British government was "often in a position to influence the economic and financial policies of the colonial governments."[21] It added that the direction in which this influence was exerted depended among other things "upon the general external financial policy which the United Kingdom decides to follow."[22] The Working Party's report confirmed that some of the restrictions that were imposed on colonial expenditure, and resulted in turn in increases in colonial sterling balances, were linked directly or indirectly to the state of the U.K. economy.[23] Nevertheless, it tried to justify the overall policy on the grounds that the accumulation of sterling reserves meant that the colonial governments were husbanding their reserves in order to cushion themselves for hard times in the future.[24]

As far as the policies governing the administration of colonial sterling assets were concerned, the Working Party assumed that the sterling balances could play an important role in reducing the strain on the United Kingdom's resources that was involved in development finance. It made four recommendations. The two most important were first, that colonial governments should be encouraged to make greater use of their own financial resources, and second, that a conservative fiduciary element in the currency systems of appropriate colonies should be approved in principle, thereby releasing funds that colonial governments could devote to development.[25] The findings and recommendations of the Working Party were, not surprisingly, endorsed by the Treasury, the Bank of England and the Colonial Office because they believed that the recommendations would assist in reducing the size of the colonial sterling balances and, with it, the threat to the welfare of sterling. Subsequently, the Working Party's recommendations formed the basis of the Colonial Office's proposals to the British government for changes in its policy toward the colonial balances.[26] In supporting the recommendation on the creation of a fiduciary issue, the Colonial Office proposed that "20 percent is quite safe as a maximum though some governments will neither want nor need to go as far as this."[27] It also suggested that a portion of the savings bank funds should be invested by the colonial governments in local securities.[28]

The changes that occurred in the colonial sterling balances policy were not due solely to the debate within government circles. At this time there was also mounting pressure on the colonial governments in Nigeria and the Gold Coast, two of the Sterling Area's main dollar earners that were well on the way to independence, to reform colonial sterling balances policy. Bangura notes that the existing colonial sterling balances policy was seen as depriving the colonies of funds that were needed for economic development. Thus, in the Gold Coast the two major political parties, the Convention People's Party and the United Gold Coast Convention, had included monetary reforms in their manifestos for the elections of 1951.[29] Nationalist agitators in Nigeria and the Gold Coast also campaigned for the establishment of central banks to replace the existing currency boards. In addition to giving colonial governments greater independence in monetary policy, nationalist agitators pressed for the creation of central banks because to them these banks were a symbol of their financial as well as their political independence and testimony to their maturity.[30] In Nigeria and the Gold Coast, therefore, political reform had also strengthened colonial demands for greater independence in fiscal and monetary matters.

By 1954 there was an unprecedented level of exigency in the imperial government's efforts to resolve the problems posed by the colonial sterling balances. This was driven by the belief among government officials that the balances of the colonies approaching independence threatened the stability of the pound. A. H. Mitchell, treasury principal and private secretary to the minister of state for economic affairs, felt that action was needed because "just over £600 million of the liabilities (more than half) of the total at the end of 1953 were liabilities to the West African colonies, and to Malaya and Singapore—the places whose independence was expected to become a live issue in the course of the next few years."[31] Sir T. L. Rowan believed that "if the colonies apply a policy of complete non-discrimination in imports on the same lines as we do, then there may be very large demands for dollars, given the size of their balances."[32] In view of the obvious dangers that this possibility presented for the U.K. economy, it was thought that steps should be taken to ensure some orderly reduction in the level of these balances before independence occurred.[33]

The anxiety over the size of the colonial sterling balances by officials in the Treasury and the Bank of England must also be seen against the background of the U.K. government's plans to restore sterling to free convertibility. By May 1953 Britain secured the agreement of Belgium, France, the Netherlands, Sweden, Switzerland, Denmark and West Germany in a scheme that authorized the banks in those countries to buy and sell sterling for current transactions. In March 1954 virtually all the sterling balances held by nonresidents of the Sterling Area (except the holders of American and Canadian accounts) were freed from British exchange controls. For the countries involved, this meant that sterling could have been converted into any currency apart from dollars. Although there was a lot more to be done before the full convertibility of the pound could be restored, these measures were clearly intended to promote confidence in sterling by giving it unlimited usefulness in the nondollar world.[34] In these circumstances a substantial colonial sterling balance, which could have been spent on goods from the Dollar Area, in the hands of territories on the verge of independence was especially alarming. To counter this threat in September 1954, after years of discussions, the principle of the fiduciary issue was finally accepted.[35] Colonies were informed that they could use a maximum of 20 percent of their currency reserve funds for local investment. The British government had therefore sent a clear signal of its intention to change its outlook toward colonial territories and prepare itself to deal with colonial independence.

CONVERTIBILITY: SETBACKS AND REFORMS, 1952–1955

In addition to the measures adopted to deal with the immediate balance of payments crisis triggered by the Korean War, the British government continued to explore broader strategies to restore sterling to full convertibility. By March 1952 the exchange reserves were "some U.S. $200 million or more above the presumed point of open crisis."[36] Although the situation was still precarious, the Treasury and the Bank of England used the respite to examine Britain's external economic policy and construct plans for returning sterling to full convertibility. The latter was also discussed in Whitehall as part of a wider debate in preparation for the Commonwealth Prime Ministers Conference in November 1952. To this end a memorandum entitled "Steps Towards Convertibility" was circulated at the end of August and a majority view emerged in favor of a "Collective Approach" to convertibility by the second half of 1953.[37] According to Fforde the primary purpose of the "Collective Approach" was to "resolve the recurrent problems of sterling as perceived by the Treasury, by the Bank of England, and by the Commonwealth governments."[38] In addition, convertibility was to be achieved by Britain in collaboration with the United States, the members of the E.P.U. and the Sterling Area. Toward the end of 1952, therefore, a time schedule was set once again for the restoration of sterling to full convertibility.

The United Kingdom's plan to restore sterling to full convertibility in 1953 was set back when the members of the E.P.U. refused to endorse the "Collective Approach" devised by Britain, primarily because they saw little advantage in abandoning the existing E.P.U. system for the one proposed by the British.[39] This reversal did not deter the U.K. government. It believed that the future conditions for convertibility were still very good.[40] Treasury officials thought also that ultimately, the question of convertibility depended very much on the prospects of the United States continuing to follow liberal trade policies or rather, perhaps, increasing trade liberalization to match the United Kingdom's stature in the world. They felt that convertibility could have been achieved in the early part of 1955, and argued that "if foreigners believed that they were playing slow on convertibility they risked a fall in confidence in sterling."[41]

As required under the terms of its membership of the E.P.U. the British government moved cautiously to end the discrimination against dollar imports and quota restrictions on nondollar imports. Between 1952 and 1954 controls were removed on imports of dollar raw materials such as cereals and animal feeding stuff, cotton, softwood, many ferrous metals, certain oils and fats and raw fur skins.[42] Overall progress was measured because dollar liberalization was fraught with difficulties for Britain. The British government was advised that in liberalized conditions it could lose about 5 percent of its export market. This loss would have been greatest in Australia and the colonies. There was a considerable suppressed demand for dollar imports in the colonies because of the tight controls that were imposed on colonial dollar expenditure. It was estimated that the United Kingdom stood to lose between £20 million and £30 million (out of a total of £390 million in 1954) if colonial trade with the Dollar Area was liberalized.

Britain's commitment on the liberalization of dollar imports and the dismantling of the quantitative trade restrictions also had serious implications for future commercial relations between Britain and its colonial territories. Colonial exports such as hardwood from Nigeria and the Gold Coast, bananas from the West Indies and citrus from Malaya, Kenya and the West Indies were all judged to be vulnerable to American competition because of the degree to which they had been sheltered from open market competition since 1939. It was anticipated that the competition from dollar goods in a liberalized trading environment would have been greater than anything encountered by the British

colonies since the end of World War II. Because of the potentially destabi-
lizing effects of loss of earnings and employment opportunities, the
immediate and/or total removal of trade restrictions was ruled out by the
British government. In the final analysis, therefore, the policy integrating
the colonial economy into that of the metropole, meant that Britain had
reserved center stage for itself in the future economic affairs of its former
colonies. Indications were that it was going to be very difficult for Britain
to extricate itself from this position, particularly since trade liberalization
and the growing international confidence in sterling had reduced the
significance of the colonial contribution to the British economy.[43]

Apart from dollar imports, by 1954 the imports of most goods from
the O.E.E.C. countries and from the majority of nondollar countries with
which the colonies traded were largely free from quantitative
restrictions.[44] While the enforcement of protective tariffs remained
necessary for some colonial products, in general Britain's commitments
on liberalization resulted in a realignment of colonial trading links, which
had major ramifications for future relations between Britain and its
colonial dependencies. Between 1952 and 1958, the United Kingdom's
share of total colonial exports fell from 30.7 percent to 23.7 percent. The
declining importance of the U.K. market was greatest in the case of the
value of exports from British West Africa to the United Kingdom. These
fell from 78 percent in 1952 to 55 percent in 1958. Exports from British
East Africa to the United Kingdom declined from 31.6 percent and 25.8
percent, and the British West Indies from 41.3 percent to 35.5 percent
during the same period. The situation was the same in the case of colonial
imports from the United Kingdom. The U.K. market share declined from
29.9 percent in 1952 to 24.4 percent in 1958. Imports into British West
Africa from the United Kingdom declined from 52.7 percent in 1952 to
44.3 percent in 1958. In British East Africa imports from the United
Kingdom fell from 47.3 percent to 37.1 percent, and in the British West
Indies from 38.2 percent to 36.7 percent during the same period.[45] By 1958
therefore, the U.K. market was no longer as important a factor in colonial
trade as it was during the war and early postwar years, and the colonial
market was also not as important to Britain as it was during the same
period. Faced with this reality, and the projected increases in the cost of
colonial development finance, Britain had to revise the mechanisms
through which it managed colonial affairs.

The realignment of colonial/metropolitan commercial relations
occurred simultaneously with continued progress toward the de facto
convertibility of sterling for nonresidents. By February 1955 the Bank of
England decided to support the rate for "transferable sterling," that is,
sterling that could not be converted into dollars. However, a market had
developed in which "transferable sterling" was traded at a discount.[46]

According to the Treasury this discount affected the exchange position of sterling in two main ways. First, it diverted dollars from the official market by encouraging the use of transferable sterling for various payments to Americans. Although the diversion of dollars through this avenue was not very large, it had a disproportionate unsettling effect on the market. Second, "the discount had a bad effect upon confidence; the fact that the transferable market was unsupported lent currency to the oversimplified belief that the transferable rate reflected the true strength of sterling."[47]

Together with the diversion of dollars from the official market, the loss of confidence in sterling made the official rate more difficult and expensive to maintain than would have otherwise been the case. Thus in February 1955, the Bank of England decided to purchase "transferable sterling" for dollars. The chancellor of the exchequer, Butler, explained that it was a "case of putting in the troops to save sterling from being sold at too great a discount."[48] Even though further steps were required to restore convertibility in the fullest sense, "no future step could be nearly so important as that one was."[49] The decision of the Bank of England reflected, among other things, the steady reduction in the sterling balances held by countries outside the Sterling and Dollar Areas and an improvement in the competitive position of the Sterling Area.[50] Official support for "transferable sterling" meant that the British authorities were willing to convert sterling held by nonresidents into gold or dollars at a very small discount (about 1 percent) on the official rate. All that remained for de facto convertibility in the fullest sense was the unification of the official and "transferable sterling" rates.[51]

The Bank of England's intervention in the "transferable market" heightened expectations that the restoration of sterling to full convertibility was likely to occur shortly. These expectations seemed justified when the British government established a Working Party (comprising officials from the Treasury, the Bank of England and the Board of Trade) to examine the effects of ending dollar discrimination in June 1955. In its report the Working Party contended that in terms of the United Kingdom's potential trade only about ⅓ of its dollar imports were completely free of control.[52] In addition as the United Kingdom's balance of payments position improved, the pressure to reduce restrictions would have increased and if sterling was made convertible, then there would not have been any justification for continuing with the controls. Furthermore, in the recent review of the General Agreement of Tariffs and Trade (GATT), countries making their currencies convertible were allowed a transitional period of about a year for dismantling the restrictions they were maintaining at the time of the convertibility operations. At the end of this period new and stricter regulations requiring all countries to justify their restrictions annually were to be inaugurated. Under the arrangements made at Geneva, the first general review of the restrictions was scheduled to occur in 1956 (independently of any move to convertibility), if there were no setbacks in world trade.[53] It was clear therefore that because of its international obligations Britain was under pressure to end trade restrictions and "if convertibility operations take place, there will be an absolute ban on our restrictions a year or so thereafter."[54]

In the first half of 1955, therefore, the British government's decision to intervene in the free market for "transferable sterling" and to sustain its exchange rate above the commodity shunting point, along with the modifications to and the review of government policy on dollar discrimination, heightened speculation that the restoration of sterling to full convertibility was at hand. Expectations intensified when the U.K. delegation which attended the O.E.E.C. meeting in July 1955 requested "the right to withdraw in the course of the next twelve months in the event of sterling becoming convertible."[55] The atmosphere of uncertainty about the future of sterling, however, led to speculation against the pound. The plight of sterling was made worse by the fact that convertibility was expected to be accompanied by a floating pound. When combined the rumors and expectations undermined confidence in sterling and triggered a drain on the United Kingdom's gold and dollar reserves. Between July and September 1955 the reserves fell by US$335 million, the biggest loss since the first quarter of 1952. At the end of September the reserves stood at their lowest level since May 1953 (Table 6.3).[56]

Table 6.3
Britain's Gold and Dollar Reserves, 1955

	1st half	2nd half	July–Sept	October	November	December
Reserves	2680	2120	2345	2297	2283	2120
Deficit	–82	–560	–335	–48	–14	–163

Source: P.R.O. T 236/4348. Key Statistics on Britain's balance of payments 1952–55

Overall Britain's gold and dollar reserves fell by US$560 million in the second half of 1955. Given the adverse circumstances, plans to restore sterling to full convertibility were shelved temporarily.

THE FINAL PHASE AND LAST WORRIES: 1956–1958

To allay fears about government policy relative to sterling and rescue its plans for returning sterling to full convertibility, the chancellor clarified the intention of the government. He told the House of Commons, "there is no doubt about the policy of the government in relation to the exchange value of the pound sterling . . . it has been, and will continue to be the maintenance of the exchange parity of 2.80 dollars to the £, either in existing circumstances or when sterling is convertible."[57] The restoration of sterling to full convertibility therefore was going to take place at a fixed rate of exchange. By the beginning of 1956 the crisis had subsided, but the relief was temporary.

The reverberations from deterioration in the British economy in 1954–1955, and the cancellation of attempts to return sterling to a freely convertible currency in 1955, prompted concerns about the viability of the Sterling Area. A secret memorandum on sterling balances and monetary policy pointed out that "the anxieties about sterling which have emerged during 1954–55 have increased the difficulties of holding the Sterling Area together."[58] Britain was also confronted by the paradox of commonwealth members of the Sterling Area without any alternative but to maintain their sterling holdings while for economic and political reasons weakening sterling by acquiring supplies of gold or dollars. Since U.K. policy by definition excluded anything along these lines the memorandum contended, "this dilemma inhibits a flexible monetary policy in the United Kingdom, is a permanent source of anxiety to H.M.G. and, in terms of the annual service, is a constant threat to the stability of sterling both on the current and the capital account, and can only be resolved by the agreement with all the parties concerned."[59] The memorandum called for a meeting between officials from the Bank of England and the Treasury to discuss the conflict between monetary policy and the policy toward sterling balances.

This prompted a group of Treasury officials to initiate a study of colonial balances to determine the reality of the danger they presented to the U.K. economy. They decided to examine the problem by looking at the sterling balances on the basis of the holdings of individual colonies. The colonial balances of the Gold Coast, Nigeria, Tanzania, Kenya, Uganda, Malaya, Trinidad, Jamaica and Bahamas were selected for this study.[60] These were the largest holders of sterling balances in West Africa, East Africa, the Malayan Area and the West Indies. The Treasury group identified the components of the colonial balances, estimated their pattern of future growth or decline and the implications of projections for the United Kingdom and the Sterling Area. The most outstanding feature in the accumulated sterling balances was the growth of the general reserves They increased from £207 million in 1952 to £345 million in 1955; overall an increase of 575 percent between 1949 and 1955. Marketing board securities were £115 million higher than the £60 million in 1949, but less than the £145 in 1952. Therefore at least 31.8 percent of the total colonial balances of £470 million were available to the colonies at short notice. This could have increased to £558 million or 38.6 percent because of the fiduciary issue authorized in 1954.

A Joint Working Party of Treasury and Bank of England officials which was set up in 1956 to examine the problems of the Sterling Area also identified the accumulated sterling balances as one of the principal dilemmas of the British government.[61] It contended that "without a [current] surplus greater than our net investments overseas it will not be possible to improve our external liquidity (whether by reducing the total of the sterling balances or by increasing the reserves)."[62] By the 1950s, the United Kingdom's assets were a quarter or less of its liabilities. Between 1952 and 1955, for example, even though the United Kingdom had a considerable current account surplus, the relationship between its external monetary assets and liabilities (the reserves and the overseas sterling balances) changed only marginally. The Working Party felt that this was not a satisfactory position for Britain. In addition, when British reserves were compared, not against liabilities, but against trade, present levels were thought to be anything but comfortable.[63] The Working Party concluded therefore that "sterling is both absolutely and relatively ill-provided with reserves."[64]

From the United Kingdom's point of view the most significant revelation about the colonial sterling balance was "that over £780 million (or more than one half) of the colonial sterling assets, involving some £700 million of the UK liabilities is attributed to the four territories most closely and rapidly moving toward independent status: Nigeria, Gold Coast, Singapore and Federation of Malaya."[65] A rapid, simultaneous drawing down of the colonial sterling assets of these territories was unlikely. But their potential threat could not have been ignored, particularly in view of the developments in what was called the underdeveloped commonwealth: India, Pakistan and Sri Lanka. The Indian Second Five-Year Plan provided for a total current external deficit of £875 million in the period 1956–1960. It was "the explicit intention of the Indian government to draw down £150 million from surplus sterling balances to finance it."[66] A new and by no means inconsiderable strain on the U.K. resources was therefore anticipated from the reduction in Indian sterling balances. Britain also expected to be hard pressed by demands for sterling balances from Pakistan and Sri Lanka. When the needs of India, Pakistan and Sri Lanka were combined with the financial demands of the rest of the Sterling Area the potential claim on the U.K. resources was approximately £100–150 million a year. In light of this the Joint Treasury/Bank of England Working Party contended that in the immediate future Britain was going to have "a heavier current burden to bear than in the past. If the United Kingdom fails to develop and maintain the necessary surplus, there is a real danger of a 'run' out of sterling by the R.S.A. (Rest of the Sterling Area) itself. A major crisis would then be unavoidable."[67] Given this forecast, the U.K. government was therefore concerned about the likely effects on the British economy of the withdrawal of the sterling balances held by existing colonies and newly independent territories in London.

The Working Party was resigned to the inevitability of colonial independence. The British government was advised to "proceed on the working assumption that the use of the bulk of these funds is under little real control from London and that their expenditure will be more and more determined by new and inexperienced governments."[68] Nevertheless, expectations were that unless the level of U.K. investment in the colonies increased, colonial sterling balances would be drawn down. The government was warned that "compared with the past years, the colonies seem likely to bring substantial new pressures to bear on the United Kingdom resources in the next few years."[69] The liquidation of the colonial sterling assets, therefore, could not solve the problems of development finance in the colonies because of the bulk of these balances were held by a few territories. As far as the Working Party was concerned, therefore, in the immediate future a significant proportion of the cost of development in most of Britain's colonies would have had to come from the United Kingdom's resources. However, it doubted whether the United Kingdom had the resource capability to satisfy colonial financial demands.

The Joint Bank of England and Treasury Working Party findings were an addition to the growing list of reports and government agencies that questioned Britain's ability to satisfy present and future demands for development finance from its colonies in the 1950s. However, the Working Party's findings were particularly significant because they were the product of an official investigation into the colonial sterling balances problem. Its revelations destroyed the British government's assumptions about the significance of the role that the colonial sterling balances could play in development financing. By 1956, therefore, there was no doubt about the reality of the problems involved in colonial development financing. The majority of the colonies lacked the resources necessary to finance their own development and, unless other sources could be found, they were going to rely heavily on Britain to satisfy their needs. Despite warning about the severe strain on Britain's resources that was likely if the development needs of the colonies were to be satisfied, the Joint Working Party did not offer any solutions to the problem. Nonetheless, the reality was that Britain could not eschew responsibility for colonial development finance as long as it had colonial dependencies. Thus, now that the difficulty it faced was officially substantiated, colonial independence was a possible solution to Britain's problem.

While Britain was struggling with the threat posed to sterling by the accumulated colonial balances, in October 1956 war in Egypt over the Suez Canal led to another run on the pound. The impact of the Suez crisis on the British economy was negligible; nevertheless, it was testimony to the general lack of confidence in sterling which prevailed internationally. As Worswick notes, "the contrast between the barely perceptible 'real' impact of the Suez upon the domestic economy, and even upon Britain's foreign trade, with the violence of the international monetary reaction is very striking."[70] In October, the month in which the crisis started, Britain's reserves fell by £100 million. Overall the deficit for the last quarter of 1956 was £275 million. Scott speculates that a large part of the latter figure was probably due to speculation against the pound.[71] A cease-fire in the Suez together with loans from the I.M.F. and the U.S. Export-Import Bank stemmed the drain on Britain's reserves, but they did not end the speculation against the pound.

In 1957 there was a run on sterling continued through the "Kuwait Gap," that is, the purchase of nonsterling securities (for example, the dollar) by U.K. residents from residents of Kuwait. This occurred because although Kuwait was a member of the Sterling Area, the authorities in Kuwait did not restrict the purchase or sale of nonsterling securities by residents. In the first quarter of 1957 an estimated £70 million was lost through this "gap." The drain reached crisis proportions when "the effective devaluation of the French franc in August, the likelihood of an upward revaluation of the German mark and the trend of wages and prices in this country [Britain] all led to fears of a possible devaluation of the pound."[72] As a consequence Britain's reserves fell by £189 million in the third quarter of 1957. The fall would have been greater "but for a special deposit made by the German government and the usual delay in settling the deficits in the E.P.U."[73]

The run on the pound in last quarter of 1956 and the first half of 1957, the granting of independence to Ghana and the impending independence of Malaya and Nigeria put the spotlight once again on the colonial sterling balances. Government officials were nervous about the danger the balances posed to the stability of sterling and wanted to determine the steps necessary to safeguard it. Calls were made for their detailed examination to establish the legal status of each fund, to facilitate an assessment of the assets that these two countries could regard as freely disposable. In August 1957, Sir T. L. Rowan, the second secretary at the Treasury, asked Sir Dennis Rickett, third secretary to the Treasury, to examine the possible consequences for the United Kingdom, if any, or all of Ghana, Nigeria and Malaya left the Sterling Area after independence. Rowan explained, "I understand that the argument is being used by the

President of the Board of Trade that this is the thing we have got to prepare for, and the best way of doing it is to ensure that if they go, they do not get all their balances in full therefore let us float [sterling] . . . this is nonsense and the best way of driving them out of the Sterling Area."[74] Rowan wanted to know what steps Britain could take to protect "our own interest, e.g. seek to procure an agreement with them that they would not put all their sterling balances on the market at once, or failing this block their balances."[75] He added, "there is a minute from the Prime Minister to the Chancellor which has not yet been circulated asking about the precise action we should take if we had to float, and whether we could not prevent drains on our currency by, for example, imposing exchange controls."[76]

The impact of Ghana's possible withdrawal from the Sterling Area upon Britain was set out some months before Rowan's call for an inquiry. Ghana's exit was deemed unlikely because the United Kingdom was its largest source of capital and inflows would have been interrupted. In addition, the abandonment of the Sterling Area would have subjected Ghana to exchange controls from the United Kingdom and probably the rest of the Sterling Area. Also, it would have taken years for Ghana to establish the kind of commercial and financial links it had with Britain with other countries, especially the United States, and the economic dislocation involved would have been detrimental to its business community. Furthermore, Ghana was heavily dependent on the Sterling Area for imports and exports, and thus a severing of links with the Sterling Area would have had adverse consequences for trade.[77] The optimists within the Colonial Office and the Treasury also took comfort in the fact that although the various advantages of membership of the Sterling Area were not very remarkable individually, collectively they provided a bond strong enough to hold the Sterling Area together. Overall, they felt that Ghana, Nigeria and Malaya would not leave the Sterling Area after independence because of the problems associated with disengaging from the sterling bloc. These included converting sterling to other currencies, the administrative alterations required in exchange controls and the fact that not all the sterling balances could have been converted immediately into other currencies.

Nevertheless, officials decided not to take any chances, so they considered measures that the United Kingdom could undertake to protect its interest if Ghana, Nigeria or Malaya decided to leave the Sterling Area. Sir Dennis Rickett, third secretary at the Treasury, advised that "they should do their utmost to avoid blocking sterling balances in any but extreme circumstances . . . the shock to the confidence of other Sterling Area territories would be so grave that some of them would be unlikely to continue to leave their reserve funds with us."[78] He added, "if we had to consider nothing worse than a threat by Ghana to withdraw a moderate proportion of her assets, we should in the last resort have to let her do so."[79] It was felt that the alternative was to seek to get the best agreement for limiting the withdrawals. However, "if we had to face decisions by say Ghana, Malaya and Nigeria to transfer more or less simultaneously a large part of their combined sterling balances it might be different."[80] Towards the end of the 1950s, therefore, imperial officials were determined to ensure that the independence of Ghana, Malaya and Nigeria did not trigger another cycle of volatility for sterling.

Despite the reassurances given in a number of reports, Rowan remained convinced that the liquidation of the colonial balances could destabilize the U.K. economy. Therefore, he called on the government to consider ways in which it could tie up "excess" sterling balances without undermining the pound. A range of options were considered once again. The blocking of the colonial balances was ruled out because it was felt that "nothing would be better calculated to precipitate a run on sterling."[81] Plans to have colonial governments sell the British government terminable annuities of ten years life bearing interest at 6 percent to the colonial governments were also opposed. Some government officials felt that it would have been extremely awkward to bring the imperial government into a relationship with the colonial governments as lenders. Mr. Armstrong, the chancellor's private secretary, a leading advocate of this view, argued that colonies were free to put their sterling where they liked. In addition the borrowing by the exchequer directly from colonial governments—"especially with a certain air of compulsion about it—seems to me to introduce a new and very unfortunate principle into our relations with the colonies."[82]

He also rejected the proposal that annuities should be exchanged for long-dated government securities held by the colonial governments, on terms that would eliminate the capital loss for colonial governments, if they sold such securities on the market. He argued that any proposal along these lines would put the United Kingdom "under intolerable pressure from all other holders of long-dated securities who faced a capital loss on realization"[83] and destroy the basis of market dealings in government securities. Moreover, encouraging colonial governments to realize their long-dated stocks was surely not the thing Britain would have wanted. As Armstrong put it, "when you are contemplating the possibility that colonial balances may be run down for development reasons over the next few years, surely one of the safeguards is the capital loss which these governments will suffer on realization,"[84] since it may make them think twice before selling. Thus, he concluded, "to remove this would surely be to encourage the very thing we fear—and the fact that the Colonial Office sees advantage in it is surely a reason why we should see disadvantage."[85]

In a subsequent letter to the Bank of England, Mr. Jenkyns, assistant secretary at the Treasury, said that although the matter of colonial balances was unlikely to arise it was down on the list of background briefs for commonwealth officials, and there may have been some pressure for them to produce a revised document. He stressed that in this document there could be no element of compulsion in any proposal. To him it was doubtful that the colonies would willingly "co-operate with Britain to resolve the problem of the accumulated sterling balances without compensation in one form or another."[86] He added that they could not agree to any scheme to fund colonial balances at anything except market rates; and contended that while "the risk of withdrawal of sterling balances by the colonies at rates which would gravely embarrass the United Kingdom, does not seem large, a funding operation would not have effectively reduced or limited the rate of withdrawal, and would introduce some highly unwelcome and new principles. In some circumstances it might well serve to aggravate the problems which it was designed to serve."[87] Despite detailed analysis and debate government officials failed to agree on measures to regulate the reduction of the colonial sterling balances.

By the end of 1957 an increase in the bank rate from 5 to 7 percent, cuts in public spending, a draw down of a loan from the U.S. Export-Import Bank, the deferral of payments due on U.S. and Canadian loans, and government assurances of its intention to maintain the existing exchange rate parity brought an end to the speculation against sterling. In the last quarter of 1957 Britain's reserves rose by £151 million. The recovery continued into 1958 and revived the imperial government's ambitions to return the pound to full convertibility in December 1958. The government's confidence was such that in September 1958 the president of the Board of Trade announced that "colonial governments are being invited to make relaxations of their restrictions on a wide range of dollar goods."[88] This was to be done in three stages by the government. The first involved the removal of controls on as wide a range of consumer goods and foodstuffs as possible. The second was the establishment of quotas for items that the cost of total liberalization was deemed to be greater than what the colonial governments could afford at that time. Stage three would have addressed the remaining items that may have presented special difficulties. In December 1958 sterling was restored to full convertibility.

CONCLUSION

Overall the economic conditions in which the British government pursued the restoration of sterling to full international convertibility between 1952 and 1958 were, comparatively speaking, the most favorable since the end of World War II. In the most difficult years, 1951–1954, there were minor adjustments to the policy that the Conservatives had inherited from Labour. Unlike the period 1945–1949, however, in the 1950s the momentum toward the restoration of sterling to full convertibility increased simultaneously with the demands for political independence, by the principal holders of accumulated sterling balances: Malaya, the Gold Coast and Nigeria. This caused alarm in government circles because it was feared that Britain would lose the political leverage necessary to preserve its economic interests and guide sterling safely to international convertibility.

Prior to 1956 British government officials assumed that if the colonies were allowed greater access to their sterling balances they could reduce the threat posed by colonial independence to the British economy. Subsequent studies demonstrated that this assumption was unfounded. They also showed that the risk to the U.K. economy from the sterling balances held in the territories close to independence was very limited. In spite of this many government officials remained very concerned that because of the size of the sterling balances held by colonial territories and the fragility of sterling, colonial independence would destabilize the U.K. economy and delay the restoration of sterling to convertibility. Their attitude epitomized the fact that toward the end of the 1950s the debate over colonial sterling balance policy and colonial independence had assumed a momentum of its own. The failure of the attempt at the restoration of sterling to international convertibility in 1947, together with the ongoing crises that had delayed convertibility, did not inspire confidence in those who were entrusted with the responsibility to achieve it. Some officials were so obsessed with ushering sterling safely back to international convertibility that they ignored the findings of studies showing the limits of the danger to the U.K. economy from the sterling balances in the hands of the colonies that were approaching independence. Ironically, the most significant revelation toward the end of the 1950s was not that the balances held by the colonies close to independence constituted a serious threat to Britain's economic stability. It was, instead, the fact that the distribution of these balances was such that even if the colonies were given greater access to their sterling reserves, the majority of them would still have had serious problems with development finance. The continuation of colonial rule in these territories, therefore, was going to be a great strain on Britain's financial resources. The best way out of this dilemma was to open the floodgates to independence throughout the British empire.

NOTES

1.   G. Means, *Malaysian Politics* (London: University of London Press, 1970), p.137. See also S. R. Ashton and S. E. Stockwell, eds., Pt. 3, *The Alliance Route to Independence, 1953–1957* (London: HMSO, 1995).
2.   Ibid., 145.
3.   Ibid., 166.
4.   Kwame Nkrumah.*The Autobiography of Kwame Nkrumah* (London: Panaf, 1957), pp. 142–143.
5.   Ibid.
6.   J. Ajayi and M. Crowder, *History of West Africa* Vol.2. (London: Longman, 1974), pp. 635–644.
7.   Ibid.
8.   A. N. Porter and A. J. Stockwell, *British Imperial Policy and Decolonisation*. Vol. 2. (London: Macmillan, 1989), p. 48.
9.   Ibid., Doc. 37. "The Future of Commonwealth Membership." Report by the Official Committee, 21 January 1954, CAB 134/786, pp. 283–298.
10.   Ibid., p. 284.
11.   *P.R.O.* T 236/3352. C. F. Cobbold to Sir Edward Bridges 6/3/53. Draft memorandum.
12.   Ibid.
13.   For the individual territories, I am using figures compiled in tables in *P.R.O.* T 236/3562. Sterling Assets of the Colonial Territories, 31 December 1952. See also the table in *P.R.O.* T 236/3562. Memorandum on the Sterling Balances of the British Colonies.
14.   *P.R.O.* T 236/3352. C. F. Cobbold to Sir Edward Bridges 6/3/53. Draft memorandum.
15.   Ibid., C. F. Cobbold to Sir Edward Bridges 6/3/53. Draft memorandum.
16.   Ibid.
17.   *P.R.O.* T 236/3352. T. L. Rowan to Sir B. Gilbert, 12/5/53.
18.   D. J. Morgan, *The Official History of Colonial Development*. Vol. 3 (London: Macmillan, 1980), p. 161.
19.   *P.R.O.* T 236/3352 "Sterling Balances and U.K. Exports." Draft memorandum by M. T. Fleet, 19/3/53.
20.   Ibid. Note of meeting held in the Treasury at 11:30 A.M. on 22/5/53.
21.   *P.R.O.* T 236/3353. Working Party on Colonial Sterling Assets. Report on the economic significance of the assets, p. 1.
22.   Ibid.
23.   Ibid., pp. 2–3.
24.   Ibid., p. 4.
25.   *P.R.O.* T 236/3353. Working Party on Colonial Sterling Assets. Report on the economic significance of the assets, p. 14.
26.   *P.R.O.* T 236/3562. Minute by A. K. Potter, 24/5/54.
27.   Ibid., E. Melville to A. K. Potter 2/7/54. The Colonial Office pointed out also that existing legislation provided for the investment of a portion of Saving Bank Funds in the colonies. It noted that many governments had not taken advantage of this provision.
28.   Ibid., E. Melville to A. K. Potter 2/7/54.

29.   Y. Bangura, *Britain and Commonwealth Africa: The Politics of Economic Relations 1951–1975* (Manchester: Manchester University Press, 1983), p. 45.
30.   Ibid., pp. 47–49.
31.   *P.R.O.* T 236/3562. A. H. Mitchell to Mr. Vinter 10/12/54.
32.   Ibid., T. L. Rowan to Mr. Armstrong 26/5/54.
33.   Ibid., A. H. Mitchell to Mr. Vinter 10/12/54.
34.   J. Polk, *Sterling: Its Meaning in World Finance* (New York: Harper and Bros., 1956), pp. 93–98. See also S. Strange, *Sterling and British Policy: A Political Study of an International Currency in Decline* (London: Oxford University Press, 1971), pp. 64–65.
35.   *P.R.O.* T 236/3562. Mr. A. H. M. Hillis to Mr. Melville 22/7/54.
36.   J. Fforde, *The Bank of England and Public Policy, 1941–1958* (Cambridge: Cambridge University Press, 1992), p. 451.
37.   Fforde, *The Bank of England and Public Policy*, p. 452.
38.   Ibid., p. 475.
39.   Ibid., pp. 451–462. See also R. Hinshaw, "Towards European Convertibility," *Essays in International Finance*, no. 31, November, 1958 pp.18–22.
40.   *P.R.O.* T 236/4359. "The Collective Approach: Where We Stand." Memorandum by the Treasury 15/6/54.
41.   Ibid.
42.   *P.R.O.* BT 230/372. Import Licensing Committee. Limited Review of Restrictions on Imports from the Dollar Area. Note by Joint Secretary R. W. Gray. 29/10/54.
43.   *P.R.O.* BT 230/390. Working Party on the effects of removing quantitative import restrictions, with special reference to dollar import restrictions. 16 July 1955.
44.   *P.R.O.* CO 852/1464. S/S Annual Report 1954/55, p. 39.
45.   For details see *Digest of Colonial Statistics* (London: HMSO, 1958), Table 4, p. 10 and *Digest of Colonial Statistics* (London: HMSO, 1960), Table 4, p. 10; and *The Commonwealth and the Sterling Area Statistical Abstract* (London: HMSO, no. 79, 1958), pp. 3–7.
46.   For details see Fforde, *The Bank of England and Public Policy*, pp. 219–249.
47.   *P.R.O.* CAB 134. Cabinet Committee on Balance of Payments Prospects. Current and Recent Developments in the Sterling Exchanges and Balance of Payments Position. Memorandum by the Treasury, 1/6/55.
48.   J. C. R. Dow, *The Management of the British Economy 1945–60* (Cambridge: Cambridge University Press, 1970), p. 86.
49.   R. F. Harrod, "The Pound Sterling, 1951–1958," *Essays in International Finance*, no. 30 (August 1958), p. 27.
50.   R. Hinshaw, "Towards European Convertibility", p. 25. He adds that several countries followed the British lead in increasing the transferability and, in some cases, the effective convertibility of their currencies. They included: Germany, Belgium, France, Italy, the Netherlands and Sweden.
51.   Ibid., p. 29.
52.   *P.R.O.* BT 230/380. Working Party on the Effects of Ending Dollar Discrimination. 10/6/55.
53.   Ibid.
54.   Ibid.
55.   Dow, *The Management of the British Economy 1945–1960*, p. 87.

56.   *P.R.O.* T 236/4349. R. L Major to Mr. Kahn and Mr. Petch 29/10/55.
57.   Dow, *The Management of the British Economy 1945–60*, p. 90.
58.   *P.R.O.* T 236/3936. Secret. "Sterling Balances and Monetary Policy." G.F.B. 4/4/56.
59.   Ibid.
60.   *P.R.O.* T 236/4253. Minute by Mrs. M. Wragge-Morley, 31/3/55. The figures used here are the ones quoted by the Treasury at this time. In preparing this study I found a lot of discrepancies in the statistics on the colonial sterling balances that were used by various government departments. To ensure consistency in the figures quoted in this chapter, I have used the statistics on colonial sterling balances that were compiled in *The Digest of Colonial Statistics*, no. 35, November–December 1957 and *The Annual Abstract of Statistics*, Vol. 93, 1956. This accounts for the difference between the figures quoted here and those quoted earlier in this chapter.
61.   *P.R.O.* T 236/5362. Problems of the Sterling Area. Report by a Working Party of the Treasury and the Bank of England. 25/6/56.
62.   Ibid.
63.   Ibid.
64.   Ibid.
65.   Ibid.
66.   Ibid.
67.   Ibid.
68.   *P.R.O.* T 236/5362. Problems of the Sterling Area. Report by a Working Party of the Treasury and Bank of England, 25/6/56.
69.   Ibid.
70.   G. D. N. Worswick, "The British Economy 1950–1959," in G. D. N. Worswick and P. Ady, eds., *The British Economy in the Nineteen Fifties* (Oxford: Oxford University Press, 1962), p.14.
71.   M. Scott, "The Balance of Payments Crisis," in Worswick and Ady, eds., *The British Economy in the Nineteen Fifties*, p. 221.
72.   Ibid. p. 222.
73.   Ibid. p. 223.
74.   *P.R.O.* T 236/3562. TLR to Sir Dennis Rickett 18/9/57.
75.   Ibid.
76.   Ibid.
77.   *P.R.O.* T 236/5362. A. W. Taylor to Sir D. Rickett 27/9/57.
78.   Ibid.
79.   Ibid.
80.   Ibid.
81.   Ibid.
82.   *P.R.O.* T 236/4776. Funding excess sterling balances. W. A. Armstrong to Ms. Jenkyns. 9/12/57.
83.   Ibid.
84.   Ibid.
85.   Ibid.
86.   Ibid.
87.   Ibid.
88.   *P.R.O.* BT 230/373. Restrictions on Dollar Imports from the Dollar Area. Undated.

7

Decolonization and Colonial Development Finance, 1952–1958

Given the economic crisis in the United Kingdom at the time the new Conservative government assumed office in November 1951, it was most unlikely that it would have had a more generous approach to colonial development finance than its Labour predecessor. Dow noted that in the process of criticizing the policies of the Labour government "the Conservatives had built up something like an alternative philosophy of economic government."[1] They saw the persistent balance of payments disequilibrium as a manifestation of the failure of the Labour government's policies. The Conservatives also felt that government expenditure was too high—perhaps much too high, and the sheer size of the budget was thus itself an inflationary force.[2] Therefore, they intended to be frugal economic managers. For them internal economic adjustments were necessary for balance of payments equilibrium and sustained economic growth. According to Holland, "such adjustments meant rigid controls on government spending; and so domestic expenditure became the crux of establishment debate to a degree not seen since the era of high Gladstonianism."[3] He added that "at some point the growth of welfare spending would have to be curtailed; meanwhile the sums meted out to colonial development represented a 'soft,' but not insignificant target."[4]

THE CONSERVATIVE AND COLONIAL DEVELOPMENT POLICY, 1952–1953

Like Labour, the Conservatives believed that colonial development was the foundation for social and political progress in colonial territories.[5] However, their approach to development continued to be heavily influenced by the state of the U.K. economy and an unyielding drive to restore sterling to full international convertibility. Except for differences in emphasis, the colonial economic policy of the Conservatives did not stray from the path set out by the Labour government. At the end of the Commonwealth Economic Conference of November–December 1952, delegates agreed that development in the Sterling Area countries should concentrate, directly or indirectly, on projects that contributed to improving the Sterling Area's balance of payments with the rest of the world.[6] This approach lacked subtlety, and thus even though the improvement of Britain's balance of payments was already a major consideration in its postwar colonial development policy, colonial governments were concerned about implications of the decisions taken at the Commonwealth Conference.

The Colonial Office moved swiftly to clarify the British government's position and allay colonial fears. It contended that the need for improvement in the social conditions in colonial territories was "fully recognized."[7] Colonial governments were also assured that abrupt changes in development policy or the abandonment of the pledges made by the British government were not being contemplated. Nevertheless, there was no escape from the balance of payments factor. Colonial governments were asked to extend their contribution to the improvement of the Sterling Area's balance of payments even further. The Colonial Office stressed that Sterling Area members were "mindful that the many claims upon the resources of the U.K. and the urgent need to restore the strength of the Sterling Area, made it essential that those resources should be utilized with due regard to the balance of payments position."[8] For this to be achieved, colonial governments were required to review their development plans to determine whether it was possible to change their priorities without distorting progress or adversely affecting their essential interest.

The Treasury agreed with the policy outlined by the Colonial Office to the colonies. However, officials such as Flett felt that the Colonial Office was still "too timid in its treatment of the need for economic as opposed to social and political investment."[9] Melville, assistant under secretary of state at the Colonial Office, explained that the colonies were not given more direct instructions to review development priorities "because we feel that there is not, in most colonies, very much room for improvement in this respect and that these governments would justifiably present a suggestion to the contrary, bearing in mind the colonial balance of payments in recent years when compared to the Sterling Area as a whole."[10] Despite reservations about the emphasis in the policy, the Colonial Office agreed with the Treasury that the balance of payments requirements of the United Kingdom, and the general Sterling Area was the criterion which ultimately determined economic development in the colonies. By the beginning of 1953, therefore, it was clear that there were not going to be any significant changes in the British government policy toward colonial development. If anything, it seemed as if the Conservatives were going to attach more importance to the Britain's balance of payments position in formulating colonial development policy than their Labour predecessors.

AMERICAN AID REEXAMINED, 1952–1953

Upon assuming office the Conservatives continued with the search initiated by Labour for a formula to fund colonial development that addressed the ever-growing colonial demands, without jeopardizing the United Kingdom's economic well-being. Thus, the question of American investment in the colonial empire was revisited. In August 1952 Oliver Lyttelton, the colonial secretary, began to consider ways and means of encouraging private American investment in the colonies.[11] Although he needed a source of funds to supplement investments from the United Kingdom, his main concern was the consequences for the British economy, of having to pay profits to American investors in dollars. The colonial secretary was worried that investors may have chosen to repatriate their capital, when such an outflow was "most embarrassing to us, e.g. by increasing the strain upon sterling at a time when sterling is weakening."[12] As a result he was reluctant to encourage colonial governments to access funds from American sources. The colonial secretary pointed out that dollar investments must be weighed against "the exchange risks to which its approval will expose the central reserves and proposals which, from this point of view, appear to be definitely bad risks should be rejected as undesirable."[13] He therefore asked colonial governments not to approve American investments that Britain felt would jeopardize the position of the sterling.

From the viewpoint of colonial territories, the difficulty with this request was that it required them to limit their access to funds from an important source, without a compensatory increase either in access to their own funds or funds from U.K. sources. This created problems for some colonies. In the Bahamas, for example, the Americans were attracted by incentives such as freedom from income taxes; however, they disliked the exchange control regulations which were placed on different types of investments.[14] The governor of the Gold Coast reported in November 1952 that American investment was "considerably hampered by such restrictive measures as exchange control, quantitative restrictions on non-sterling imports and immigration quotas."[15] He noted that "the first two restrictions stem from the policy to conform with the general

Sterling Area requirements, and are necessitated by the desire to limit non-sterling expenditure."[16] The acting governor of Uganda said the main problem for his government was to give guidance on what was the right type of investments, and to set out the conditions that the Treasury would have most likely attached to a company's right to repatriate profits and capital. He told the colonial secretary, "if you find it necessary to insist that any undertaking must either be a dollar earner or a dollar saver to qualify as the 'right type,' then you might find it difficult to leave it to my discretion to determine which industries should qualify."[17] The governor of Kenya wanted colonies to be given more discretion to approve investment projects involving American capital "even where there was a balance of payments loss, provided that the local economy benefitted."[18]

Despite the protest from some colonial governments, the colonial secretary remained steadfast in his opposition to a change in policy, and made it clear that colonial needs were subordinate to those of the wider Sterling Area. He pointed out, "while I entirely agree that local benefits can best be assessed on the spot, [the] extent to which these justify a loss to the Sterling Area involves a judgement of factors going beyond the purely local situation . . . and in my view warrants reference to me in order that the wider Sterling Area considerations can be fully allowed for."[19] In the final analysis, although foreign investment in the British colonial empire was not prohibited, it was not actively pursued. The policy enunciated by the colonial secretary underscored once again the fact that the state of the British economy, in particular its balance of payments position, was ultimately the most critical factor that shaped colonial economic policy toward U.S. capital in particular, and foreign capital in general.

INCREASING DEMANDS AND INCREASING RELUCTANCE: COLONIAL DEVELOPMENT FINANCE, 1953–1958

In 1953 colonial governments were asked to submit their needs for external finance for the 1955–1960 period. In drawing up their requirements the colonial governments were advised to consider the following: their estimated physical capacity; economic projects that would strengthen the territories' resources and meet the commonwealth balance of payments criteria; and the maximum utilization of local resources including local loans and balances held in London.[20] Their submissions were scrutinized by a Colonial Development Working Party (which Treasury representatives attended as consultants) which presented its report in August 1954. The report of this Working Party had serious ramifications for Britain's relations with its colonial territories. It claimed that with few exceptions colonial plans were reasonably balanced among economic development, basic services and social services. After evaluating the proposals submitted by colonial governments, the C.D.W.P. reduced the projected costs for their development programs for the period 1955–1960 from £693.40 million to £630.34 million.[21] These funds were to be drawn from local resources, colonial development and welfare funds and external loans. Of the total sum required (£630.34 million) 51.5 percent was to come from local resources in the colonies, 17.6 percent from colonial development and welfare funds and 30.9 percent from external loans. As far as the latter were concerned, the C.D.W.P. noted that even if assistance from the International Bank for Reconstruction and Development and the United States were taken into consideration, the greater part of the external funds required by the colonies would have to be raised on the London money market.[22] In the colonial governments' estimation for development finance the contribution from local sources was less than that of the Working Party, 38.3 percent as opposed to 51.5 percent. The colonial governments also expected more funds from colonial development and welfare grants and external loans than were proposed by the Working Party, 61.7 percent as opposed to 48.5 percent (Table 7.1).

Table 7.1
Financing Colonial Development Programs, 1955–1960

	Colonial Governments' Proposals		Working Party's Proposals	
	£ million	%	£ million	%
Local Resources	265.46	38.3	324.62	51.5
C.D.W. (includes carry over)	190.19	27.4	110.93	17.6
External Loans	237.75	34.3	194.79	30.9
TOTAL	693.40	100.0	630.34	100.0

Source: P.R.O. T 230/249. Report of the Colonial Development Working Party 1954.

The new funds required under colonial development and welfare were estimated by the C.D.W.P. at about £90 million. Of this sum about £61.6 million or nearly 70 percent was accounted for by the needs of six territories—Kenya, Tanganyika, Nigeria, the Federation of Malaya, British Guiana and Jamaica. Similarly, of the loan figure of £194.79 million (C.D.W.P.'s proposals), Kenya, Tanganyika, East Africa Railways and Harbour (E.A.R.H.), Nigeria, Northern Rhodesia, Cyprus and Trinidad accounted for about £146 million.[23]

In spite of the disagreement between the C.D.W.P. and the colonial governments over the amount that was required for colonial development between 1955 and 1960, there was consensus between them on two important issues. To begin with, just under half of the development funds needed by colonial territories had to come from external sources. Moreover, the United Kingdom's resources in the form of colonial development and welfare allocations and the London money market were going to be the most critical sources of external funds for the development of colonial territories. The report of the Colonial Development Working Party was based on the principle that "the colonies ought to finance as much as possible of their own development themselves, and have taken into account the level of reserves held by colonial governments and the other public bodies."[24] It warned against "an over-simplified conception of the sterling assets and the degree to which they are available for development."[25] The use of these funds was governed by their distribution; therefore, the territories with the largest reserves, for example, the Gold Coast and Uganda, did not need external assistance. The report of the Working Party concluded that based on the information provided by the colonial governments and departments of the Colonial Office "the amount of desirable development (i.e. development which is both useful in itself and bearable as regards the burden of residual recurrent expenditure) which could be undertaken in the period 1955/60, if the necessary finance were available, is of the order of £650 million."[26] This represented an average annual investment of £130 million for the next five years, or ⅕ of 1 percent of the United Kingdom's national income.

According to the Working Party's calculations for the period 1955–1960, the colonies would have been unable to obtain all the loans needed to fund colonial development. The Working Party believed that about half of the estimated £650 million for colonial development could have been obtained from local colonial resources and the colonies could safely raise a maximum of about £200 million in loans. The remainder would have had to come from direct external grants, of which £115 million would have been additional to what was already available from the carryover from the existing Colonial Development and Welfare Act.[27] Overall, the Working Party believed that external aid was going to be more important between 1955 and 1960 than it was between 1950 and 1955. It pointed out that "at present grants represent some 15% of total development expenditure and external loans some 20%. In our calculations the proportion will rise to about 25% and 30%, respectively."[28] This was mainly because the period 1955–1960 was not expected to be boom years for primary producers.

In the context of the problems confronting the British economy at this juncture the shortfall in the colonial loan requirement cited by the C.D.W.P. was sure to create problems for Britain. If indeed the colonies were unable to secure a substantial part of the loans required for development from existing sources, they would have turned quite naturally to Britain, the colonial overlord, for assistance. There were no easy solutions here either. To begin with the state of the British economy did not allow Britain to provide generous financial assistance to its colonial dependencies. In addition, the bulk of the colonial sterling balances were held by a few colonies, some of which were going to be independent shortly, and Britain still had not worked out how best to neutralize the threat that these balances posed to its economic stability. This apart, the British government was reluctant to encourage foreign investments, especially from the United States, and domestic consider-ations were making it difficult for the colonies to obtain access to the London money market.

The true nature of the financial problem confronting Britain and the colonies was evident in the fact that the development program on the scale proposed by the Working Party did not represent a significant expansion in the existing rate of development. In fact, it would have done little more than maintain the current momentum. The Working Party warned the British government that if the sums actually provided were appreciably less than their calculations "development will not merely not proceed as rapidly as desirable but may actually slacken."[29] Having accepted the inevitability of independence in Ghana, Malay and Nigeria in 1954, therefore, the British government was advised that without its ongoing financial support colonial development and welfare would be in jeopardy.

The Treasury was in general very critical of the report of the Colonial Development Working Party. It claimed that the chief value of the work "has been in bringing out the character of the problems involved, and in determining the direction in which different colonies can best aim in their development policy, rather than in the arithmetic of the exercise."[30] It contended that the figure for the external needs of the colonies (£150 million) was based on varying data and more or less arbitrary adjustments to those figures; thus it must have contained a very wide margin of error. It also questioned the Working Party's claim that the figures represented no more than the sum required for the maintenance of the existing momentum in colonial development.[31] As far as the Treasury was concerned, it was impossible to estimate the actual rate of development at any given point in time.

Despite the fact that the problems of sterling were a critical factor in preventing the colonies from fully utilizing the funds allocated for colonial development and welfare schemes, the Treasury used colonial underspending as an example of the inaccuracy and over-optimism that always governed colonial estimates. Moreover, it concluded that past experience always pointed to the fact that, except when specially stimulated by sudden internal prosperity, colonial development was a slow, long haul. In most colonies the technical and administrative base for development was narrow, thus the Treasury contended that even though material shortages had been largely overcome, "finance is still not the only limiting factor in progress."[32] It saw attempts to break the steady rhythm in the rate of colonial development with artificial injections of large amounts of cash as dangerous, because colonies could have very easily become overburdened with capital and thus unable to meet growing recurrent commitments. Unlike most contemporary observers, the Treasury believed that "there is virtue in the discipline imposed by a shortage rather than an over abundance of finance."[33] It argued that what the colonies needed to enable them to make permanent progress along the right lines was not a sudden artificial spurt "but a steady rhythm to which the U.K. will contribute as necessary until the growing prosperity enables the colonies to maintain themselves."[34]

The Treasury's rebuttals were rather spurious. To begin with, there was nothing virtuous about the sacrifice forced upon the colonies by the shortages in capital goods and supplies which accompanied the stringent measures which were adopted to protect sterling. The reality was that the pace of development in many poverty-stricken colonies was being delayed because of these financial constraints. The Treasury did not produce any valid arguments to support the suggestion that the rate of colonial development expenditure forecasted by the Colonial Office for the period 1955–1960 was unrealistically high. Nor was there any economic explanation or justification for the policy of keeping colonial governments short of funds for development apart from the need to resolve Britain's balance of payments problems. Despite the Treasury's general criticisms of the report, there was consensus between the Treasury and the C.D.W.P. on two important issues relative to colonial development finance. First, only a few colonies would have been in a position to finance their own development after 1960. Second, the existing development programs would not have expanded the colonial resource base appreciably for more than five years.[35] Thus, in the short run it was highly unlikely that the capital injections for the period 1955–1960 would have relieved the United Kingdom of its responsibilities for colonial development finance. In spite of the colonies' predicament, the chancellor claimed that he would have had the greatest difficulty in contemplating an average expenditure of more than £18 million on the Colonial Development and Welfare Vote for the period 1955–1960.[36] The reality was therefore that even though the Treasury was very critical of the cost of colonial development presented in the C.D.W.P.'s report, the provision for financial support for colonial development for the period 1955–1960 was not, in the final analysis, one of its priorities.

In September 1954 the colonial secretary used the findings of the Colonial Development Working Party as the basis for an application to the chancellor of the exchequer for approval of development and welfare assistance totaling £150 million for the period 1955–1960. He also asked for the introduction of a system of direct exchequer loans to the colonies, to safeguard them against possible failure to raise a further £150 million which they needed for external loans for the same period, on the London loan market.[37] Given the Treasury's reactions to the report of the C.D.W.P., it was clear that it was not going to countenance the level of financial assistance sought by the Colonial Office. Under the Colonial Development and Welfare Act of 1955 the provisions for expenditure were extended to March 1960. The amount allocated was increased from £140 million to £220 million, an additional £80 million in new funds. This was £70 million less than the Colonial Office asked for, and £10 million less than the maximum the Treasury itself claimed was possible because of budgetary constraints and external stringency. Thus, there was a major shortfall in the funding provided by the British government for colonial development and welfare.

The colonies' chances of receiving adequate monetary aid were exacerbated by the combined effects of two factors. The first was the steady decline in the surplus in colonial transactions with the Dollar Area. The size of this surplus had symbolized the importance of the colonies to the United Kingdom and the general Sterling Area in the postwar era. The second was the rapid advance toward independence by the principal dollar-earning colonies. The colonial surplus with the Dollar Area decreased steadily from a peak of US$480 million in 1951 (Table 3.4) to US$260 million in 1954. By 1956 it fell further to US$218 million.[38] In 1954 the Malayan Federation together with Britain's West African territories (mainly Nigeria and Ghana) accounted for about 82 percent of the dollar surplus in colonial transactions.[39] In 1955 the Malayan Federation alone accounted for 65.4 percent of the colonial dollar.[40] The advance to independence in the key dollar-earning colonies (Malaya, Ghana and Nigeria) therefore destroyed a critical part of the foundation upon which Britain had constructed its economic relations with the colonies in the postwar era and left it with financial obligations to dependencies from which it derived very little benefit.

Thus, it was not at all surprising that the chancellor saw the expenditure requested for colonial development as a serious burden on the United Kingdom's resources. He pointed out:

the total amounts authorized to be paid from the Exchequer for Colonial Development and Welfare in ten years have risen from £50 million by the Act of 1940, to £120 million under the Act of 1945 and £140 million under the Act of 1950. The Colonial Office now proposes that assistance should be raised to £150 million in five years. . . . Admittedly costs have been rising during the period under review; but when and how do [sic] the Colonial Office see the process of constantly increasing grants being arrested? What do they anticipate is likely to happen in 1960, when the period of grants which we are now considering come [sic] to an end?[41]

Toward the end of 1954, therefore, the Treasury appeared to be growing tired of the continued appeals for assistance that came from the colonies. Although sterling grants and loans could have stimulated expenditure on U.K. goods and services and thereby could contribute to its balance of payments surplus, this was dependent on too many variables for it to be an attractive option. In addition, colonial development and welfare grants were a charge on the United Kingdom's current account and an increase in their levels at this time would have added even further to the United Kingdom's financial difficulties.

The chancellor pointed out that "in many important services expenditure by U.K. Departments is being held at present levels or reduced; desirable developments in national health, education and social services cannot be made for financial reasons. . . . A contribution by the U.K. to CD and W must have regard to the limits being imposed by other forms of expenditure."[42] Budgetary and external stringency also made it hard for the United Kingdom to afford more than £90 million over the period. According to the Treasury a "greater increase than this is in fact most unlikely to be achieved, and that it is undesirable as well as unnecessary to provide for more."[43] For a government that was bent on cutting costs and controlling spending, without the dollar surplus of the Malayan Federation, Ghana and Nigeria, the scale of expenditure in the colonies, proposed by the Colonial Office, could not be justified. The British government was also worried about its obligations with respect to development expenditure after 1960, because only a few colonies were expected to be able to finance their own development.

In explaining its inability to satisfy the funding requirements of the colonial territories, the Treasury placed the claims on the United Kingdom's financial resources against the position of the United Kingdom as a whole. It pointed out that since the war the United Kingdom's short-term liabilities had been many times its short-term assets. From experience this was normally a recipe for a balance of payments crisis. The Treasury felt that it was quite impossible to forecast what the current balances were going to be for the next five years, and thus the British government had to be cautious about accepting commitments for long-term financing. Consequently, the chancellor could not guarantee that colonies would be allowed to raise a specific sum of money on the London market in any one year.[44] Direct borrowing from the exchequer by colonial governments was ruled out because to the Treasury it was a sign of desperation which was unnecessary in the present circumstances. However, if the situation arose in a particular colony faced with grave difficulties in raising the money it needed on the London market "the Chancellor of the Exchequer would be prepared to consider with the Secretary of State [Colonial Office] what steps might be appropriate at that time to deal with the matter."[45]

The move toward colonial independence was an unequivocal declaration that the nationalists had rejected the United Kingdom's prescription for political reform. On the other hand, it presented opportunities for savings in colonial expenditure that Britain could employ without being accused of abandoning its colonial obligations. Development and welfare grants were inconsistent with the "hitherto accepted conception of independent status within the Commonwealth."[46] By the end of 1954 the Treasury was already looking to the benefits that were to accrue to it from colonial independence. The Colonial Office was reminded that many of the larger colonies that were approaching independence "should be encouraged to become less, not more dependent on the U.K. for development finance. From this angle one would have expected a tapering down of development grants in the case of the larger colonies, and not increases."[47]

THE LONDON CAPITAL MARKET: THE PROS AND CONS, 1955–1958

Although the Colonial Development and Welfare Act of 1955 set the British government's targets for colonial development and welfare expenditure, the issue of colonial loans was not settled. The British government's policy on colonial loan financing was outlined in detail in June 1955 by W. G. Wilson, principal at the Colonial Office.[48] The main sources of colonial loans were local and external. Generally speaking imperial policy was that "local sources were to be fully explored before the colonies sought external loans."[49] On the other hand, the money raised through local loans was always marginal to the total capital requirements of colonial governments and quasi-governmental institutions. Thus, local capital had to be supplemented by external capital to stimulate economic activity in colonial dependencies. However, raising funds externally was a major problem for most colonies, because their needs were usually in excess of the capacity or willingness of external sources.

In terms of sources of colonial finance the London loan market was "next to local reserves, the most important single source of development finance."[50] These loans were an important supplement to the funds provided under the Colonial Development and Welfare Act. Therefore, shortfalls in finance from the London money market would have added to the problems already created by the reduction in colonial development and welfare funds which the Colonial Office sought for the period 1955–1960. The colonies found London market funds attractive because they were controlled by private investors, rather than by the British government. Money market loans were the main channel through which overseas capital was fed into the colonial territories. They provided a basis for the expansion of economic and social services and, by extension, the standard of living and national income essential to balance and support rapid political advance. Moreover, London market loans were also, generally speaking, the cheapest source of loan funds, and the use of the monies raised was subject to fewer restrictions and administrative complexities than loan funds derived from any other external source.[51] Consequently, the preservation of the credit that they enjoyed in this market was important to colonial governments. The main problem for colonies seeking loans on the London market was the Treasury's reluctance to guarantee specific annual amounts because of the instability in the U.K. economy.

The British government controlled the number of colonial applications for loans on the London market to avoid saturating it. It also monitored the market to ensure that funds available in London were not diverted to other external borrowers to an extent that would have reduced the amount available for colonial and commonwealth investors. Between 1949 and 1954 colonial governments raised £130 million in loans on the London market, or a yearly average of about £21 million. The highest amount for any one year was £27 million and the lowest was £16 million.[52] Although no general commitment could have been given, Wilson believed that it was reasonable to expect that the market would be able to supply the colonies with about £20 million to £25 million annually over the next few years. He added also that it was imperative that the limited funds be fully absorbed and applied where they were most urgently needed, and could be most usefully employed, in the development of colonial territories and, equally important, contribute to the stability of the Sterling Area as a whole.

Wilson pointed out that "the pattern of colonial borrowing must be such that heavy borrowing from any one region or territory, or frequent applications for small amounts, must be avoided, and the borrowing programme for any one year must include issues from the territories well-spread geographically."[53] This implied some kind of collaboration among colonial territories with regard to applications on the London loan market. The supply of money on the London market was limited and the calls on it so great that potential borrowers had to demonstrate the existence of an actual cash need for the funds sought at the time of issue. This provision was disadvantageous to many colonies. As a result, in November 1954, the chancellor of the exchequer promised to act in consultation with the colonial secretary, in circumstances where a colony was experiencing grave difficulty in raising loans on the London money market.[54] The colonies were allowed to raise £25 million per year on the London market for the period 1955–1960.[55] The Treasury's guarantee was based on the assumption that they would supplement these loans with their own resources and the provisions made in the Colonial Development and Welfare Act of 1955.

The Colonial Office was not satisfied with the support the colonies received from the Treasury. From its account of the loans raised by the colonies on the London market, it was clear that the target set for the colonies was not being met. In the two years 1955 and 1956 colonial governments were only able to raise a total of £20.9 million on the London money market, £9.7 million in 1955 and £11.2 million in 1956.[56] In November 1956 the Colonial Office complained that "taking the 1954 estimate of the product of the London market and comparing it with the actual results of 1955 and 1956 a short fall of £29 million has already occurred: if this is added to the £25 million expected for 1957, on the basis of the 1954 estimate, there is a presumption that the total amount of London loan finance to be found by the end of 1957 would be of the order of £54 million."[57] The Colonial Office contended that in light of this problem it had to raise £22.5 million in London by the end of 1957, to discharge commitments already incurred, and which could not be avoided even if an immediate embargo was placed on all continuing capital development, scheduled to be financed from the London money market in that period. Despite the assurance given by the Treasury in 1954, therefore, the colonies were unable to fulfill their loan requirements on the London market. To solve this problem the Colonial Office claimed further that "special measures are now urgently needed to ensure that colonial governments can be provided with the loan finance they need . . . the minimum product of such special measures would have to be £13.5 million and the maximum £33 million up to the end of 1957."[58] Therefore, the Colonial Office asked the British government to take steps to provide special support which strengthened the standing of colonial stock, so that more private funds would be attracted to new issues, and the amounts of dealing in them would increase. The Colonial Office also wanted the government to find a source of funds that, while not reducing the amount of money flowing from private investors, would ensure that the established needs of colonial borrowers were met.[59]

In December 1956 a Colonial Office memorandum on colonial loans on the London market was considered at a meeting of Treasury and Colonial Office officials chaired by Sir E. Compton, third secretary at the Treasury.[60] A. H. Poynton, deputy under secretary at the Colonial Office, argued that one alternative to raising the required sums for the colonies on the London market was to reduce the size of colonial development programs. He pointed out, however, that "this would be an admission of defeat and was unlikely to be acceptable either to Ministers or to Parliament."[61] For Poynton the constructive alternatives were to authorize the national debt commissioners to invest in colonial government stock, direct loans from the exchequer or an extension in the functions of the Colonial Development Corporation (C.D.C.). Poynton added that while there were objections to each of these alternatives, the colonial ministers were pressing for an early resolution of the problem, and it was therefore necessary to think in terms of the least objectionable alternatives.

The Colonial Office complained that "one of the dangers at present was that the colonies always had to have an 'emergency' in order to get more loans from H.M. Government."[62] It claimed that the colonies were not prepared to delay their development needs to accommodate Britain's financial difficulties much longer and eventually they would have sought help from other sources. It was difficult for the Colonial Office to accept that the United Kingdom was unable to find what it termed "an infinitesimal proportion of total United Kingdom investment"[63] for colonial development. It was convinced that the problems surrounding colonial development were not related to a lack of funds, but rather to the arrangement for transferring financial resources to the colonies.[64] The Colonial Office was being rather naive; the reality was that the British government was strapped for cash and colonial development was not one of its priorities.

The Treasury was much more pragmatic. It claimed that since 1954 there were two fundamental changes, that affected both the estimates that had been made initially and the pledge given by the former chancellor. First, the economic climate in the United Kingdom had changed profoundly, and to counter inflation the British government had embarked on an active monetary policy involving a credit squeeze that reduced the funds available for all borrowers. In short, the measures needed to resolve the United Kingdom's economic problems were impacting negatively on the disbursement of loans from the London money market to the colonies. As a result it was more difficult for the colonies to access money market funds. Second, there was an increase in the unpopularity of colonial stocks relative to others. Thus, the Treasury explained, it "could not exclude the possibility of recommending to

Ministers that colonial development programmes should be cut down."[65] The Treasury added further that "the reason for the drying up of the market was partly the unwillingness of private bodies to make their savings available to colonial borrowers; and the Exchequer itself had a major problem on hand in trying to finance the vast loans to which it was already committed."[66] As far as the Treasury was concerned, therefore, colonial development was not sacrosanct. Faced with the need for stringency, the Treasury was prepared to cut development finance to the minimum sums, and even lower if necessary.

The Treasury and the Colonial Office agreed that in 1957 colonial governments could expect to raise about £12 million on the London money market. Since the amount required was about £19.5 million for inescapable needs, and between £35 million and £40 million to finance the expansion of development that had been decided before 1954, this left a gap of between £7.5 million and £28 million.[67] The reduction in provisions for colonial development finance from the London money market was consistent with the approach adopted by the British government relative to other sources of development funds which were available to colonial territories. Moreover, in addition to the shortfall in the provision under the Colonial Development and Welfare Act, the colonies had to manage with further reductions in finance from the London money market, their second most important source for development finance. It is clear, therefore, that in the latter years of the 1950s Britain had lost its enthusiasm for colonial development—tell-tale sign that it was no longer interested in retaining its colonial territories.

Despite the accord between the Treasury and the Colonial Office relative to loan finance from the London market, officials continued to explore possible alternatives to the London money market for colonial development finance. In this regard Treasury officials were reluctant to add direct loans to the colonies to the financial commitments already facing the exchequer. However, they believed that if ministers took the view that money for the colonies had to be found from somewhere, exchequer loans were preferable to the other alternatives which had been suggested.[68] Thus, in December 1956 direct loans to colonial governments from the exchequer were accepted as a possible alternative to loans from the London money market for the period 1957–1960. If all else failed, therefore, the exchequer was the colonial governments' lender of last resort. These loans could only be accessed if an independent board set up to assess applicants was satisfied that they were unable to raise the money they required from their own resources or from the London market.[69] In addition, the sum involved was subject to a statutory limit, which was to be reduced if the governments were eventually successful in raising loans on the London money market.[70]

The Colonial Office, on the other hand, believed that colonial governments should have been authorized to increase the proportion of their
currency reserves that was invested in locally issued government
securities from the present 20 percent to 50 percent.[71] The latter figure
was the maximum which was recommended by the Working Party on
Colonial Sterling Balances in 1954. Although this suggestion was noted
for further consideration there were two difficulties with it. First, it may
not have provided enough money in areas like East Africa where it was
most needed, if currency boards were unwilling to cooperate. Second, it
may have been inadvisable for underdeveloped colonies to take such a
large step away from an automatic currency system.[72]

The possibility of obtaining capital from outside the Sterling Area,
including aid from the government of the United States, was reexamined
once more. W. Armstrong, under secretary at the Treasury, noted, "on the
question itself, my recollection is that it has been from time to time
examined with the Colonial Office but difficulties have always been
produced—and not only on the American side."[73] It was also pointed out
that the Colonial Office had tried to obtain loan finance from several
sources outside the Sterling Area "but that recently, the only one which
has yielded substantial sums is the International Bank."[74] Although
Jamaica and other West Indian islands were able to raise a few million
dollars from Canada and New York, it was felt that these markets were
not likely to prove a source of funds for African colonies. There were also
doubts whether the Canadian and American markets could supply funds
on the scale required to bridge the gap between what was required by the
colonies and what the colonies could raise on the London market.[75]

Direct loans from the U.S. government were in a different category
altogether, and two points stood out. First, this source had not hitherto
yielded much on terms acceptable to the United Kingdom. Second, there
did not seem to be any existing form of U.S. aid that Britain believed was
suitable for the colonies.[76] According to J. Forsyth, Treasury principal,
special negotiations with the U.S. government were required before any
funds were forthcoming, and this would have taken time. Therefore, it
was unlikely that any sums would be produced in 1957. Despite
considering a number of possibilities to the London money market for
colonial development finance, therefore, by 1957 the British government
was yet to decide on alternatives. By 1957, therefore, the British
government did not give any priority to colonial demands for financial
assistance from their two most important sources, colonial development
and welfare funds and the London money market. The British government was adamant that its own needs took precedence over those of the
colonies and seemed resigned to the fact that independence would
eventually put an end to its misery.

CONCLUSION

The economic problems in the United Kingdom, that were evident in balance of payments difficulties and an unstable pound, and a rapid advance to independence in Britain's principal dollar-earning territories provided the main backdrop against which British policy governing colonial development finance evolved during the period 1952 to 1958. The under-lying premise of the Conservative government's approach to colonial development finance was fundamentally the same as that of the Labour. Colonial development was intended not only to advance the welfare of colonial people, but also to facilitate economic recovery in Britain. In terms of the latter, the value of the colonies was seen primarily in relation to their contribution to the correction of the United Kingdom and the Sterling Area's deficit in trade with the Dollar Area. Therefore, the independence of the principal dollar earners, Malaya and the Gold Coast, and the impending independence of Nigeria destroyed a critical part of the foundation upon which the United Kingdom had constructed its economic relations with its colonial territories in the postwar era. The British government was left with the unattractive prospect of having to maintain at tremendous cost an empire shorn of its most valuable assets.

By 1955 it was clear that the British government was unable to finance the level of development that the Colonial Office regarded as necessary to maintain the momentum toward progress in colonial territories. The C.D.W.P. had estimated that development finance for the period 1955–1960 would be 30 percent more than it was in 1950–1955. Worse still, the Treasury was not very confident that current development programs would have increased the colonies' productive capacity appreciably for more than five years. It also doubted whether many colonies would have been able to finance their own development after 1960. The uncertainty about the political and economic viability of the colonies enhanced the argument for cuts in colonial expenditure. This was evident in the inflexibility and lethargy that governed colonial development finance, especially after the mid–1950s. This approach was in sharp contrast to the vitality with which the United Kingdom promoted the development of resources in tropical Africa and other parts of the British empire between 1946 and 1952. The colonies were valuable to Britain because they contributed to the correction of its trade deficit with the Dollar Area. Without this, there was no inducement for Britain to develop or maintain the majority of its colonial dependencies. Colonial demands for independence at the end of the 1950s were therefore welcomed because Britain was unwilling and unable to satisfy colonial requirements for development finance.

NOTES

1.   J.C.R. Dow, *The Management of the British Economy 1945–1960* (Cambridge: University Press, 1970), pp. 66–67.
2.   Ibid.
3.   R. Holland, "The Imperial Factor in British Strategies from Attlee to Macmillan, 1945–1963," *Journal of Imperial and Commonwealth History*, Vol. XII, no. 2 (January 1984), p. 181.
4.   Ibid.
5.   *P.R.O.* CO 852/1365. Draft circular dispatch for the Treasury and Commonwealth Relations Office concurrence. January 1953.
6.   Ibid.
7.   Ibid.
8.   Ibid.
9.   Ibid. Flett to Emmanuel 10/2/53.
10. Ibid. Melville to Flett 26/2/53.
11. *P.R.O.* CO 852/1420. Circular 835/52. Confidential O. Lyttelton 22/8/52.
12. Ibid.
13. Ibid.
14. *P.R.O.* CO 852/1420. Gov. of the Bahamas to Rt. Hon. Oliver Lyttelton 5/12/52.
15. Ibid. Gov. of the Gold Coast to S/S 19/11/52.
16. Ibid.
17. Ibid. Ag. Gov. of Uganda to S/S 5/5/53.
18. Ibid. Gov. of Kenya to S/S 5/8/53.
19. Ibid. S/S to O.A.G. Kenya 1/9/53.
20. *P.R.O.* T 230/249. N. W. Hemmings to Sir Robert Hall. Colonial Development Finance. colonial secretary's Proposals 30/10/54.
21. *P.R.O.* T 230/249. Report of the Colonial Development Working Party August 1954.
22. Ibid.
23. Ibid.
24. Ibid.
25. Ibid.
26. Ibid., para. 98. The programs for the Gold Coast, the Bahamas, Bermuda and the Central African Republic were not included in this figure.
27. Ibid.
28. Ibid., para. 103.
29. Ibid., para. 100.
30. *P.R.O.* T 230/249. Memorandum on Colonial Development Finance 27 October 1954.
31. Ibid.
32. Ibid.
33. Ibid.
34. Ibid.
35. Ibid.
36. Ibid.
37. *P.R.O.* T 230/249. Memorandum on Colonial Development Finance 27 October 1954.

38. *Parliamentary Papers*, 1956–1957, Vol. X (Cmd. 194), Appendix VII.
39. *Parliamentary Papers*, 1957–1958, Vol. IX (Cmd. 451), Appendix VII.
40. *Parliamentary Papers*, 1956–1957, Vol. X (Cmd. 194), Appendix VII.
41. A. N. Porter and A. J. Stockwell, eds. *British Imperial Policy and Decolonisation*, vol. 2, 1951–1964 (London: Macmillan, 1989), pp. 349–350.
42. Ibid.
43. *P.R.O.* T 230/249. Memorandum on Colonial Development Finance 27 October 1954.
44. Ibid.
45. Ibid.
46. Porter and Stockwell, *British Imperial Policy and Decolonisation*, p. 350.
47. Ibid.
48. *P.R.O.* T 236/4961. W. G. Wilson to A. K. Rawlinson (Treasury) 20/6/55.
49. Ibid
50. Ibid.
51. Ibid.
52. Ibid. Circular dispatch to all Colonies. Loan Finance. Annex 1. Loans raised by public subscription in London.
53. Ibid.
54. *P.R.O.* T 236/4961. Draft Secret. Colonial Loans on the London Market. Annexure to E. P. Undated. This document was written sometime in November 1956.
55. Ibid.
56. *P.R.O.* T 236/4961. J.H.V. Davies to Mr. Peck 19/11/57. See also Loan Finance for colonial governments. Note of a meeting held at 3:00 P.M. on 13 December 1956 at H.M. Treasury, Great George Street, SW.1.
57. *P.R.O.* T 236/4961. Draft Secret. Colonial Loans on the London Market. Annexure to E. P. Undated. This document was written sometime in November 1956.
58. Ibid.
59. Ibid.
60. *P.R.O.* T 236/4961. Loan Finance from Colonial Governments. Note of a meeting held at 3:00 P.M. on 13 December 1956 at H.M. Treasury.
61. Ibid.
62. Ibid.
63. Ibid.
64. Ibid.
65. Ibid.
66. Ibid.
67. Ibid.
68. Ibid.
69. Ibid.
70. Ibid.
71. Ibid.
72. Ibid.
73. Ibid. W. Armstrong to Mr. Jenkyns 24/1/57.
74. Ibid. J. Forsyth to Mr. Jenkyns 14/2/57.
75. Ibid.

76.   Ibid. F. W. Gloves-Smith, private secretary to the president of the Board of Trade, told Sir Leslie Rowan in June 1957 that while the Colonial Office was always willing to use U.S. financial assistance, the conditions imposed on U.S. loans had always created difficulties. The most significant were demands that U.S. aid must have matched equal contributions from the receiving territory and the delays in approving the loans. See *P.R.O.* T 236/4961. Minute by F. Gloves-Smith 27/6/57.

Conclusion

The declining role of sterling as an international currency and the continuous instability in the British economy had by the 1930s precipitated the start of a profound transformation in Britain's colonial economic policy. In the emerging economic relationship between the metropole and its colonial territories, Britain became increasingly dependent on the colonial territories' resources to stabilize its balance of payments and safeguard the position of sterling as an international currency. This development played an important role in helping shape the United Kingdom's reaction to the changes in the international economy in the 1930s. Its effect was evident in Britain's decision to employ discrimination in its trade with hard currency areas, create the system of imperial preferences and to establish the Sterling Area.

In the late 1930s there was widespread unrest in the British empire and grim warnings from a number of publications about the likely consequences of the British government's failure to arrest social decay and improve the economic conditions in colonial territories. This culminated in the passage of the Colonial Development and Welfare Act of 1940, under which the social and economic development of colonial territories was made a precondition for their political advancement. By 1940, therefore, the foundation for the postwar economic relationship between Britain and its colonial territories was established. It was built upon two main pillars. First, the value of colonial territories was linked to the nature of their contribution to the British economy, especially the stabilization of its balance of payments and the preservation of the role of sterling as an international currency. Second, Britain was responsible for the social and economic development of its colonies. Its declared objective in undertaking this commitment was to prepare colonial territories for political advancement. In theory this relationship was mutually beneficial, but in reality it was not. A wide range of discriminatory trade practices and other restrictive measures were instituted to ensure that colonial economic policy gave top priority to the correction of Britain's trade imbalance, particularly its deficits with the Dollar Area. However, the level of funding and the goods and services required to develop the colonies were not given priority treatment by the British government.

Between 1939 and 1945 the exigencies of war and the need to safeguard sterling and stabilize the British economy had a major influence on colonial economic policy. These factors led to the integration of colonial fiscal and monetary policy into that of the United Kingdom, and the introduction or enhancement of measures that allowed Britain to exercise an unparalleled amount of control over the resources of its colonial empire and those of the Sterling Area. However, as the war took its toll and Britain's economic fortunes deteriorated, the British government was forced to give in to U.S. pressure to alter its trade and monetary policy in order to obtain urgently needed financial aid from the Americans. Thus, Britain entered the postwar era committed to liberalizing its trade practices, abandoning discrimination against the Dollar Area, reducing its holdings of accumulated sterling balances and restoring sterling to full international convertibility by July 1947. Britain's endeavor to honor its obligations to the United States had major consequences for postwar colonial economic policy. The Second World War also had an impact on the nature of political relations between Britain and its colonial territories. In India, Burma and Sri Lanka, imperial rule was weakened considerably, in retrospect irretrievably. However, elsewhere in the British empire political reforms were limited and unsystematic and at the end of the war colonial rule was still firmly entrenched. In these territories Britain entered the postwar period convinced that social and economic progress was necessary for political advancement and that it could dictate or at least regulate the process of political reform.

Between 1945 and 1949 the British government battled resolutely to resolve the complications involved in economic reconstruction, honoring its commitments to the United States, maintaining the viability of the Sterling Area, restoring the pound to full international convertibility and catering to escalating colonial demands for political and economic reform. These difficulties were constricted further by the dynamic nature of the domestic, colonial and international circumstances in which Britain functioned. Between 1946 and the first quarter of 1947 the mobilization of colonial resources was not an important part of Britain's strategy for economic recovery. However, as the problems with sterling convertibility emerged, the British government became convinced that the expansion of commodity production in the colonies and the maximization of their exports would make an important contribution to rectifying its own trade deficit, and that of the general Sterling Area, with the Dollar Area.

The collapse of convertibility in July 1947 represents a landmark in Britain's postwar colonial economic policy. As a result of this, its trade deficit with the Dollar Area became a pivotal aspect of colonial economic policy and the value of the colonies to the United Kingdom increased immeasurably. An elaborate program was devised to systematically ascertain and increase the export production of colonial products that were either dollar earners or alternatives to supplies that were obtained from hard currency sources. This program became the prototype for the strategies that Britain employed in the aftermath of the crises that followed the devaluation of sterling in 1949 and the outbreak of the Korean War in June 1950. At the zenith of the process of colonial resource mobilization, 1947–1952, the benefits accruing to Britain from colonial development were easily justified. Consequently, the program for resource mobilization was energetically pursued, more financial resources were placed at the disposal of the colonies and colonial economies were integrated further into that of the metropole.

Paradoxically, the transfiguration in economic relations between Britain and its colonies took place simultaneously with the genesis of a momentous nationalist challenge to colonial rule in three of Britain's most valuable dollar-earning colonies: the Gold Coast, Malaya and Nigeria in 1948. In view of the importance of their contribution in assisting the United Kingdom to redress its trade deficit with the Dollar Area, the British government was in no mood to capitulate. Yet, repression was alone not sufficient to neutralize the nationalist forces, so the British government was compelled to make political concessions. At the onset of its struggles with the nationalists, British government officials were not alive to the full significance of the nationalists' challenge, especially the threat posed to the foundations of metropolitan/colonial economic relations. However, there was potential danger for Britain. Between 1946 and 1949 it allowed its dependencies to continue to accumulate sterling reserves, because it was unable to satisfy the demand for goods and services which a release of these balances would generate. As long as its authority was intact, Britain was in a position to enforce policies to deal with the problems created by the growth of these balances. However, by 1949 about 37 percent of the colonial sterling reserves were held by the three colonies in the vanguard of an accelerating drive toward self-government and independence. As the pace increased the economic implications of the political challenge to

colonial rule began to dawn on British government officials.
The economic recovery that followed the devaluation of sterling in
1949 did not last long. By the middle of 1951 Britain was again embroiled
in a crisis, triggered on this occasion by the aftermath of the Korean War.
At this time the colonial surplus in transactions with the Dollar Area was
at its peak and the challenge from the nationalist forces in the Gold Coast,
Nigeria and Malaya was continuing. Next to the guerrillas who were
fighting in Malaya, Nkrumah's C.P.P. provided the most serious threat to
British colonial rule in these three colonies. Because of the importance of
their contribution to resolving its trade deficit with the Dollar Area and
the need to restore sterling to full international convertibility, Britain tried
desperately to safeguard its economic interest. However, the C.P.P.'s
victory in the general elections of 1951 was a clear indication that militant
nationalists in the Gold Coast were in the ascendancy in their struggle
with Britain for self-government.

In Nigeria the balance of power was also tilting in the direction of the
nationalist elements. Despite the general absence of the militancy that
characterized the transition in the Gold Coast, in an effort to control the
process of change in Nigeria, Britain had to ensure that political changes
here were in keeping with those in its neighbor the Gold Coast. In
Malaya, Britain reacted positively to the nationalists, who used the
emergency to press their claims for independence. Therefore, even
though it was still hanging on tenaciously, by 1951 Britain was clearly
losing political control in its most valuable colonies.

Throughout the period under review the British government faced
two major problems in relation to colonial development finance. First, the
majority of the colonies were unable to meet their needs from their own
resources and were dependent on the United Kingdom for assistance. In
many cases the socioeconomic position of colonial peoples had deteriorated further because the war had hindered the progress of the
development and welfare schemes. Second, Britain did not have the
resources to fund development at a level sufficient to resolve the pressing
social and economic problems in the colonies. Moreover, Britain was
reluctant to seek help from foreign sources, particularly the United States,
because it wanted to avoid interference in its colonial affairs. Thus, the
pressure placed by the colonies upon Britain's resources increased
further.

The position of the colonies was not helped by the fact that their needs
were subordinate to those of the United Kingdom. The colonies
experienced serious shortages both in the supply of consumer goods and
in the capital goods and services required for development projects. Their
problems were especially acute between 1946 and 1948. The postwar
shortages in the colonies were exacerbated by the restrictions imposed by

Britain on colonial trade with the Dollar Area and Britain's failure to prioritize their needs. This reduced the rate of expenditure of the funds allocated for development and welfare and delayed the projects themselves. This was a serious setback for the political objectives that were at the center of Britain's development and welfare plans in the colonies. Thus, by 1951, the demands for political reform had outstripped the levels of economic development that Britain envisaged were necessary before major political concessions could be made.

There were also a number of other important developments that affected the United Kingdom's future relations with the colonies at this time. As a result of the continuing cycle of economic instability and the internal adjustments necessary in the metropolitan economy, it was becoming progressively more difficult for the British government to justify its expenditure on development in the colonies. On the other hand, the demands for finance in the colonies were projected to increase. Although the outlook for the colonies was grim, the colonial surplus in transactions with the Dollar Area was still large enough to sustain Britain's interest in the development and welfare of its colonies.

Overall the developments that culminated in the widespread decolonization in the British empire after 1956 unfolded rapidly. The advance toward political independence by Malaya, the Gold Coast and Nigeria after 1951 occurred simultaneously with a concerted push by Britain to restore sterling to full international convertibility. By 1953 alarm bells were sounded by officials from the Bank of England and the Treasury, who feared that with the independence of Ghana, Malaya and Nigeria Britain would lose the political leverage necessary to preserve its economic interests and guide sterling safely to international convertibility. The officials' main concern was how to limit the damage to the British economy, which they believed was going to occur if these three colonies decided to spend their sterling reserves in hard currency areas after independence. Studies subsequently revealed that there was a threat, but it was a bit exaggerated. Nevertheless, because of the strain on the United Kingdom's reserves anticipated from withdrawal of reserves by India, Pakistan and Sri Lanka between 1956 and 1960, additional withdrawals by Ghana, Nigeria and Malaya would have created problems for Britain. Official concern was also evidence of the level of anxiety that prevailed relative to sterling toward the end of the 1950s. The abortive attempt at the restoration of sterling to international convertibility in 1947, together with the crises that had hampered subsequent attempts at restoring convertibility, left officials understandably nervous. Some were so consumed by the need to return sterling to international convertibility that they were not satisfied with studies showing the limits of the danger to the U.K. economy from the sterling balances in the hands of the colonies that were approaching independence.

Despite the anxiety which they provoked the sterling balances were never an obstacle to political independence in the colonies. By 1954 it was clear that Britain had become resigned to the independence of Ghana, Nigeria and Malaya. These were still its three most important dollar-earning colonies. As a result, Britain accepted the destruction of a critical part of the structure upon which it had built its economic relations with its colonial territories in the postwar era. The economic questions governing colonial preparedness for independence were now totally irrelevant to political reform. However, without Ghana, Malaya and Nigeria, the colonial surplus in transactions with the Dollar Area was not very substantial. The independence of these states therefore was going to leave Britain with an empire devoid of its most valuable assets.

To compound matters, by 1955 it was clear from the cuts to the sum requested by the Colonial Office for colonial development and welfare that the British government was not able and not willing to finance colonial development at the level that the Colonial Office and the Colonial Development Working Party felt was necessary to maintain the momentum in economic progress in colonial territories. Worse still, the Treasury itself was doubtful whether current development programs would have increased the colonies' productive capacity significantly for more than five years. The Treasury also wondered whether many colonies would have been able to finance their own development after 1960. Therefore, the independence of Ghana, Nigeria and Malaya was not only going to rob Britain of its most valuable colonies, it was also going to leave Britain with the prospect of having to maintain at tremendous cost colonial territories that did not provide Britain with any reciprocal economic benefits. For Britain the best solution to this problem was to reduce its liabilities by withdrawing from the colonies. By demanding political independence the colonies had rejected the path to political advancement which to Britain was the driving force behind its expenditure on colonial development and welfare. Also, Britain could not now be accused of abandoning its colonies to escape the burden of its financial obligations to them. After 1957, therefore, Britain rapidly granted independence to most of its colonial territories.

Select Bibliography

PRIMARY SOURCES

The Public Record Office (P.R.O.), London
CAB 129/47 and CAB 129/48
CO 537, CO 583, CO 847 and CO 852
PREM 8/977, PREM 8/1187, PREM 11/140, PREM 11/1324 and PREM 11/1367
T 220, T 229, T 230 and T 236

National Archives Ibadan (N.A.I.), Nigeria
Ib. Min. Agric. 1–509
Oyoprof 2/3/1-204

Private Papers

Papers of Arthur Creech Jones
Papers of the Fabian Colonial Bureau
Rhodes House Library, Oxford

Official Publications

Annual Reports
Nigeria Cocoa Marketing Board, 1947–1951
Nigeria Cotton Marketing Board, 1949–1951
Nigeria Eastern Region Production Development Board, 1949–1951
Nigeria Groundnut Marketing Board, 1949–1951
Nigeria Local Development Board, 1947–1948

Nigeria Northern Region Production Development Board, 1949–1951
Nigeria Oil Palm Produce Marketing Board, 1949–1951

Colonial Development Corporation (C.D.C.)
Parliamentary Papers 1948–49. XIII (188), 471. C.D.C. Annual Report and Statement of Accounts for the year ending 31 December 1948.
Parliamentary Papers 1950. VIII (105), 171. C.D.C. Annual Report and Statement of Accounts for the year ending 31 December 1949.
Parliamentary Papers 1950–1951. IX (161), 571. C.D.C. Annual Report and Statement of Accounts for the year ending 31 December 1950.
Parliamentary Papers 1951–1952. IX (167), 95. C.D.C. Annual Report and Statement of Acccounts for the year ending 31 December 1951.
Parliamentary Papers 1952–1953. VIII (158), 685. C.D.C. Annual Report and Statement of Accounts for the year ending 31 December 1952.

Colonial Development and Welfare
Parliamentary Papers 1939–40. X (Cmd. 6175). Statement of Policy on Colonial Development and Welfare. Secretary of State to Parliament, February 1940.
Parliamentary Papers 1942–1943. IX (Cmd. 6442), 601. Report on the operation of the Colonial Development and Welfare Act to 31 October 1942.
Parliamentary Papers 1944–1945. XIX (105), 597. Report on the operation of the Colonial development and Welfare Act 1 April 1944 to 31 March 1945.
Parliamentary Papers 1945–1946. XIX (Cmd. 6713). Colonial Development and Welfare: Dispatch dated 12 November 1945, from the Secretary of State for the Colonies to Colonial Governments.
Parliamentary Papers 1955–1956. XIII (Cmd. 9462). The Colonial Development and Welfare Act, 1955
Parliamentary Papers 1958–1959. X (Cmd. 672), 107. Report on the Use of Funds Provided Under the Colonial Development and Welfare Acts and an Outline of the Proposal for Exchequer Loans to the Colonial Territories.
Parliamentary Papers 1970–1971. VIII (Cmd. 4677), 575. Colonial Development and Welfare Acts 1929–70: A Brief Review.

Return of Schemes under the Colonial Development and Welfare Act
1 April 1943 to 31 March 1944. *Parliamentary Papers 1943–1944,* VII (6532), 601.
1 April 1945 to 31 March 1946, *Parliamentary Papers 1945–1946,* XIX (150), 1.
1 April 1946 to 31 March 1947, *Parliamentary Papers 1946–1947,* XIX (127), 73.
1 April 1947 to 31 March 1948, *Parliamentary Papers, 1947–1948,* XXI (166), 11.
1 April 1948 to 31 March 1949, *Parliamentary Papers, 1948–1949,* XXIX (211), 1.
1 April 1949 to 31 March 1950, *Parliamentary Papers, 1949–1950,* XIX (107), 9.

Reports of Committees, Commissions, et cetera
Parliamentary Papers 1918. XVII (Cmd. 9183), 365. Colonies' War Contribution. Treasury Minute.

Parliamentary Papers 1937–1938. IX (Cmd. 5845). Report of the Commission on Cocoa Marketing in West Africa, 1938

Parliamentary Papers 1940–1941. VII (Cmd. 6299). Dispatch from the Secretary of State for the Colonies to the Colonial Governments Regarding Certain Aspects of Colonial Policy in Wartime.

Parliamentary Papers 1943–1944. III (Cmd. 6554). Report on Cocoa Control in West Africa 1939–1943 and a Statement on Future Policy, 1944.

Parliamentary Papers 1945–1946. XIX. (Cmd. 6707). Statistical Material Presented during the Washington Negotiations, 1945.

Parliamentary Papers 1945–1946. XX. (Cmd. 6785). World Food Shortage, 1945.

Parliamentary Papers 1945–1946. XX (Cmd. 6879). Second Review of the World Food Shortage, July 1945–1946.

Parliamentary Papers 1946–1947 X (Cmd. 7030). A Plan for the Mechanised Production of Groundnuts, 1946.

Parliamentary Papers 1946–1947. X (Cmd. 7167), 403. Report on the Colonial Empire 1939–1947.

Parliamentary Papers 1947–1948. VIII (181-1). Fifth Report of the Select Committee on Estimates, Colonial Development, June 1948.

Parliamentary Papers 1947–1948. X. (Cmd. 7314). The East African Groundnut Scheme, 1948.

Parliamentary Papers XI (Cmd. 7433), 47. Report on the Colonial Empire, 1947–1948.

Parliamentary Papers 1948–1949. XIII. (Cmd. 7715), 641. Progress report on the Colonial Territories, 1948–1949.

Report of the Mission appointed to inquire into the production and Transport of Vegetable Oils and Oilseeds in West African Territories (HMSO, London, 1947).

The Colonial Empire, 1949–1950 (Cmd. 7958), 415.

The Colonial Territories 1950–1951 (Cmd. 8243).

The Colonial Territories 1951–1952 (Cmd. 8553).

The Colonial Territories 1952–1953 (Cmd. 8856).

The Colonial Territories 1953–1954 (Cmd. 9169).

The Colonial Territories 1954–1955 (Cmd. 9489).

The Colonial Territories 1955–1956 (Cmd. 9769).

The Colonial Territories 1956–1957 (Cmd. 194).

The Colonial Territories 1957–1958 (Cmd. 451).

The Colonial Territories 1958–1959 (Cmd. 780).

The Sterling Area: An American Analysis. The United States Economic Cooperation Administration Special Mission to the United Kingdon, London, 1951.

Economic Report: Salient Features of the World Economy 1945–1947. New York: United Nations Department of Economic Affairs, 1948.

World Economic Report 1948. United Nations.

World Economic Report 1949–50. United Nations.

Statistical Abstracts

The Commonwealth and the Sterling Area Statistical Abstract nos. 78–79, 1958. London: HMSO, 1959.

The Commonwealth and the Sterling Area, 73rd Statistical Abstract, 1949–1952. London: HMSO, 1953.
The Digest of Colonial Statistics 1952–1958. London: HMSO, 1959.

Newspapers
The Nigerian Citizen
The Nigerian Daily Times
The West African Pilot

SECONDARY SOURCES

Books

Addison, P. *The Road to 1945.* London: Jonathan Cape Ltd., 1975.
Ajayi, J.F.A., and M. Crowder. *History of West Africa.* Vol. 2, London: Longman, 1974.
Akinsuroju, O. *The Nigerian Political Theatre 1923–1953.* Lagos: City Publishing Association, 1953.
Albertini, R. von. *Decolonisation: The Administration and the Future of Colonies, 1919–1960.* New York: Africana Publishing Co., 1982.
Aldcroft, D. H., *The Inter-War Economy: Britain 1919–1939.* London: B. T. Batsford, 1970.
Alford, B. W. E. *Britain in the World Economy since 1880.* London: Longman, 1996.
Allen, C. and W. Johnson. *African Perspectives.* Cambridge: Cambridge University Press, 1970.
Amery, L. S. *The Washington Loan Agreements: A Critical Study of American Economic Foreign Policy.* London: MacDonald and Co. Ltd., 1946.
Ananaba, W. *The Trade Union Movement in Nigeria.* London: Hurst, 1969.
Anderson, D. M., and D. Killingray, eds. *Policising and Decolonisation: Politics, Nationalism and the Police, 1917–1965.* Manchester: Manchester University Press, 1992.
Argy, V. *The Postwar International Money Crisis: An Analysis.* London: George Allen and Unwin, 1981.
Arikpo, O. *The Development of Modern Nigeria.* London: Penguin, 1967
Ashton, S. R. and S. E. Stockwell. *Imperial Policy and Colonial Practice.* London: HMSO, 1996.
Austin, D. *Politics in Ghana 1946–1960.* London: Oxford University Press, 1964.
Awa, E. O. *Issues in Federalism.* Benin City: Ethiope Publishing Co., 1976.
Azikiwe, N. *My Odyssey: An Autobiography.* London: Hurst, 1970.
Azikiwe, N. *Zik: A Selection from the Speeches of Nnamdi Azikiwe.* London: Cambridge University Press, 1961.
Baldwin, K. D. S. *The Niger Agricultural Project.* Oxford: Basil Blackwell, 1957.
Baldwin, K. D. S., et al. *The Nigerian Cocoa Farmers.* London: Oxford University Press, 1956.
Bangura, Y. *Britain and Commonwealth Africa: The Politics of Economic Relations 1951–1975.* Manchester: Manchester University Press, 1983.

Bauer, P., and B. S. Yamey. *Markets, Market Control and Marketing Reform.* Great Britain: Weidenteld and Nicolson, 1968.

Bauer, P. *West African Trade.* London: Routledge and Kegan Paul Ltd., 1969.

Bell, P. W. *The Sterling Area in the Post-War World: Internal Mechanism and Cohesion 1946–1952.* Oxford: Clarendon Press, 1956.

Belof, M. *Imperial Sunset: Britain's Liberal Empire, 1897–1921 (2nd edition).* London: Methuen, 1987.

Boyce, R. W. *British Capitalism at the Crossroads, 1919–1932: A Study in Politics, Economics and International Relations.* Cambridge: Cambridge University Press, 1987.

Brown, I., ed. *The Economies of Africa and Asia in the Inter-War Depression.* London: Routledge 1989.

Burnham, P. *The Political Economy of Postwar Reconstruction.* London: Macmillan, 1990.

Burns, A. C. *In Defence of Colonies.* London: George Allen and Unwin, 1957.

Cairncross, A. *The British Economy since 1945: Economic Policy and Performance.* Oxford: Basil Blackwell, 1992.

———. *Years of Recovery: British Economic Policy, 1945–1951.* London: Methuen, 1985.

Cairncross, A., and B. Eichengreen. *Sterling in Decline: The Devaluations of 1931, 1949 and 1967.* Oxford: Basil Blackwell, 1983.

Cain, P. J., and A. G. Hopkins. *British Imperialism: Crisis and Deconstruction 1914–1990.* London, New York: Longman, 1993.

Capie, F., and G. Wood. *Financial Crises and the World Banking.* London: Macmillan, 1986.

Clarke, R. *Anglo-American Economic Collaboration in War and Peace.* Oxford: Clarendon Press, 1982.

Cohen, A. *British Policy in Changing Africa.* Evanston: Northwestern University Press, 1959.

Cohen, B. J. *The Future of Sterling as an International Currency.* London: Macmillan, 1971.

Cole, G.D.H. *The Postwar Condition of Britain.* London: Routledge and Kegan Paul, 1956.

Coleman, J. *Nigeria: Background to Nigerian Nationalism.* Berkeley: University of California, 1958.

Conan, A. R. *The Problem of Sterling.* London: Macmillan, 1966.

———. *The Sterling Area.* London: Macmillan, 1953.

Constantine, S. *The Making of British Colonial Development Policy 1914–1940.* London: Frank Cass Ltd., 1984.

Darwin, J. *Britain and Decolonisation: The Retreat from Empire in the Post-War World.* London: Macmillan, 1988.

———. *The End of the British Empire: The Historical Debate.* Oxford: Basil Blackwell, 1991.

Day, A. C. *The Future of Sterling.* London: Oxford University Press, 1954.

Dell, E. *The Schuman Plan and the British Abdication of Leadership in Europe.* London: Oxford University Press, 1995.

Dobson, A. P. *The Politics of Anglo-American Economic Special Relationship 1940–1987.* New York, St. Martin's Press, 1988.

Dow, J. C. *The Management of the British Economy, 1945–1960.* Cambridge: Cambridge University Press, 1970.

Drummond, I. M. *British Economic Policy and the Empire 1919–1939.* London: Harper and Row Publishers Inc., 1972.

Eichengreen, B. J. *Golden Fetters: The Gold Standard and the Great Depression, 1919–1939.* Oxford: Oxford University Press, 1992.

Emerson, R., and M. Kilson, eds. *The Political Awakening of Africa.* Englewood Cliffs, NJ: Prentice-Hall, 1965.

Feavearyear, A. *The Pound Sterling: A History of English Money.* Oxford: Clarendon Press, 1963.

Fforde, J. *The Bank of England and Public Policy 1941–1958.* Cambridge: Cambridge University Press, 1992.

Fieldhouse, D. K. *Black Africa, 1945–1980: Economic Decolonisation and Arrested Development.* London: Allen and Unwin, 1986.

Foot, H. M. *A Start to Freedom.* London: Hodder and Stoughton, 1964.

Foreman-Peck, J. *A History of the World Economy.* NJ: Barnes and Noble, 1983.

Frankel, S. H. *Capital Investment in Africa.* London: Oxford University Press, 1938.

Furedi, F. *Colonial Wars and the Politics of Third World Nationalism.* London: I B Publishers, 1994.

Gallagher, J. *The Decline, Revival and Fall of the British Empire.* Cambridge: Cambridge University Press, 1982.

Gardner, R. N. *Sterling Dollar Diplomacy in Current Perspective.* New York: Columbia University Press (new expanded edition), 1980.

Gifford, P. and W. R. Louis, eds. *The Transfer of Power in Africa: Decolonisation 1940–1960.* New Haven: Yale University Press, 1982.

Goldsworthy, D. *British Documents on the End of Empire, pts. 1–3.* London: HMSO, 1994.

———. *Colonial Issues in British Politics 1945–1961.* Oxford: Clarendon Press, 1971.

Greaves, I. *The Colonial Sterling Balances.* Princeton: Princeton University Press, 1956.

Gupta, P. S. *Imperialism and the British Labour Movement 1914–1964.* London: Macmillan, 1975.

Hailey, W. M. *An African Survey.* London: Oxford University Press, 1957.

———. *The Future of Colonial Peoples.* London: Oxford University Press, 1944.

———. *Native Administration and Political Development in British Tropical Africa.* Liechenstein: Krus Reprint Corporation, 1979.

Hancock, W. K., and M. M. Gowing, *British War Economy.* London: HMSO, London, 1949

Hargreaves, J. *The End of Colonial Rule in West Africa.* London: Macmillan, 1979.

Harrod, R. F. *The Life of John Maynard Keynes.* London: Macmillan, 1951.

Hathaway, R. M. *Ambiguous Partnership: Britain and America 1944–1947.* New York: Columbia University Press, 1981.

Havinden, M. and D. Meredith. *Colonialism and Development: Britain and Its Tropical Colonies, 1850–1960.* London: Routledge, 1993.

Hawtrey, R. G. *Towards the Rescue of Sterling.* London: Longmans, 1954.

Helleiner, G. K. *Peasant Agriculture, Government and Economic Growth in Nigeria.* Homewood, Illinois: Richard D. Irwin, Inc., 1966.

Hennessy, E. *A Domestic History of the Bank of England 1930–1960*. Cambridge: Cambridge University Press, 1992.

Hirsch, F. *The Pound Sterling: A Polemic*. London: Victor Gollancz, 1965.

Hogan, M. J. *The Marshall Plan: America, Britain and the Reconstruction of Western Europe, 1947–1952*. Cambridge: Cambridge University Press, 1989.

Holland, R. F. *Britain and the Commonwealth Alliance*. London: Macmillan, 1981.

———. *European Decolonisation 1918–1981: An Introductory Survey*. New York: St. Martin's, 1985.

Holtfrerich, Carl-Ludwig, ed. *Interactions in the World Economy*. New York: Harvester Wheatsheaf, 1989.

Hopkins, A. *An Economic History of West Africa*. New York: Columbia University Press, 1973.

Howe, S. *Anticolonialism in British Politics: The Left and the End of Empire 1918–1964*. Oxford: Clarendon Press, 1993.

Howson, S. *Sterling's Managed Float: The Operations of the Exchange Equalisation Account, 1932–1939*. Princeton: Princeton University Press, 1980.

Hutchinson, T. W. *Economics and Economic Policy in Britain 1946–1966*. London: George Allen and Unwin Ltd., 1968

Hyam, R., ed. *The Labour Government and the End of Empire 1945–1951*. London: Institute of Commonwealth Studies, 1992.

Ingham, B., and C. Simmons, eds. *Development Studies in Colonial Policy*. London: Frank Cass, 1987.

Jay, D. *Sterling, Its Use and Misuse: A Plea for Moderation*. London: Sidgwick and Jackson, 1985.

Jefferies, J. C. *Transfer of Power—Problem of the Passage to Self-Government*. London: Pall Mall Press, 1960.

———. *Whitehall and the Colonial Service: An Administrative Memoir, 1939–1956*. London: The Athlone Press, 1972.

Jewsiewicki, B., and D. Newbury, eds. *African Historiographies; What History for What Africa?* Beverly Hills: Sage Publications, 1986.

Jones, C. A., ed. *New Fabian Colonial Essays*. London: The Hogarth Press, 1959.

Judd, D. *Empire: The British Imperial Experience from 1765 to the Present*. New York: Basic Books, 1996.

Kahler, M. *Decolonisation in Britain and France: The Domestic Consequences of International Relations*. Princeton: Princeton University Press, 1984.

Kahn, A. E. *Great Britain in the World Economy*. New York: Columbia University Press, 1946.

Kaplan, J. J., and G. Schleiminger. *The European Payments Union*. Oxford: Clarendon Press, 1989.

Kapur, D., et al. *The World Bank: Its First Half Century*. Washington: Brookings Institute Press, 1998.

Kesner, R. M. *Economic Control and Colonial Development: Crown Financial Management in the Age of Joseph Chamberlain*. Oxford: Clio Press, 1981.

Kilby, P. *Industrialisation in an Open Economy: Nigeria, 1945–1966*. Cambridge: Cambridge University Press, 1966.

Killingray, D., and R. Rathbone, eds. *Africa and the Second World War*. New York: St. Martin's Press, 1986.

Kindleberger, C. *The World in Depression 1929–1939*. Berkeley: University of California Press, 1987.

Kirk-Greene, A. H. M. *The Principles of Native Administration: Selected Documents 1900–1947*. Oxford: Oxford University Press, 1965.

Kirk-Greene, A. H. M., ed. *The Transfer of Power: The Colonial Administrator in the Age of Decolonisation, Proceedings of a Symposium Held at St. Anthony's College*. Oxford: Oxford University InterFaculty Committee for African Studies, 1979.

Kunz, D. B. *The Battle for the Gold Standard*. London: Croom Helm, 1987.

Lee, J. M. *Colonial Development and Good Government*. Oxford: Clarendon Press, 1967.

Leubuscher, C. *Bulk Buying from the Colonies*. Oxford: Oxford University Press, 1956

Leys, C. *Underdevelopment in Kenya: The Political Economy of Neo-colonialism, 1964–1971*. London: Heinemann, 1975.

Louis, W. R. *Imperialism at Bay: The United States and the Decolonisation of the British Empire*. Oxford: Clarendon Press, 1977.

Mackenzie, J. *Propaganda and Empire, the Manipulation of the British Public Opinion*. Manchester: Manchester University Press, 1984.

Mason, E. S., and R. E. Asher. *The World Bank since Bretton Woods*. Washington: The Brookings Institute, 1973.

Means, G. P. *Malaysian Politics*. London: University of London, 1970.

Meyer, F. V. *Britain's Colonies in World Trade*. London: Oxford University Press, 1948.

Milne, R. S. *Government and Politics in Malaysia*. Boston: Houghton Mifflin & Co., 1967.

Milward, A. S. *The Economic Effects of Two World Wars on Britain* (2nd ed.). London: Macmillan, 1984.

———. *War, Economy and Society 1939–1945*. London: Allen Lane, 1977.

Moggridge, D., ed. *The Collected Writings of John Maynard Keynes*. Vols. XXIV and XXVI, London: MacMillan, 1980.

Morgan, D. J. *The Official History of Colonial Development*. Vols. 1 and 2. London: Macmillan, 1980.

Morgan, K. O. *Labour in Power 1945–1951*. Oxford: Clarendon Press, 1984.

Morris-Jones, W. H., and G. Fischer, eds. *Decolonisation and After: The British and French Experience*. London: Frank Cass, 1980.

Neillands, R. *A Fighting Retreat: The British Empire 1947–1997*. London: Hodder and Stoughton, 1996.

Newlyn, W. T., and D. C. Rowan. *Money and Banking in British Colonial Africa*. Oxford: Clarendon Press, 1954.

Newton, S., and D. Porter. *Modernisation Frustrated: The Politics of Industrial Decline in Britain since 1900*. London and Boston: Unwin Hyman, 1988.

Niculescu, B. *Colonial Planning: A Comparative Study*. London: George Allen and Unwin Ltd., 1958.

Nkrumah, Kwame. *The Autobiography of Kwame Nkrumah*. London: Panaf, 1957.

Oliver, E. *Economic and Commercial Conditions in Nigeria*. London: HMSO, 1957.

Oliver, R. W. *International Economic Co-operation and the World Bank*. London: Macmillan, 1975.

Olusanya, G. O. *The Second World War and Politics in Nigeria 1939–1953*. London: Evans Bros. Ltd., 1953.

Padmore, G. *Africa: Britain's Third Empire*. London: Dennis Dobson Ltd., 1949.

Pearce, R. *The Turning Point in Africa: British Colonial Policy 1938–1948*. London: Frank Cass, 1982.

Peden, G. C. *Keynes, the Treasury and British Economic Policy*. Basingstoke: Macmillan, 1988.

Pedler, F. *Main Currents of West African History 1940–1978*. London: Macmillan, 1979.

Pelling, H. *Britain and the Marshall Plan*. London: Macmillan Press, 1989.

———. *The Labour Government 1945–1951*. New York: St. Martin's Press, 1984.

Perham, M., ed. *Mining, Commerce and Banking in Nigeria*. London: Faber and Faber, 1948.

Petter, M., and J. M. Lee. *The Colonial Office, War and Development Policy*. London: Maurice Temple Smith, 1982.

Polk, J. *Sterling: Its Meaning in World Finance*. New York: Harper and Bros., 1956.

Pollard, S. *The Development of the British Economy 1914–1967*. London: Edwin Arnold Publishers Ltd., 1962 .

Porter, A. N., and A. J. Stockwell, eds., *British Imperial Policy and Decolonisation, 1938–1964*. Vol. 2. London: Macmillan, 1989.

Pressnell, L. S. *External Economic Policy since the War, Vol. I: The Postwar Financial Settlement*. London: HMSO, 1987.

Prest, A. R. *War Economics of Primary Producting Countries*. Cambridge: Cambridge University Press, 1948.

Pritt, D. N. *The Labour Government 1945–1951*. London: Lawrence and Wishart, 1963.

Rendell, W. *The History of the Commonwealth Development Corporation*. London: Heinemann, 1976.

Rowland, B. M., ed. *Balance of Power or Hegemony: The Interwar Monetary System*. New York: New York University Press, 1976.

Schenk, C. R. *Britain and the Sterling Area: From Devaluation to Convertibility in the 1950's*. London: Routledge, 1994.

Shonfield, A. *British Economic Policy since the War*. Baltimore: Penguin Books, 1958.

Short, A. *The Communist Insurrection in Malaya 1948–1960*. London: Muller, 1975.

Sklar, R. *Nigerian Political Parties*. New York: NOK Publishers, 1963.

Sokolski. *The Establishment of Manufacturing in Nigeria*. London: Frederick A. Praeger, 1965.

Stahl, K. M. *The Metropolitan Organisation of British Colonial Trade*. London: Faber and Faber, 1951.

Stockwell, A. J. *British Policy and Malayan Politics*. Kuala Lumpur: Arts Publishing Works, 1979.

Stockwell, A. J., ed. *The Malayan Union*, pts. 1–3. London: HMSO, 1995.

Strange, S. *Sterling and British Policy: A Political Study of an International Currency in Decline*. London: Oxford University Press, 1971.

Tarling, N. *The Fall of Imperial Britain in South East-Asia*. Oxford: Oxford University Press, 1993.

Thurston, A. *Records of Colonial Office, Dominions Office, Commonwealth Relations Office and Commonwealth Office*. London: HMSO, 1995.

Triffin, R. *Gold and the Dollar Crisis: The Future of Convertibility*. New Haven: Yale University Press, 1960.

Vanthoor, W. F. V. *European Monetary Union Since 1948: A Political and Historical Analysis*. London: Edward Elgar, 1996.

Whitaker, C. S. *The Politics of Tradition: Continuity and Change in Northern Nigeria, 1946–1960*. Princeton: Princeton University Press, 1970.

Wickizer, U. D. *Coffee, Tea and Cocoa: An Economic and Political Analysis*. Stanford: Stanford University Press, 1951.

Worswick, G. D. and P. H. Ady, eds. *The British Economy 1945–1950*. Oxford: Clarendon Press, 1952.

Zupnick, E. *Britain's Postwar Dollar Problem*. New York: Columbia University Press, 1958.

Articles

Abbot, G. C. "British Colonial Aid Policy during the Nineteen Thirties," *Canadian Journal of History*, vol. 5 (1970), pp. 73–89.

Adamthwaite, A. "Britain and the World, 1945–9: The View from the Foreign Office," *International Affairs*, vol. 61, no. 2 (1985), pp. 223–235.

Ady, P. "The Future of the Sterling Area: Ghana," *Bulletin of Oxford University Institute of Statistics*, vol. 21, no. 4 (1959), pp. 313–324.

Bigland, A. "The Empire's Assets and How to Use Them," *Journal of the Royal Society of Arts*, LXV (1917), pp. 355–365.

Booth, A. "Britain in the 1930's: A Managed Economy?" *Economic History Review*, XL (1987), pp. 499–522.

Brown, G. A. "The West Indies," *Oxford University Institute of Statistics Bulletin*, vol. 21, no. 4 (1959), pp. 357–371.

Buckley, S. "The Colonial Office and the Establishment of an Imperial Development Board: The Impact of World War I," *Journal of Imperial and Commonwealth History*, II, 3 (1974), pp. 308–315.

Butlin, M. W., and P. M. Boyce. "Monetary Policy in Depression and Recovery," *Working Papers in Economic History*, no. 44 (August 1985).

Caine, S. "Collaboration in Development in the New Africa," *The Africa Bureau Anniversary Address* (1958).

———. "Some Doubts about Sterling Area Policy," *Lloyds Bank Review*, no. 32 (April, 1954), pp. 1–18.

Cell, J. W. "On the Eve of Decolonisation: The Colonial Office's Plans for the Transfer of Power in Africa, 1947," *Journal of Imperial and Commonwealth History*, no. 3 (1980), pp. 235–257.

Choyce, M. A. "A Review of Cotton Development in Nigeria," *Samaru Agricultural Newsletter*, no. 10 (1968)

Clauson, G. L. M. "The British colonial currency system," *Economic Journal*, LIV (1944), pp. 1–15.

Conan, A. R. "The Changing Pattern of International Investment in Selected Sterling Countries," *Essays in International Finance*, no. 27 (December 1956).

Cowen, M. P. "Early Years of the Colonial Development Corporation: British State Enterprise Overseas during Late Colonialism," *African Affairs*, vol. 83 (1984), pp. 63–76.

Cowen, M. P., and N. J. Westcott. "British Imperial Economic Policy During the War," in D. Killingray and R. Rathbone, eds., *Africa and the Second World War* (New York: St. Martin's, 1986).

Cripps, S. "Colonies: Contribution to World trade stability," *Crown Colonist* (January 1948).

Darwin, J. "British Decolonisation since 1945: A Pattern or a Puzzle?" *Journal of Imperial and Commonwealth History*, vol. 12 (1984), pp. 187–209.

———. "Imperialism in Decline: Tendencies in British Imperial Policy between the Wars," *History Journal*, no. 23 (1980), pp. 657–679.

Drummond, I. M. "Britain in the World Economy, 1900–1945," in R. Floud and D. McCloskey, eds., *The Economic History of Britain since 1700, vol. II, 1860 to the 1970's* (Cambridge: Cambridge University Press, 1981).

———. "More on British Colonial Aid Policy in the 1930's," *Canadian Journal of History*, no. 6 (1971), pp. 189–195.

Dumett, R. "Africa's Strategic Minerals during the Second World War," *Journal of African History*, vol. 26 (1985), pp. 381–408.

Faulkner, R. C. "Cotton Seed Multiplication in the Northern States of Nigeria," *Samaru Research Bulletin*, no. 163 (1972).

Flint, J. E. "Critics of Empire and Colonial Reform, 1919–38," seminar paper presented at the History Department, Dalhousie University (18 January 1985).

———. "Governor versus Colonial Office: An Anatomy of the Richards Constitution for Nigeria, 1935–1945," *Historical Papers/Communications Historiques*, Canadian Historical Association (1981).

———. "Planned Decolonisation and Its Failure in British Africa," *African Affairs*, vol. 82, no. 328 (1983), pp. 389–411.

———. "The Origins of Decolonisation in Nigeria," seminar paper presented at the African Studies Centre, Dalhousie University (2 February 1978).

Ford, A. G. "Notes on the Working of the Gold Standard before 1914," *Oxford Economic Papers*, vol. 12, no. 1 (1962), pp. 52–76.

Frankel, S. H. "Some Conceptual Aspects of International Economic Development of Underdeveloped Territories," *Essays in International Finance*, no. 12 (May 1952).

Goldsworthy, D. "Keeping Change within Bounds: Aspects of Colonial Policy during the Churchill and Eden Governments, 1951–1957," *Journal of Imperial and Commonwealth History*, vol. XVIII (1990), pp. 81–108.

Graham, R. W. "American Perspectives on Decolonisation: The Case of Nigeria 1941–1960," paper presented at the History Department seminar, University of Maiduguri (1984).

Greaves, I. "Sterling Balances and the Colonial Currency Systems: A Comment," *Economic Journal*, vol. 63 (1953), pp. 921–923.

———. "The Colonial Sterling Balances," *Essays in International Finance*, no. 20 (1954).

Harrison, M. "Resource Mobilization for World War II: The U.S.A., U.K., U.S.S.R., and Germany, 1938–1945," *Economic History Review*, vol. XLI, no. 2 (1988), pp. 171–192.

Harrod, R. F. "The Pound Sterling," *Essays in International Finance*, no. 13 (February 1952).

———. "The Pound Sterling 1951–1958," *Essays in International Finance*, no. 30 (August 1958).

Hawkins, E. K. "The growth of a money economy in Nigeria and Ghana," *Oxford Economic Papers*, vol. 10, no. 3 (1958), pp. 339–354.

Hazlewood, A. "Sterling Balances and the Colonial Currency System," *Economic Journal*, vol. 62 (1952), pp. 942–945.

———. "The Economics of Colonial Monetary Arrangements," *Social and Economic Studies*, no. 3 (1954), pp. 291–315.

Helleiner, G. K. "The Fiscal Role of Marketing Boards in Nigerian Economic Development, 1947–1951," *Economic Journal*, vol. 74, no. 195 (1964), pp. 582–610.

Hinden, R. "Imperialism Today," *Fabian Quarterly* (April 1945).

Hinds, A. E. "Colonial Policy and Nigerian Cotton Exports," *International Journal of African Historical Studies*, vol. 29, no. 1 (1996), pp. 25–46.

———. "Government Policy and the Nigerian Palm Oil Export Industry, 1939–1949," *Journal of African History*, vol. 38 (1997), pp. 459–478.

———. "Imperial Policy and the Colonial Sterling Balances," *Journal of Imperial and Commonwealth History*, vol. XIX, no. 1 (1991), pp. 24–44.

———. "Sterling and Imperial Policy, 1945–1951," *Journal of Imperial and Commonwealth History*, vol. XV, no. 2 (1987), pp. 149–169.

Hinshaw, R. "Towards European Convertibility," *Essays in International Finance*, no. 31 (November 1958).

Holland, R. F. "The Imperial Factor in British Strategies from Attlee to Macmillan, 1945–1963," *Journal of Imperial and Commonwealth History*, vol. XII, no. 2 (1984), pp. 165–186.

Hopkins, A. G. "Accounting for the British Empire," *Journal of Imperial and Commonwealth History*, XVI, no. 2 (1988), pp. 234–242.

Hyam, R. "Africa and the Labour Government," in A. Porter and R. F. Holland, eds., *Theory and Practice in the History of European Expansion Overseas* (1988).

Jones, Creech, A. "British Colonial Policy with Particular Reference to Africa," *International Affairs*, vol. 27, no. 2 (1951), pp. 76–183.

———. "Colonial Policy and the Labour Government," digest of a speech delivered by Rt. Hon. A. Creech-Jones, M.P., at a meeting held at Conway Hall, London, 14 December 1946.

———. "Labour's Colonial Policy: A Survey," *Fabian Colonial Bureau Colonial Controversy Series*, no. 3 (1947).

Jones, M. E. F. "The Regional Impact of the Overvalued Pound in the 1920's," *Economic History Review*, 2nd series, XXXVIII (1985), pp. 393–401.

Katz, S. I. "Sterling Instability and the Postwar Sterling System," *Review of Economic and Statistics*, XXXI (1954), pp. 81–87.

———. "Sterling's Recurrent Postwar Payment Crises," *Journal of Political Economy*, LXIII(1955), pp. 216–226.

Lee, J. M. "Forward Thinking and War: The Colonial Office during the 1940's," *Journal of Imperial and Commonwealth History*, vol. 6 (1977), pp. 64–79.

Lewis, W. A. "Colonial Development," *Manchester Statistical Society* (1948–49), pp. 1–30.

Louis, Wm. "American Anti-colonialism and the Dissolution of the British Empire," *International Affairs*, vol. 61, no. 3 (1985), pp. 395–420.

———. "The Imperialism of Decolonisation," *Journal of Imperial and Commonwealth History*, vol. 22, no. 3 (1994), pp. 462–511.

Mackie, J. "The Possibilities of Increasing Cotton Production in Nigeria," *Empire Cotton Growing Review*, vol. 25 (1948).

Maiden, R. L. "A Survey to Ascertain the Possible Expansion of Cotton Production in the Northern Region of Nigeria during the Next Five Years," Gaskiya Corporation (1956).

Meredith, D. "The British Government and Colonial Economic Policy 1919–1939," *Economic History Review* (1975), pp. 484–498.

Milewski, J. J. "The Great Depression of the Early 1930's in a Colonial Country: A Case Study of Nigeria," *Africana Bulletin*, no. 23 (1975).

Newton, C. S. "The Sterling Crisis and the British Response to the Marshall Plan," *Economic History Review*, vol. 37, no. 3 (1984), pp. 391–408.

Newton, S. "Britain, the Sterling Area and European Integration, 1945–1950," *Journal of Imperial and Commonwealth History*, vol. 8 (1985), pp. 163–182.

Opie, R. "Anglo-American Economic Relations in Wartime," *Oxford Economic Papers*, vol. 9, no. 2 (1957), pp. 15–151.

Pearce, R. "The Colonial Office and Planned Decolonisation in Africa," *African Affairs*, vol. 83 (1984), pp. 79–94.

Rooth, T. "Britain's Other Dollar Problem: Economic Relations with Canada, 1945–1950," *Journal of Imperial and Commonwealth History*, vol. 27, no. 1 (1999), pp. 81–108.

Sargent, J. R. "European Free Trade the Choice for Britain," *Oxford Economic Papers*, vol. 10, no. 3 (October 1958), pp. 265–276.

Schenk, C. "Decolonisation and European Economic Integration: The Free Trade Area Negotiations, 1956–1958," *Journal of Imperial and Commonwealth History*, vol. 24, no. 3 (1996), pp. 444–463.

Scott, M. Fg. "What Should Be Done about the Sterling Area?" *Oxford University Institute of Statistics Bulletin*, vol. 21, no. 4 (1959), pp. 213–251.

Shannon, H. A. "The Evolution of the Sterling Exchange Standard", *International Monetary Fund Staff Papers*, Vol. 1, no. 3 (April 1951), pp. 334–354.

United Africa Company. "The West African Currency Board," *Statistical and Economic Review*, no. 8 (1951), pp. 1–19.

———. "Produce Goes to the Market, Nigeria: Palm Produce and Groundnuts," *Statistical and Economic Review*, no. 3 (1949), pp. 1–39.

———. "Produce Goes to the Market, Nigeria: Cotton," *Statistical and Economic Review*, no. 7 (March 1951), pp. 16–47.

Wescott, N. J. "Sterling and British Policy: The British Imperial Economy 1939–1951." Seminar paper, Institute of Commonwealth Studies, University of London (1982).

Wicker, E. R. "Colonial Development and Welfare, 1929–1957: The Evolution of a Policy," *Social and Economic Studies*, vol. 7 (1958), pp. 170–192.

———. "The Colonial Development Corporation 1948–1954," *Review of Economic Studies*, Vol. 23/24 (1955–1957), pp. 213–228.

Windel, D. "Developments in the World Raw Cotton Statistical Situation during the First Half of the 1946–47 Season," *Empire Cotton Growing Review*, vol. 24, no. 2 (1947), pp. 103–110.

———. "The 1946–47 World Raw Cotton Situation," *Empire Cotton Growing Review*, vol. 24, no. 4 (1947), pp. 269–275.

Wright, K. M. "Dollar Pooling in the Sterling Area, 1939–1952," *American Economic Review*, vol. 44 (1954), pp. 559–576.

Wright, Q. "Post-War Reconstruction of the Colonies and Protectorates of British West Africa," prepared under the auspices of the West African Press Delegation to Great Britain (August 1943).

Zachernuk, P. S. "Nigerian Critics of Empire: Economic Ideas among the Educated Elite, 1939–1945," seminar paper presented at the Centre for African Studies, Dalhousie University, 26 November 1982.

Unpublished Theses

Adesimi, A. A. "The Prospects and Potential of Groundnut Cultivation as a Means of Enhancing Economic Opportunity in the Rural Economy of Northern Nigeria." Ph.D. thesis, Wisconsin, 1973.

Adeyeye, S. O. "The Western Nigerian Cooperative Movement, 1935–1964." M.A. thesis, Ibadan University, 1967.

Bello, S. "State and Economy in Kano 1894–1960: A Study of Colonial Domination." Ph.D. thesis, Ahamadu Bello University, Zaria, 1982.

Bowden, J. H. "Development and Control in British Colonial Policy, with Special Reference to Nigeria and the Gold Coast, 1935–1948." Ph.D. thesis, Birmingham, 1980.

Emudong, C. P. "The Evolution of a new British Colonial Policy in the Gold Coast 1938–1948: Origins of Planned Decolonisation or NeoColonialism." Ph.D. thesis, Dalhousie University, 1982.

Hinds, A. E. "British Imperial Policy and the Development of the Nigerian Economy, 1939–1951." Ph.D thesis, Dalhousie University, Halifax, Nova Scotia, Canada, 1985.

Njoku, J. "African Marketing Schemes: Peasant Agriculture and Marketing Schemes in Southern Nigerian Societies 1914–1964." Ph.D. thesis, New School for Social Research, U.S.A., 1974.

Nordman, C. "Prelude to Decolonisation in West Africa." Ph.D. thesis, Oxford, 1976.

Ukegbu, B. "Production in the Nigerian Oil Palm Industry, 1900–1954." Ph.D. thesis, London, 1974.

Zachernuk, P. S. "Nigerian Critics of Empire: Political and Economic Ideas among the Nigerian Educated Elite, 1920–1950." M.A. thesis, Dalhousie University, 1983.

Index

Abadan oilfields, seizure of, 72
Accra Riots, 55
Accumulated balances, an enigma for the British government, 20
Accumulated sterling balances: Americans' position, 20; conundrum for Britain, 16; growth of, 15–16; most outstanding feature, 164–165. *See also* Accumulated balances, Colonial balances and Colonial sterling balances
Action Group, The, party in western Nigeria, 152
Agricultural production in Europe, 91
American capital: British government's consideration to, 141–142; investment in colonial empire revisited, 177–178
Anglo-American Loan Negotiations, the first formal session, 14–15
Anglo-American Negotiations, contentious issue in, 12
Armstrong, W. A.: private secretary to the chancellor of the exchequer, 169; under secretary at the Treasury, 190
Ashanti Pioneer, commented, 105
Atlantic Charter, 12
Attlee, Prime Minister Clement, 47; responded, 48; was informed, 119

Azikiwe, Nnandi, 78, 104

Bank of England: and potential threat to Britain's balance of payments, 156; decision to purchase transferable sterling, 162; dissatisfaction with colonial governments, 25; rejected Colonial Office's contentions, 19
Bauer, P. T., 115–117
Bevin, Ernest, foreign secretary, 47; on colonial development plans, 105
Board of Trade, one of main concerns, 93–95
Bourdillon, Bernard, governor of Nigeria, 27
Bourdillon, H. T., assistant under secretary of state, Colonial Office, 81
Bridges, Sir Edward, permanent secretary to Treasury, 154
Britain: abandoned Gold Standard, 8–9; and Allied forces, 6; balance of payments crisis of 1951, 76–77; between 1946 and July 1947, 38–39; and choice to make, 52; committed to free conversion of sterling, 14; concerns about potential problems, 129–130; confronted by political development, 53–56; dilemma made

About the Author

ALLISTER HINDS is Lecturer in the Department of History at the University of the West Indies—Mona Campus. He has published a number of articles on the impact of the sterling on colonial economic policy in general and the Nigerian economy in particular.